TotalRecall Publications, Inc.
1103 Middlecreek
Friendswood, Texas 77546
281-992-3131 281-482-5390 Fax
www.totalrecallpress.com

Cover Photo by
—See Page 190 for information on Front Cover
—See Page 75 for information on Back Cover
ISBN: 978-1-59095-132-3
UPC: 6-43977-41323-9

FIRST EDITION
1 2 3 4 5 6 7 8 9 10

Colophon is trademarked 1,000 Years Of Medicine In Nevada's Great Basin is made possible by a grant from NEVADA HISTORY OF MEDICINE FOUNDATION, INC.

The Straight and Narrow

Anton P. Sohn MD

This Book is Dedicated

In Memory of My Parents,
Anton Peter and Ruth Marie Sohn

Because strait is the gate,
and narrow is the way,
which leadeth unto life,
and few there be that find it.
Matthew 7:14.

This Edition is Dedicated to
Arlene, My Loving Wife for over 59 Years

Anton Paul Sohn MD

Reno, Nevada, 2022

Contents

Acknowledgements

First and foremost I'd like to acknowledge my immediate family, Arlene, Phillip, Eric, and Kristin, who have given purpose to my life. In addition, Kristin has edited this book and my previous books. I was motivated to write this book by my longtime friend Louis "Gene" Toole whose influence dates to the 1950s. Bruce Moran of TotalRecall Press provided tremendous help and motivation to publish this edition. His skill is obvious in the format and design of this book. Others who were important are mentioned in the Introduction.

Information from the following books:

1. *The Straight and Narrow, A.P. Sohn, 1992.*
2. *Idaho Wildflowers in the River of No Return Wilderness at Pistol Creek,* R. Montgomery, W. Payne, A.P. Sohn, W.J. Thompson, and L.E. Toole; 5th edition, 2018
3. *With These Hands: A lifetime of Art and Crafts,* A.P. Sohn, 2020
4. *Growing up in Irvington,* A.P. Sohn, 2020
5. *Traveling the Globe,* A.P. Sohn, 2020
6. *Addendum to Traveling the Globe,* A.P. Sohn, 2020
7. *My Honor to Serve Mankind,* A.P. Sohn, 2020
8. *Call of the Mountain,* A.P. Sohn, 2020
9. *Vietnam War* (Sohn, Myers, Brady, and Ganchan), TotalRecall Press, A.P. Sohn, 2022)
10. *1,000 Years of Medicine in Nevada's Great Basin* (TotalRecall Press, A.P. Sohn, 2022)

Introduction

This edition was motivated by my desire to update the original edition to include newly discovered Sohn/Fulton genealogy, add details to original information, and include personal events up to the present. This effort was aided by over 10,000 photographs and videos in my possession, which presented a daunting task in selecting representing copies. I was also aided by numerous books, which are enumerated in Acknowledgements.

To understand my motivations, it is necessary to know my background and family circumstances. Heredity, family, moral discipline, and unpredictable circumstances molded my personality. In addition, growing up in Indiana in a hardworking, middle-class family shaped my life and philosophy. Early religious training and family life had a profound influence on my values and, ultimately, my choice of a career. Growing up revolved around church attendance and religious activities.

Abraham Lincoln said, "All that I am or hope to be, I owe to my mother." To paraphrase Lincoln, "All I am or hope to be, I owe to my parents, Anton Peter and Ruth Marie." Dad, a small businessman, lived through the Great Depression, and his economic principles were imbued in his children. Many a time I heard him say, "If you can't afford to pay cash you can't afford it." This advice cannot be applied across the board, but to pay one's way, up front, is good strategy for everyday living. Just as important was my mother's influence; her attitude about self-confidence and determination became a major philosophy in the life of the Sohn children. She consistently stressed, "You can do anything anyone else can do"

To put Sohn family philosophy in its simplest form—decency counts. If I had to give advice learned from my Indiana years—do what is right. Dad related to me on one occasion when we discussed education, "I don't sit down and think about something, I just do what is right." Dad and Mom observed and emphasized strict moral principles. In the true sense of the word, Dad was a good person and had excellence of character. My brother, Bill, had Psalms 37:23 and :27 inscribed on my father's tombstone: "The steps of a good man are ordered by the Lord and the end of that man is peace."

Education—in addition to religion—was emphasized in our home. My father only went through the sixth grade in German-speaking school, but there was no question that my siblings and I would go to college and get a "solid" education. Our parents were determined to educate their children. I observe this principle and pay for the education of my children and grandchildren.

Mother's side of the family, the Fultons, had a history of pursuing education: her grandfather, William Hays Fulton, attended business college and her father taught school. Her grandmother, Martha Ann (McCarty) Fulton, went to college at Saint Mary of the Woods Academy in Terra Haute, Indiana.

Mom obtained an RN from the Protestant Deaconess Hospital in Indianapolis and took postgraduate work in nursing. Her brother, William, after he worked his way through school, practiced dentistry in Indianapolis for thirty–seven years. He told me that he became a dentist because he couldn't afford medical school. He was an inspiration to our family, and continued the family tradition of *service to humanity.* The youngest Fulton sister, Madonna (Stanley), also became a nurse at the Deaconess Hospital.

I am writing this manuscript to record family history and tradition, an important part of family pride and awareness. Furthermore, I have enjoyed the opportunity to revisit family and, in some instances, meet relatives for the first time. This document will also create a factual record, although not all information could be verified, and tell a story that is typically American. The story is about families leaving Europe and the British Isles to escape war and famine and to search for and find opportunity in America.

The Sohns, Faveys, Fultons and Pecks—my grandparents and their families—blended the physical toughness and virtues of farmers, soldiers, and skilled laborers to become businessmen and middle–class professionals.

There is some irony in my endeavor to write this historical and biographical sketch. Through high school and later in college, I concentrated on science, mathematics, and the arts to the detriment of the humanities, English and literature. A problem with premedical education is neglect of the humanities. This is predictable and understandable since students must do well in the biological sciences to get admitted to medical school. Unfortunately medicine is not the only profession with this problem: engineering, architecture, and other professional schools concentrate on highly technical subjects to the detriment of a liberal education. Now, looking back, I can say that my memorable educational experiences were the inspirations I gained from grade schoolteachers: art—Mrs. Martha Barber, woodworking—Mr. Hershel Whitaker, and high schoolteachers: mechanical drafting—Mr. Wathen Leasor and art—Mr. F.M. Howard. I was also inspired by poetry that I memorized in high school:

Forbearance

Hast thou named all the birds without a gun?
Loved the wood rose, and left it on its stalk?
At rich men's tables eaten bread and pulse?
Unarmed, faced danger with a heart of trust?
And loved so well a high behavior,
In man or maid, that thou from speech refrained,
Nobility more nobly to repay?
O, be my friend, and teach me to be thine!
—Ralph Waldo Emerson

Thanatopsis

So live, that when thy summons comes to join
The innumerable caravan, which moves
To that mysterious realm, where each shall take
His chamber in the silent halls of death,
Thou go not, like the quarry slave at night,
Scourged to his dungeon but, sustained and soothed
By an unfaltering trust, approach thy grave,
Like one who wraps the drapery of his couch
About him and lies down to pleasant dreams.
—William Cullen Bryant

The Chambered Nautilus

Build thee more stately mansions O my soul,
As the swift seasons roll!
Leave thy low-vaulted past!
Let each new temple, nobler than the last,
Shut thee from heaven with a dome more vast,
Till thou at length art free,
Leaving thine outgrown shell by life's unresting sea!
—Oliver Wendel Holmes

To complete this book I used family records and other sources compiled by my uncle, William Roy Fulton, DDS. He also wrote and recorded Fulton heritage. If other predecessors were as diligent in recording their experiences, this work would be twice as long and twice as interesting. Too frequently, everyday occurrences are thought to be commonplace and therefore not recorded. Accordingly, if I shed some light on the past, I will exceed my purpose.

To my brother, William Peter Sohn of Indianapolis, I give credit for preserving and developing the Sohn history. I wish I had space to reproduce the genealogy charts and information he researched. Also, bits and pieces of our history, including newspaper articles and letters were sent to me by my mother.

Some of the information in this edition may be difficult to understand. I caution the reader to remember that some events were over eighty years ago, and our opinions have changed. This 2022 edition also has been edited from the 1992 original. In addition, it records my life history up to the present.

I—Sohn History, Across the Ocean, Down a River

DISCHARGE—NIKOLAUS SOHN

His Excellency the Grand–Duke of Hessen and Near Rhein ETC

The appointed Colonel and commander of the Life–guard Regiment documents and acknowledges herewith; after the rifle–man Nikolaus Sohn, born in Reissen, District Lindenfels, 31 years of age, 6 feet 5.3 inches tall with blond hair and blue eyes who has served honorable for 9 years and 2 months with the rifle company of the 11th battalion of the life–guard Regiment under the command of Major Pfaff has asked for his discharge and that such should not be refused after his term of service. Thus I grant him herewith his discharge and request all military men and civilians who may be presented with this paper to let pass safely and without impediment the discharged rifle–man Nicolaus Sohn of Lutheran belief, by profession a skilled laborer and give him all necessary assistance.

Dated Darmstadt on 1 April 1823 signed by me and the Battalion Commander and affixed with our family seal.

During his time of service he did not receive any regimental punishment.

DISCHARGE—JOHANN ADAM SOHN

Grand–Duke of Hessen

After the discharge due to substitution permission was granted to Musketeer Johann Adam Sohn from the 7th Company of the 3rd Hessian Infantry Regiment born in Reissen, district Lindenfels whose description is added below and who has served for 10 years and 3 and 3/6 months in the Hessian military of the 3rd Hessian Infantry Regiment and sealed with the regimental seal.

Worms, 12 July 1857.
The commander of the 3rd Hessian Infantry Regiment Gerlach, Colonel

Birth date: 14 Jan 1826.
Nose: strong.
Height: 6 feet 0.8 in.
Mouth: average.
Build: Medium. Chin: sharp.

Face: oval. Beard: none.
Color of face: healthy. Other signs: none.
Color of eyes: grayish brown.
Color of eyebrows: blond. Religion: Lutheran.
Color of hair: blond.
Profession: Bricklayer.
Forehead: high and arched
Marital Status: None.
Signature of Holder-----
Other Remarks: None.
Participation in Campaign: 1849 in Baden.
Wounded, how, when, and what occasion: none.
Decorations received: 12 November 1849 Field Service and
Grand–Duchy Memorial Medal. 14 June 1856 Military Service Medal Class I
Behavior: Good

In place of Captain Schimpff, Lieutenant

During the time of Wilhelm I (1797-1888) many families fled Prussia to escape war. Wilhelm put down the revolution of 1848 when the all-German constitution was established in Frankfurt. In 1861, he became King of Prussia with Prince Otto von Bismarck's help. During the Franco-Prussian War in 1871, he became Kaiser of a united Germany. As a result of the constant war, the Sohns, who were soldiers and skilled laborers, emigrated from Prussia. The fact that all Prussian males over 12 years old served in the military for one year probably stimulated the Sohns to leave their home country. Michael Sohn, who was eligible had not served in the military, but his brother, Anton, was the first to emigrate.

In 1853 Anton, age 25, sailed on the *Bark Stanislaus* from Antwerp to New York. Listed on the ship's manifest was his future wife, Catherine Schmidt, age 24. After they arrived in the New World, Anton and Catherine proceeded down the Ohio River with many other German emigrants. They settled in New Albany, Indiana.(1) In 1850, New Albany, across the river from Louisville, with 8,181 inhabitants was the largest city in Indiana.(2) There were no major cities in Indiana. Although the foreign born were less than ten percent of the Hoosier state's population, more than half were German. In some communities the German language was more often heard than English.(3)

At that time, the first railroads were being built into Indiana and Kentucky, but Anton, a blacksmith, and Catherine traveled by flatboat to their frontier home. Four years later, his father, Nikolaus, left their home in Reissen, Prussia (near Darmstadt, Germany) to join his son in the new world.(4) Anton's mother, Eva Katherine (Sattler) Sohn (1801–1852), had been dead five years and his grandfather, Johann Nikolaus (1765–1832), had been dead for 25 years. Most likely Anton provided a new home and money.

The 1870 Census shows that Anton was successful. He owned real estate valued at $4,000 and was a partner with Casper Fiock in the Spring Brewery.

The Sohn relatives of Anton arrived in New York on 9 November 1857. They had sailed three months from London and disembarked from the *Amazon*, a three–mast sailing vessel. In the party were three of Anton's brothers: Johann Adam, age 31, Johann Nikolaus, age 17, and Michael, age 27, who was not listed on the passenger manifest.(5) Also on board were his sisters, Eva Elisabetha, age 14, and Anna Elisabetha, age 23. Johann Adam's wife, Anna Margaret Doersam and their children, Georg Peter (my grandfather), age five, and Elizabetha, age three, were in the party.(6) Archive records from Germany indicate that Anton had a brother, Valentin, who emigrated, but no record could be located in America.(7)

Nikolaus, Anton's father, was uneducated and had served for nine years and two months in the Prussian army with a rifle company of the 11th battalion of the Life-guard Regiment.**(8)** He helped defeat Napoleon in the Leipzig (1813) and Waterloo (1815) battles. His son, Johann Adam, had served over ten years as a Musketeer in the 7th Company of the 3rd Hessian Infantry Regiment.(9) He served with distinction under Wilhelm I when the Baden uprising was brought under control in 1848 and received the Field Service and Grand Duchy Memorial Medal and the Military Service Medal Class I. The discharge papers state that Nikolaus was 6 feet 5.3 inches; Johann Adam was 6 feet 0.8 inches.(10) Ironically, the Sohns left Prussia because of war, but after they arrived at their new home they were soon caught up in another war. Several served in the army during the American Civil War.

One can't help wondering what Anton and Catherine's home was like when his parent, siblings, nephew, and niece showed up to start their new life in America. Little is handed down by family oral history or written documents other than birth and marriage certificates. My brother, William, accounted for all the Sohn immigrants.(11) Nikolaus died in 1882, and even though he was uneducated he had learned to write. Johann Nikolaus went away to the Civil War and never returned; we assumed that he was killed in battle. One hundred and twenty years later it was determined that he had been wounded in the Battle of Chickamauga while serving as a soldier. He settled in Missouri where he died in 1932.(12) It is unknown if he communicated with his family in Indiana.

His brother, Michael, had not served in the military and left Prussia without authorization. "Grandma, Anna Margaret Doersam, who was on the passenger list and wife of Johann Adam said they put one of Grandpa's brothers [Michael] in a barrel and bored holes in it so he could breathe."(13) Independently, Delphia Hasty who was married to Johann Nikolaus's son, Albert, in Missouri recounted that one of the brothers was smuggled aboard ship and drowned in a fishing net while attempting to swim to shore in New York Harbor.(14)

Johann Adam Sohn, stone mason, lived for 35 years at 437 Beeler Street in New Albany. He was the Street Commissioner in 1882 and had been the president of the Jaeger's Lodge for many years when he died on 16 March 1905.(15) His son, Georg Peter—addressed as Peter—was also a Jaeger, however it is unknown if he hunted wild game in Southern Indiana. On the other hand, he is known to have hunted a man. Once after a bank robbery, he went home, got his pistol, and joined the posse.(16)

In the manner of the old world, George Peter followed in his father's footsteps and became a stone mason. Later, he owned a saloon at Forth and Market in New Albany. He was over six feet tall and was not afraid to bounce an unruly customer out of the saloon. He was an erect and proud man. In 1877, he married Mary Elizabeth Favey. Her family emigrated from Switzerland and France. Grandma Mary Elizabeth was a kind and gracious lady, a marked contrast to her strict and severe husband. The children were raised in her Catholic faith. The immigrant Sohns were Lutheran. Of Georg Peter and Mary Elizabeth's eight children, including twins, only three lived beyond childhood: Celina Mary Roth (1880–1938), Anton Peter (my father), and Amelia Anna Weber (1890–1978).

Aunt Celina was the oldest of the three children. She and her husband, Uncle Joe Roth, operated a dry goods store in New Albany. Her funeral was one of the few times—in nearly thirty years—that Dad closed the store and traveled to New Albany. Her store had a front porch with a swing, but what was more important to me as a child, it faced the street where the Monon train ran down the middle. They had seven children; five—Joseph, Wilhemina, Coletta, Mary Elizabeth, and Imelda—lived to become adults. Cousin Joe—born in 1908—and his wife, Frances, had children my age. We sometimes stayed with them when we made our annual trip to the banks of the "Ohio." Cousin Joe died of Hodgkin's Disease, as did Wilhemina and "Mary Elizabeth."(17)

Usually, when we made trips to Dad's hometown we stayed with his sister, Aunt Amelia, and her children. Her husband, Herbert Weber, died in 1943 from fungal empyema contacted during the war. With the head of the family gone, life was not easy for the Webers. Melvin assumed the responsibilities of supporting the family. When we visited them, Dad always took groceries. Melvin Herbert Weber and Mary Edith (Weber) Grantz, live in New Albany with their families.

In September 1937, Melvin came to stay with us for a high school graduation trip. He related to me that this was his last vacation until he retired. He remembers walking from Dad's store to the Monument Circle. His mother, Aunt Amelia, died in 1978. During the funeral, the rosary I bought in 1958 at the Vatican (in St. Peter's Cathedral) was placed in her hands. She was a kind and gentle lady. Her death brought her generation to an end, one hundred and forty years since the original emigrant Sohns came to America. Their descendants are thoroughly American.

REFERENCES:

(1) William Peter Sohn, *SOHN GENEALOGY,* 1765-1979, (Filed with the Indiana Historical Society).
(2) James H. Madison, *The Indiana Way: A State History* (Indiana University Press, 1986), p. 96.
(3) *Ibid.*, p. 173.
(4) Nikolaus, 1797-1882, is buried in Fairview Cemetery, New Albany, where most of the early Sohns are interred. Tomb stones were erected over his and his children's graves in 1983 under William Sohn's guidance.
(5) Michael belonged to the 93rd Reg. Indiana Volunteers, Co. C during the Civil War. He was discharged on 14 June 1865 and is buried in the Fairview Cemetery.
(6) Johann Adam and Anna Margaret were married in a civil ceremony on 6 February 1858 in New Albany, Indiana. The religious ceremony performed in Prussia was not recognized.
(7) Valentin was born in 1836 and named after his grandfather, Valenin Slatter.
(8) See appendix for translation of the discharge.
(9) *Ibid.*
(10) *Ibid.*
(11) Sohn, *Genealogy.*
(12) Correspondence in William Peter Sohn's possession.
(13) Letter from Eva H. Lingle, Carey, Kansas, to William Peter Sohn.
(14) Conversation between Delphia Hasty and William Peter Sohn at the Sohn Reunion, Washington State Park, Missouri, June 21, 1981.
(15) New Albany Newspaper, March 16, 1905.
(16) *Jaeger* is "hunter" in German. The story is from personal communication with Melvin Weber, his grandson.
(17) Hodgkin's Disease is a malignancy of the lymph tissue.

II—Favey History, Across an Ocean, Down a River

Emigration records indicate that Francis Favie (Faivet) arrived in New York in 1846 as a child of four years.(1) His father, Francois Xavier Faivet (1810–1852), a hewer of wood and son of Pierre Joseph Faivet (1779–1854) was from Froidevaux, Switzerland.(2) His mother, Rosine (Cerf) Faivet was from Surmont, France, a short distance from Froidevaux. The family settled in Vincennes, Indiana, on the Wabash River, a tributary feeding the Ohio River. Francis' siblings were Celestin Joseph (1838) Celestine Eugenia (1844–1922), Marie Josephine (1846–), Magdeleine Zeline (1847–1918) and Mary Elizabeth, my grandmother, who was the first Faivet child born in America. Mary Elizabeth was born in Vincennes, Indiana, on 23 March 1853, six months after her father had died. She could read and write French. She read the mail to the residents at the old folks' home in Vincennes, Indiana.(3)

For unknown reasons the family moved east to Floyds Knobs, a small Catholic village west of New Albany, Indiana. The area was originally settled by soldiers of George Rogers Clark after the final capture of Vincennes from the British in 1779. After the War of 1812, settlers of French, German and Belgian origin moved into the Ohio River Valley around Floyds Knobs. Many of the settlers had been soldiers in Napoleon's Army.

Family history indicates that Eugenia and Mary Elizabeth (Sohn) moved to New Albany after the death of their mother and did servant work. Magdeleine Zeline (Celina) married Clements Bruet. Their daughter, "Cousin" **Lizzie** married into the Kaiser family. Many of our trips to New Albany included a visit with "Cousin" Lizzie who lived upstairs above their tobacco store.

The Kaisers had been in the New Albany area since, at least, 1834, when the family founded the Kaiser Tobacco Store. The store grew and established a wholesale division with vending routes in Southern Indiana. It became a classic American success story, "A business that has survived the Industrial Revolution, the Civil War, the coming and going of the steamboat age, two world wars, a depression and several recessions, and the 1937 flood."(4) It originally was on Pearl Street, the main street of a bustling riverboat town, but the growth of the business forced a move to Fifth and Oak streets.

REFERENCES:

(1) The names were Anglicized. Faivet became Favey. Francis died in 1929 of tuberculosis and is buried at St. Mary of the Knobs, Floyds Knobs. Credit goes to Mary Soos, granddaughter of Celina (Sohn) Roth, for her help in researching the early Sohns and Faveys.

(2) Pierre Joseph's parents were Joannis Baptiste (Fevet) Faivet and Maria Magdalena (Choffat) of Soubey, Switzerland. This information was supplied by the *Commune de Soubey (Jura)* to Betty Hooker and Mary Soos.

(3) Told to me by my father, Anton Peter Sohn.

(4) *The New Albany Courier-Journal,* 1987.

Sohn Reunion Glenwood Park, July 10, 1927. *Row 1:* Tom Hartley, Danny Engnehl, Mary Helen Engnehl, Marshal Humphery, Dorothy Buchman, Charles Buchman, Mary E. (Roth) Schrader, Lucille (Houpt) Oster, Imelda (Roth) Wehrmann. *Row 2:* Elizabeth (Walter) Hartley, --, Harry Engnehl, Margaret Engnehl, Louise (Engnehl) Humphrey, Frances (Engnehl) Buchman, Arch Buchman, Fletcher Bush, Lula (Payton) Bush, Celina (Sohn) Roth. *Row 3:* Mabel (Sohn) Austin, Margaret Houpt, Carrie (Walter) Hartley, --, --, Margaret (Hartley) Pierson, Lizzie (Sohn) Walter, Louisa (Sohn) Engnehl, Annie (Sohn) Payton, Clara Walter, Virginia (Dieckmann) Campbell, Louise Walter Dieckmann. *Row 4:* George Peter, Mary E. Sohn, --, Andrew Sohn, Carrie (Sohn) Perkins, Morris Engnehl, Shirley Dieckmann, --. *(Courtesy of Mary E. Grantz)*

(Photo Names are not Indexed)

III—Sohn Genealogy

Johann Nicholas Sohn (1765-1832)—**Anna Elizabeth Springel**

↓

Nicklaus Sohn, Prussian Army (1797-1882)—**Eva Katherine Sattler** (1801-1852)

↓

Johann Adam Sohn (1/14/1826-3/16/05)—**Anna Margaretha Doersam** (4/5/1827-8/22/16)

↓

George Peter Sohn (4/1/1852-1/9/33)—**Mary Elizabeth Faivet** (3/23/1853-4/4/28)

↓ ↓ ↓

Anton Peter Sohn (1887-1961) **Amelia Sohn Weber** (1890-1978) **Celina Sohn Roth** (1880-1938)

==========

NOTE: There are three separate unrelated Sohn clans in the U.S. 1) My German Lutheran relatives (listed above); 2) Jewish Sohns who live on the east coast of the United States; and 3) South Korean Sohns who live on the west coast.

Anton Peter Sohn (1/12/87-10/12/61)—**Goldia May Shepard** (1885-1967)

↓

Elizabeth Antonette (Betty) Sohn Hooker (1922-2015)

==========

Anton Peter Sohn (1/12/87-10/12/61)—**Ruth Marie Fulton** (3/2/03-9/12/86)

↓ ↓ ↓ ↓

Annlouise (1934-2018) **Anton Paul** (10/1/35) **William P.** (12/2/36) **Robert F.** (7/31/41)

==========

Annlouise Sohn (Parke) Walker (1934-2018)—**Robert S. Walker** (3/3/25-6/28/74)

↓ ↓

David (6/17/63)—**Geralyn** (9/7/60) **Laurrie** (1961-92)

↓ ↓

Patrick (2/6/95) **Victoria** (3/14/98)

==========

William Peter Sohn (12/2/36)—**Harriett Bell** (10/22/37)

↓ ↓

Craig Sohn (7/29/68)—**Yolanda** (12/25/67) **Suzanne** (12/25/66)—**Greg Carr** (4/4/65)

↓ ↓ ↓

Grace (2/28/00) **Nicholas** (7/9/96) **Kathryn** (7/9/96)

==

Robert Fulton Sohn (7/31/41)—**Millicent (Mimi) Hosp** (4/15/42)

↓ ↓

Robert (Rob) (8/3/65)—**Jill Reves** (4/19/65) **Christopher** (7/2/67)—**Beth Woolridge** (12/8/68)

↓ ↓ ↓ ↓

Cassidy (4/4/96) **Sintra (9/11/98)** **Valerie Pearson** (5/7/94) **Jessica Parsons** (3/25/97)

==

Anton Paul Sohn (10/1/35)—**Arlene Ann Hedegard** (4/23/39)

↓ ↓ ↓

(4/28/66) (1/13/60) (3/24/69) (5/20/69) (3/24/69) (2/1/75) (3/20/71) (6/12/70)

Anton Phillip—Eliz. Gleason **Eric—K. Siron** **Eric—M. De Souza** **Kristin—Mark Fermoile**

↓ ↓ ↓ ↓ ↓ ↓

(11/29/94) (8/24/97) (3/10/97) (6/9/99) (9/27/00) (2/27/11)

Anton Peter **Alexander** **Kerry** **Brady** **Sierra** **Isabella**

Amelia, Anton Peter Sohn, 1897

Anton Peter Sohn, 1893

IV—Fulton History, Across an Ocean

My mother's relatives, the Fultons, were Scotch-Irish Presbyterians who came from Northern Ireland and emigrated to the New World in the 1700s. Like the Sohns and other Americans they followed the rivers to their eventual destination. According to family tradition, two sons of William F. Fulton (1600-1667) from Kilkenny, Ireland, emigrated: one received a land grant in Nova Scotia, only to lose it because of pro-colonial activities; the other brother, William (1648-1741), settled in Lancaster County, Pennsylvania, and became the patriarch of my mother's family.(1)

One of William's sons was Robert Fulton (1730-1771), a tailor and the father of Robert Jr., the artist-inventor of the steamboat. Another was William Fulton Jr. (1734-1781) who, with his sons, William (1759-1781) and David (1761-1781) fought with "Mad Anthony" Wayne in the Indian Wars.(2) Father and both sons contracted the "fever" during a campaign and returned home; all three died within one week. Then, the "germ theory" or bacterial and viral cause of diseases was not known. The most prevalent diseases were epidemic and included "camp fever," usually typhoid fever or typhus.(3) Medical care was also inadequate in the military service and most of the participants—like the Fultons—returned home to get medical and home care.(4)

After their mother died, William and David's brothers, including Elijah (1766-1813) and his wife, Elisabeth, left Pennsylvania and traveled to Limestone (now, Maysville) Kentucky. After Wayne signed a treaty on 4 August 1795 at Greenville ending the Indian wars, they went up the Scioto River, from the Ohio River, to the Whetstone (Olentangy) junction near Columbus, Ohio. In approximately 1800 they were able to capitalize on their military service and "took up" military land.(5)

One of Elijah's sons, William, married in the spring of 1820 and moved to Clinton, Indiana, near the Illinois border on the Wabash River. Then, Clinton was a rural trading post, but it became a coal mining community. Shortly thereafter, he wrote his uncle, "I have met with great misfortune since I went to the Wabash. I lost my wife and child and am destitute of all my family."(6) His situation improved, he married Jane Nice and in 1824 he was appointed sheriff of Vermillion County. He received $35 and an extra $2.50 for obtaining a copy of the laws regulating sheriffs in a new county. At that time Indiana was a new state, eight years old.

The movement for Indiana to become a state collapsed during the War of 1812, but after the war the pioneers came over mountain trails, and mostly along the rivers like William Fulton to settle in Indiana. Indian troubles were now eliminated in the

Northwest Territory. The population of the territory in 1800 was 5,641; by 1820 the state had a population of 147,178.(7) Most came looking for a new life, a fresh start, and free land where they could carve out a new home—by the sweat of their brow—in the wilderness.

Fundamental to pioneer life was a strong, large, cohesive family with basic religious tenets, and the ability to cope with hardship and early death. The first home was usually a log "lean-to" with three walls and a fire at the open end. The furniture was simple, crude, and homebuilt. Food was usually plentiful and consisted of home-grown crops and native foods such as grapes, pawpaws, and persimmons. Wild game, such as deer and turkey, was available, but bear and Indians were a threat. For early pioneers, life was not easy, but freedom and opportunity were important.

Mary Eliz. Favey Sohn, 1915

Geo. Peter Sohn, Eliz. Sohn Walter, Andrew Sohn
Annie Sohn Payton, Caroline Sohn Perkins,
Louisa Sohn Engnehi, 1927

William and Jane's first son, my great–grandfather, William Hays Fulton (1827–1905), was born on 17 August 1827 in the new state of Indiana. He started the Fulton family tradition of education; he began his formal education at a subscription school in Clinton, attended the Paris Academy at Paris, Illinois, and then obtained a business education at the Bryant's and Stratton's Business College in Indianapolis. He moved to New Albany (later, renamed Camargo), Illinois, where he built a home and a store in 1854. The store was a simple frame building—horizontal wood siding, a covered board walk, and a false front—typical of frontier general stores. The material for the house was cut and shipped from Chicago—total cost, $2,500. The wood in the upper rooms was solid walnut. "At each side of the front door were beautiful panes of colored glass.... The parlor was arranged with the organ at one side, a love seat on another.... Upstairs was a large hallway that opened into the three bedrooms."(8)

In 1858, Derexa Brown became his bride.(9) Her mother was the sister of James Whitcomb, the governor of Indiana during the Mexican War, 1843 to 1848. Derexa attended the Paris Seminary in Paris, Illinois and the Saint Mary of the Woods Academy in Terra Haute, Indiana. The academy, founded in 1840, is the oldest women's Roman Catholic liberal arts college in the United States. She had musical talent. She sang, played the piano, and wrote poetry.(10) She was also a member of the Women's Christian Temperance Union (WCTU).

Amelia, Dad, L. Kaiser, E. Kaiser, 1942.

May Shepard Sohn, Betty, Dad, 1923.

George Peter, Dad, Mary Eliz., Amelia, Celina, 1924

Mae Smith Sohn, Dad, 1906.

William Hays was elected Justice of the Peace on 14 December 1861 and became Notary Public; then, he was commissioned Postmaster and was a member of the school board. A responsible citizen, he was also a member of the election board. His first son,

William Everett, my grandfather was born 19 February 1860 in Camargo, but the town was too small for a high school; accordingly, he completed two years of high school in Newman, Illinois. On 1 March 1879 the superintendent of schools wrote a letter stating that William was qualified to teach, but as the result of unspecified health conditions and a roaming instinct he headed west to Wyoming to try his hand at ranching. "He...enjoyed the outdoor life...his cowboys...the cattle [and] singing the lullabies."(11) After several months his father's store business had increased, and he came home to help. The operation included a general country store—meat, butchering, dry goods, kerosene, farm supplies—and a huckster wagon.

In 1887 at the age of 27, William Everett married Jennie Caroline Peck, age 20. They resided with his parents next to the store. Two years later, they purchased one acre north of town from his father for $50 and built a small house with two rooms and kitchen "lean-to" on the rear. In the spring of 1889, William started a painting and decorating business, but he returned to the general store in partnership with his father. After a fire destroyed the building in 1901, he gave the $1,000 insurance to his father and started his own store in Hindsboro. The family was growing: Mabel, Ernest, Martha, William Roy, and Raymond—five more were to come.

By 1905, William Everett was prosperous and restless; the West was still exciting. He and a friend headed to Southeast Missouri with horses and a covered wagon. William bought 160 acres (cost—$1,320 for 120 acres and $330 for 40 acres), seven miles from Malden, Missouri. He worked for $10 a day blasting stumps to clear land for a drainage ditch. Before he returned for his family, he built a large two-story house on the newly purchased land.

He disposed of his interest in the store in Illinois and loaded the furniture, a horse, and a cow into a box car. The family, including my mother—Ruth Marie, age two—occupied a passenger car and started toward the Mississippi River in 1905. A ferry transported the train across the river, and they continued by rail to their new home on the Missouri prairie.

Shortly after they arrived all the family was involved in clearing the land. In the summer, the children picked cotton and helped with the chores. When school started, during the week, they walked two miles to school. On weekends, the Fulton home became the center for neighborhood social activities; they owned the only organ in the area. Singing bees were a popular diversion in rural America at the turn of century.

Also, at that time, in Missouri wild game was plentiful—deer, squirrel, and panther—and the wild call of the wolf was heard. Although the stay in Missouri was enjoyable, their home was surrounded by swamp and the climate was the cause of the family's health problems. Malaria was common in the Mississippi River Valley and Martha had "brain fever," a form of malaria. Mabel, also, was sick and had her tonsils removed. It cost $10 for a doctor to visit from Malden. Due to these problems the family returned to Hindsboro, Illinois, on Robert's first birthday, 27 March 1907.(12)

In Hindsboro, William Everett purchased a drug and general store on the east side of Main Street, north of the printing office. Shortly thereafter, he moved his business across the street to the Merrill Building and added school supplies and textbooks to the inventory. In 1913 he was elected Justice of the Peace, a position he held for many years.

William became a member of the Democratic Party. (The Sohns were also Democrats. Southern Indiana, in contrast to the rest of the state, was strongly Democratic. Dad voted for every Democratic presidential candidate, including Kennedy.) In 1913, William purchased the Merrill Building and the adjacent house from the Merrill estate.

In 1926, he retired from the store business; one year later, on 27 January 1927 he died from a stroke and was buried in the VanVoorhis Cemetery near his Illinois home.(13)

REFERENCES:

(1) Dr. William Roy Fulton, *THE HISTORY OF THE FULTON FAMILY,* The History of William Fulton and descendants of Fulton Township, Lancaster County and Fawn Township, York County, Pennsylvania, 1952.

(2) William and David's sister, Mary wrote that her father and brothers fought in the Revolution, but a search of the records reveals no evidence to verify her assertion. It is concluded that they fought in the Indian wars.

(3) John Duffy, *The Healers,* (University of Illinois Press, Urbana, and Chicago, 1979), pp. 77–79. The first yellow fever epidemic was in 1793 and cholera didn't occur in epidemic form until 1832.

(4) *Ibid.,* p. 207.

(5) *Ibid.*

(6) *Ibid.*

(7) Madison, *The Indiana Way*, p. 59.

(8) Dr. William Roy Fulton, *William Hays Fulton (1827-1905)* See Appendix.

(9) Dr. William Roy Fulton, *FULTON FAMILY.*

(10) See appendix.

(11) Dr. William Roy Fulton, *FULTON FAMILY.*

(12) Dr. William Roy Fulton, *William Everett Fulton* (1860-1927).

(13) *Ibid*

V—Fulton Genealogy

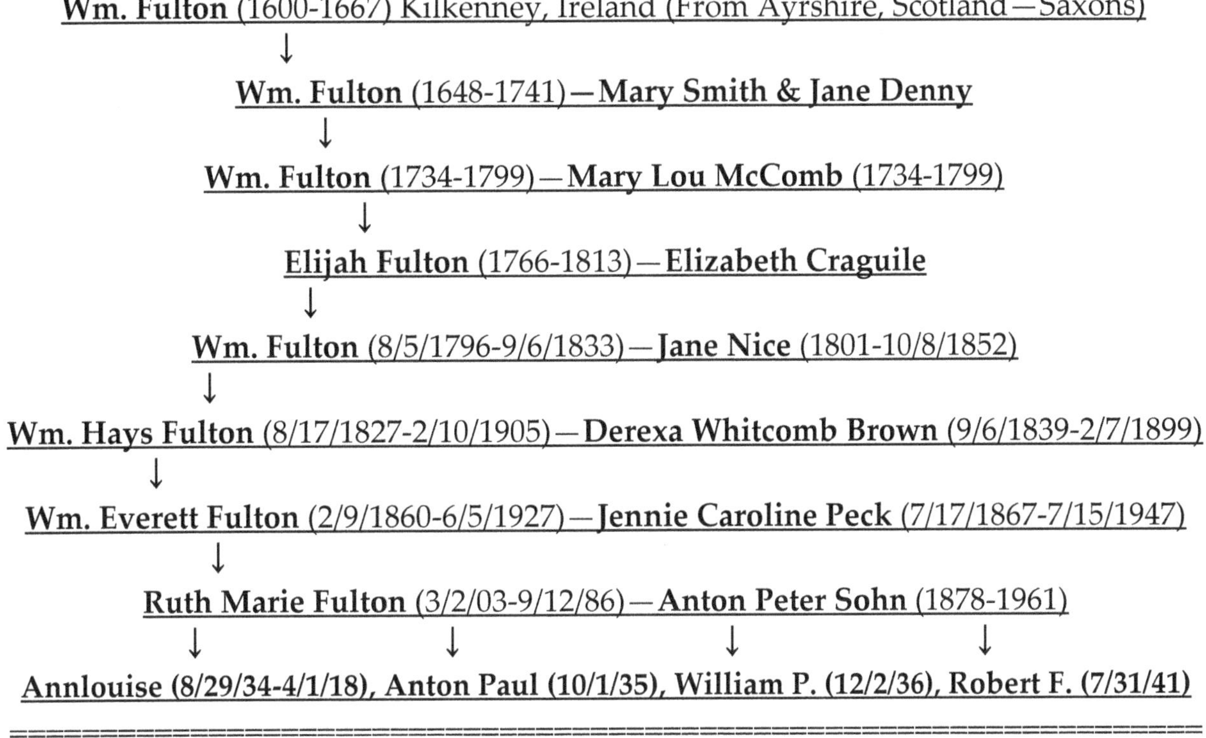

NOTE: Page 22-23 lists etc. Wm. Everett and Jennie Caroline Peck Fulton's ten children and Twenty grandchildren.

VI—Peck History, Across an Ocean, Down a River

William Everett Fulton's future wife and my grandmother, Jennie Caroline Peck, came from the Illinois prairie; earlier, her family had moved west from Pennsylvania and Kentucky. The Pecks came from Germany, probably originally from Poland, and emigrated to America in the 1700s.(1) Records indicate that Daniel Peck was born 15 June 1753 in Stuttgart, Germany. He was a member of the Frontier Rangers in Pennsylvania from 1775 to 1783.(2) He settled near Strausburg (Lancaster County), Pennsylvania, where their first son, Jacob, was born 4 June 1782.

During the western expansion, the family—transporting a feather bed, rocking chair, and blanket chest—joined the Washburnes, Plaucks, Hursts, and Hilligosses to travel down the Susquehanna River to the Ohio River, then, to Maysville, Kentucky. On the evening of their arrival was an Indian attack.

Daniel Peck Sr. settled inland near Flemingsburg (Flemings County), Kentucky, cleared land for a homestead and in 1818 owned slaves and one thousand acres of land. He died on 26 February 1867 and was buried on the Hobson Dudley farm; a stone slab marked the grave. It was a custom in Kentucky to place field stones at the head and foot of a grave and carve the initials or name on the headstone.

After his father's death, Jacob and several of his siblings moved north to Putnam County, Indiana, purchased land and built a house; unfortunately, it burned down in 1938 due to a defective flue. The farm is a mile and half east of Putnamville, Indiana, on the south side of the National Road (Old U.S. Highway 40).

Jacob Peck married Matilda Knight, the daughter of Dr. Lenox Knight, the first doctor in Manhattan (a small village in Putnam County) on 26 March 1808. Matilda died after her thirteenth child, Jacob Knight, Jr. was born on 6 November 1836. In the nineteenth century, childbirth was fraught with many hazards: infection, breech delivery, post-partum hemorrhage, and birth trauma.

According to family tradition, a colored lady named Thomas nursed young Jacob Knight Peck. Unknown to the parents she sedated him with whiskey. When her actions were discovered, she was terminated.

The elder Jacob Peck died 23 March 1857 of typhoid fever. He is buried a half mile east of the family home, on a hill in the Old Bethel Cemetery in Putnam County, several hundred feet north of the National Road.

On 14 January 1858, Jacob Knight Peck married Martha Ann McCarty. Her brother, William Elijah, was the father of Dr. Thomas Lloyd McCarty who settled in Dodge City,

Kansas. "Doc" McCarty was on the way to Denver in 1872 when he was asked to treat a cowboy wounded in a gun fight. The citizens of the town persuaded him to stay in Dodge City. The doctor in the popular television program during the 1960s, *Gunsmoke*, was modeled after him.

Jacob and Martha Peck moved to Bowdre Township, Douglas County, Illinois, and settled on 80 acres on the Scattering Forks Creek. The fifth of their ten children, Jennie Caroline (my grandmother), was born on 17 July 1867.

Jacob built a kiln and constructed the first brick house in Douglas County, Illinois. It burned approximately 15 years ago. The building was a county landmark. My mother obtained a brick from the ruins and brought it to Reno where it rests in my wine cellar.

Jacob Knight Peck (1836-1904)

Fulton Store, Camargo, Ill, 1890

Wm. Hays Fulton (1827-1905)

Fulton Store, Hindsboro, Illinois, ca. 1912

By 1885, 27 years of farm life was enough for the Peck family. They moved to Tuscola, Illinois, and bought a general store. The following year he traded it for a dry goods store and a grocery store. Two years later, he sold the stores and bought a restaurant at Camargo, Illinois. Over the next two years Jacob Knight Peck owned stores, in Newman and Fairlands, Illinois. At the time of his death on 16 January 1904 Jacob was living with his son, William, in Hindsboro.

Fulton family reunion at Christian Park, ca. 1938. *Row 1:* Tom Stanley, Dick Stanley, Annlouise Sohn, Ruth Ann Barker, Jack Barker, William "Sonny" Fulton, Helen Jane Fulton, —. *Row 2:* Madonna and Patty, Ruth and Bill, Helen, Martha, Mabel, Grandma (Fulton) Dixon, Ernie, William, Raymond, Charlie. *Row 3:* Anton Peter and Anton Paul, Elmer, Sol, Grandpa Dixon, Alice, Dove, Raymond's wife, Pearl, Charlie's wife, Polly. *Row 4:* John Kibler, Jenette (Cook) Kibler, Donald, —, —, —, —. *(Courtesy of W. R. Fulton)*

Fulton Reunion, Christian Park, Indpls.., 1938 (Photo Names are not Indexed)

REFERENCES:

(1) See letter dated 12/18/75.

(2) Dr. William Roy Fulton, *THE PECK FAMILY,* 1778 Pa. Archives, 3rd Series, Vol XXIII, Page 207, Lancaster Co. Pa.

VII—Jennie Carolyne Peck Fulton's Life

This was written November 1, 1937, by Jennie Carolyne Peck.

Note: The spelling and grammar are not changed from the original.

Seen the light of day July the 17 1867 year in Duglos Co Bodry town ship Illinois near the ashland school house and the Mont giled church of Jacob Knight Peck and Martha Ann McCarty Peck they both came from Greencastle, Indiana I was born in a log cabin on a farm of 160 acers I had seven brothers and two sisters one sister died one year old and one Brother at three years old his name was Benjamin Smiley My sister name was Anna Mae. My brother names were Franklin Orlando, William Eliga, Charles Abel, Roberthida, Stephen Lafette, Seymours Benjmine Smiley. My sisters were Emmily, Florence, Anna Mae, My father came to Illinois When he Was first maried and bought 160 acers of land Was in timber and hazel brush and watter watter every Where and he drained and tiled the land and cleared the land and built a log cabin on the land I was Born in a log cabin My father improved his farm untill he had one of the best farms in Duglos Co My father always Wanted a Brick house and so he went to mafacuring[?] Brick and built himself a Brick house of eight rooms and Brick smoke house and basement under the Smoke house We had watter runing though the seler all sommer around the milk my it was so coold milk My father was a lover of Bees he built them litle Bee houses and When I was a littl girl he would say tuts you can have your play house in the Bee house he always had a nick name for us children he always Called me tutes I went to school at ashland My father helped build the ashlan school house and furnished the Brick and material to build the school house.

My father bought the eighty 80 acers of land and built the log cabin I was born in then he bought the 80 a cross the road it Was all timber and river ran through the Back end of it that made 160 acers farm he told Mother when he got his first 80 acers payed for now I have got the 80 acres payed for and we will gover and See Mother MCarty and there Sisters and Brothers then when they drove in a big Wagon to Indiana to See My grand Mother MCarty and my aunts and Uncls My father and Mother came back from Indiana My Uncl MCarty said Jacob how would like to by that land a cross the road my father said, O I don't now I have Just got out of det but My Uncl said it is mine land it would be so nice for you and Martha to have it I wont to Sell it to you I will give you plenty time to pay for the land and so my father bought the land and paid for the North 80 acer he called[?] My Uncle MCarty said all I want is som of the timber so you see My uncl MCarty Ws true friend and Uncle of ours.

My grand Mother McCarty lived with our family When I was a little and she would say Jennie Will you bring grand Mother a drink I can remember with that lace Cap she always Ware they she Was a good Woman, and I knew she lived to be an old Woman 83 years old our grand Mother McCarty the Montgiled giled Church was built by my father and othor men of the neighborhood he furnish the Bick and other Material for the Chuch My sistere Ema and Myself would ride horce back to sunday school and Church many time We have Went in the big sled to the school house and Church and My Brother would take me and my sister to parties and appl pealing O how we would peal apples and core them Just Barels of then then we would get to play skip ma lou and old Dan tucker ans all of the party pray till late hour and go home all tired out.

My father bought us a nice side sadle Myself and sister Emma would ride behind me I was 14 years old sister Emma was 7 years old We was getting nicley so my Mother was an invalad for about one year and half I would try to go to school but any day they would come to the school house and say my Mother worce and for me to hurry home then in the year of 1881 October 6 day I was 14 years old When she died and my sister Emily was 7 years old O I was so yung and it looked like evry thing fell on my shoulders to do the cooking and washing My sister Was so much yunger than I was O When my mother Went to heaven it was so dreary a round that home I would go off somewhere and cry I wouldent Want anyone to see me. My father seemed like a different Man after my mother left O it seemed like things went from better to worst for him My little Brother Seymour Was only two and half years old When Mother died, he never was very strong when he was a child I usted to think if Mother could just be sitting there in her rocking chare but she has gon to heaven Where her trobles are no More and parting.

My father raised to orphant boys they lived with us for years there names was george Sharit and John Rittiner they Were like Brothers to me they Worked on the Brick yard I can remember when they drove a too wheled Cart to bring the mud for the Brick Keel I would run to ride with them they would take me up on the seat and I would ride all round with the boys they like Brothers to me When garge growed up he said I will go out and get me som Woark to do it Was not Very long that garge cam back home and said to my father Uncle Jake I have com back I wondered if you Will let me stay I will do anything you Want me to do Cut weeds or anything or wood he would say all right gorge we need som wood for the fire place I have heard My father say when he was a little boy Crackers was raety they w not made very much he would try make them he Would make the dought and rool it and try to make crackers he liked them so well that he never trids to make them a gain.

Charles Abel Peck died Februrary 17 – 1837....

My father farmed for a year or to then he traded his farm for a general store in Tuscola Ill then he mooved his store to Lovington Ill and run the store at Lovingto Ill for a bout too years then he sold out and bought a resturent at Camargo Ill then he went to Newman Ill and Kept a resturent in Newman Ill then after he left Newman Ill and he com to Hindsboro Ill and lived With my brother he Was one of the oldest setlers in Bowdrie town Ship having settle on scatern fork in January 1861 whare he improved a splended farm and recided till untill January 1885.

Jacob Knight Peck was Born November 6, 1836, 5 miles South of greencastle Indiana he was married to Martha Ann January 14, 1868, his Wife was Born in the same neighborhood May 18, 1839, he made his home with his son in Hindsboro Ill except one year With his Daughter at Camargo Ill that was me Elder Reed preached his funeal was at the Brodas Cemetry for Moth and father.

My father was buried at Brodas cemetry bsid My Dear mother wher parting is no more My father was a man with great honesty and was always chartible to evry one.

My father Kept resturent in Camarg Ill and I helped my father in the resturent that was I met William Fulton maried at Newman Ill and maried him May 17, 1887 year We lived With Mother and Father Fulton for that Winter and My husband bought som land and built us a house and then in Febuary 29 1888 leep year I thought I had a litle new house. and pretty baby girl I was well off with golden hair When I was Maried I took my little Brother to live with me and I raised him as my one My husband has laughted about the first time he saw me my father was a directer at the ashland school Mr WE Fulton teached school and he came to my father's house to apply for a school he said I was standing behind the door and wouldent come out from behind the dore but just peeked around the door he said he had thought about me a lot then he said after we Were maried he nowed why he looked for me more and more untill he found me Mr WE Fulton Kept store at Camargo Ill with his father they had the Post Office and miet market the burent down and then Mr WE Fulton bought my sister in law out store in Hindsboro Ill september 1898 year and he Kept that store for several years then sold his store to my Brother Charles Peck then My husband Bought a farm im Missouri[?] near Maldin south eastern Mouossri(?) that was the 17 day of July he built a big house on his farm most of his land was timber land he cleared and did(?) most of the land I liKed the comunity and the people Was good neighbors and good neighbors they all was Went to church You Would think it Was a 4 Jult celebration there so many people at Church but it Was so unhelthy we decided that we would mooved back to Hindsboro Ill and he bought a Drug store and school soply in 1914 the war broke out the World War two of My sons inlisted and marched off to war. Their names Wer Ernest [and] Willian Fulton Raymond wanted to go but his eys was not so good so he could not go William Fulton in listed I joined the Christain Church the 14 day of December and five of My Children faled me to the alter Raymond Ruth Helen Madonna Willian Brother Abner Cox was the pasier of the Church joined the church and was babtisid William Erest(?) Fulton pased a way on the 5 of June 1927 year he Kept store for so many year and Was justed peace for nine years he was Justis of pease when he Died he loved his Children Dearley and alwayis wanted to see then to get a good edication(?) and music and see them started in life he always Wanted to help evry body he could our Children Were by Name at home.

My Children	Born	Died
1. Mabelle Florence Fulton (Howard)	2/29/88	1/1/76
2. Ernest Hays Fulton	5/20/90	12/23/68
3. William Roy Fulton	5/5/95	3/12/97
4. Martha Ester Fulton (Cook)	10/14/92	12/16/75
5. Raymond Vernon Fulton	12/6/96	1/18/87
6. Helen Mae Fulton (Barker)	3/25/99	5/1/93
7. Ruth Marie Fulton (Sohn)	3/2/03	9/12/86
8. Robert Evert Fulton	3/27/06	3/30/82
9. Madonna Luise Fulton (Stanley)	11/17/08	7/15/59
10. Charles Roland Fulton	5/16/11	5/10/73

My children and my husband was all I had to live for. I thought now they are all grown up and doing fine.

Robert and Charles [were] Boy Scouts and Madonna was a Girl Scout.

My Grandchildren	**Born**
1. Jenette Cook Kibler	9/26/14
2. Byron Barker	9/7/21
3. Carolyn Barker	12/23/22
4. Clarence Fulton Barker	6/4/25
5. Jackie Barker	2/27/30
6. Ruthie Barker	9/8/32
7. Donald Howard	5/28/21
8. William Fulton	8/5/33
9. Annlouise Sohn	8/29/34
10. Anton Paul Sohn	10/1/35
11. William Peter Sohn	12/2/36
12. Robert Fulton Sohn	7/31/41
13. Helen Jane Fulton	3/7/34
14. Rovine Edith Fulton	6/19/32
15. Dorothy Jane Widner Fulton	Step granddaughter
16. Tommy Stanley	10/27/31
17. Richard Stanley	11/19/33
18. Patricia Carolyn Stanley	11/28/36
19. Cinda Lou Fulton	11/1947 Born After Jennie C. Fulton died
20. Bob Tom Fulton	1949 Born After Jennie C. Fulton died

I stayed at my daughter's house while they took a trip to Florida. Mr. and Mrs. Anton Sohn and Mr. and Mrs. Elmer Cook went....I stayed with Ruth Sohn's children...(January 28, 1939). This autobiography was typed July 1991 from the original.

VIII—Anton Peter Sohn (My Dad, 1887-1961)

Raised on a River

Anton Peter was born on 12 January 1887 in New Albany, Indiana, a steamboat town on the Ohio River. He attended St. Mary's Catholic school where German was the primary language. Dad's schoolteacher, *Herr Ross,* was strict and in keeping with the times administered corporal punishment. Like most young schoolboys Dad was mischievous, but astute enough to keep a "look out" for *Herr Ross*. My father, recalling his school days, would shout their student warning, *"Heraus, Ross ist gekommen!"*(1) The family was frugal, and money was in short supply. Dad quit school at the age of 11 to go to work.

He was raised in fear of his father. He and his sisters spoke only when recognized at the dinner table because the threat of a backhand was always present. Strick discipline was more common up through the turn of the century than at present. Children were "seen and not heard." Christmas in the Sohn family meant receiving a toy from the previous year with new paint. Christmas morning, oranges and nuts were found in the stockings. It was a tradition for my grandpa to dress up like St. Nicolaus and make an appearance. When the children were bad or had been in trouble—watch out! St. Nicolaus dealt out punishment.

At age eleven, Dad was a water boy on the Monon Railroad making $1.50 per day after school. The money earned was given to his dad, but he was allowed to keep $5 of his last pay and he purchased an overcoat with a velvet collar in Louisville for $4.50. By the age of twelve he had been a helper on a coal oil wagon with Eddie Schmitt, a cousin, at $3 per week and had worked for the Red Fox Tobacco Company.

In 1902, young Anton Peter was a clerk for the J.T. Krementz butcher shop. The store was cold, unheated, and sold fare such as wild duck, rabbit, and quail. By 1905, Dad was working across the Ohio River in Louisville at the Theodore Klare slaughterhouse. The starting pay was $5 per week, later it was increased to $9. During this time, he came down with rheumatic fever. Years later, Dad would say that his heart disease was due to diphtheria.(2) The next job—he ran a grocery for a streetcar conductor—paid the magnificent sum of $12 per week.

Later in 1905, while working in his father's saloon, he had a confrontation with his dad that would change his life. One night he forgot to ice the beer and was jerked out of bed at 4:00 a.m. He made the decision to leave home. His mother, with tears in her eyes, slipped him a $5 gold piece behind her back. He took the Monon excursion train north to Indianapolis where he would spend most of his adult life. The only exception was the seven years he spent on a farm in Jackson County, Indiana.

By 1907, Dad owned his first grocery at 1744 Brookside Avenue. He built up the business and sold it in six months. Then, he bought properties at 1727 and 2134 Northwestern Avenue. From 1908 until 1910, Dad owned a grocery at 1303 Senate Avenue. He bought his first house up the street at 1508. He worked hard and was successful. Money came easily. At Donner's Grove, Illinois, he married Mae Smith, a divorced woman 15 years older who had two boys. Although they were married for over ten years, they had no children. She died in 1919.(5) Her name was never mentioned when I was growing up in Irvington. According to Dad, "It wasn't important." He did pay for her two boys college education.

An incident happened, at that time, that Dad would relate to me more than 40 years later. He was asleep upstairs when he heard someone in the chicken coop. Grabbing his pistol he ran to the window and fired at the fleeing thief. Although he always had a handgun (unloaded) at the store when I was growing up, he said he would never shoot at another person. (He also kept a blackjack, with a wrist loop, given to him by my Uncle Harry Stanley, a detective on the Big Four RR.) Dad related, "What if I killed a man for a chicken." The story ended when the police came on bicycles and captured the thief.

By 1911, Dad had saved enough money to buy Indianapolis Manhattan Theater, on Washington Street, west of Illinois Avenue where the Indiana Theater now stands. The Manhattan was a five-cent nickelodeon with silent movies and a band or piano player hired to provide appropriate sound. On 18 April 1912 the Titanic sank, shortly thereafter the marquee proclaimed: *Extra—Special—Today—Moving Picture Of Steamer—Titanic—Leaving Liverpool—Showing Capt. Smith On Board—Titanic—10 Minutes Before Sailing—Making Inspection And Leaving Dock, Other Interesting Incidents.*(6) Dad recalled how he served as a barker and showed dubbed pictures of championship boxing matches with live improvised music and made "buckets" of nickels.

A favorite activity at the time, Dad recalled, with a twinkle in his eye, was to stand on a corner of Washington Street and watch the ladies get off the streetcar exposing their ankles.

During this period he considered trading his property in Indianapolis for land in Texas. After a long train ride he was shown acres of desolate land; later, oil would be found on the property. The "chance of a lifetime" was gone.

In 1913, Dad moved to Jackson County, Indiana, with $10,000 in his pocket. He decided to try his hand at farming. He purchased the Ed Rodert farm of 120 acres, one-

and one-half miles north of Tampico, Indiana. After six years Dad had enough, "It was the hardest work I ever did, everything was by hand." The farm equipment sold at public auction on 10 August 1920. The announcement stated: "15 head of cattle, 60 head of hogs, 25 head of sheep, 3 head of horses, and implements and misc. articles."(7) The miscellaneous articles included an Overland Touring car and a Continental Truck. Dad traded the farm for 20 acres of land in Indianapolis: ten acres on East Raymond Street and ten acres on West Raymond Street.

He returned to Indianapolis in 1920 with $10,000, the same amount he had when he left. We owned the parcel of land on West Raymond until after Dad died in 1961. It is now part of the Fletcher Industrial Park. The property on East Raymond was lost in his second divorce.

After the wife that "wasn't important" died, Dad married May Shepard in 1921. In 1923 he built a house on East Raymond Street property and two stone pillars, built by Grandpa Sohn, were added at the junction of the drive and the road. Father and son had made up. Years after my grandpa died, we would drive out Raymond Street to view the stone pillars. The interest in the grocery business was still present and Dad bought a store, the Blue Grass Meat Market, at 2402 East Washington Street, near State Street. The next year, his first child, Elizabeth Antonette (Betty), was born.(8) The new family resided at 3816 Bryam and Dad now owned a store at 749 Southeast Street.

During the next four years stores were owned at 917 North New Jersey, 2548 North Capital, and 28th Street & Sherman. In 1926, after the rapid succession of grocery acquisitions, Dad bought *1035 Fletcher Avenue,* the store he owned until he retired. After a bitter divorce, six years later in 1932, he was living behind the store at 1035 in a two–room apartment.

Then, two events occurred that would change his life forever: he met Ruth Marie Fulton and he converted to the *"straight and narrow"* Apostolic faith. In 1933, Anton and Ruth were married in the house where I was raised, 378 South Downey Avenue, purchased in 1931 for $4,000.

REFERENCES:

(1) Lookout Ross is coming.

(2) He died of aortic insufficiency probably due to rheumatic fever that began in 1905.

(3) Information on card given to visitors after 1936.

(4) Hester Anne Hale, Indianapolis: The First Century (Indpls., Marion Co./Indpls. Historical Soc. 1987)

(5) Letter from Ruth Marie Sohn, 11/1/66.

(6) Ind. Historical Soc. and Indpls. Star Magazine 6/4/72.

(7) Public Sale. Having decided to quit farming and relocate to the city, I will offer for sale at Public Auction at my farm known as the Ed Rodert farm, one and one/half miles northeast of Tampico on Tuesday, August 10, 1920, beginning at 10:00 o'clock a.m. the following described property to-wit: 15 Head of Cattle, One full stock Jersey Cow: 7 Fresh Milk Cows, all fresh in June and giving good flow of milk, and all with second or third calves; 4 Yearling Steers, 3 Heifer Calves. 60 Head of Hogs. Consisting of 3 Brood Sows, 2 Sows and 13 pigs; 1 Poland China Male Hog; 40 Head of Shoats weighing from 50 to 110 pounds.

25 Head of Sheep. Ranging from One to Three Years old. 3 Head of Horses. One three-year-old Bay Horse, 161/2 hands high; Brown Horse 8 years old, 15 3/4 hands high; Big Bay Mare, 10 years old and bred; all good workers. Implements and Misc. Articles. One new Manure Spreader, Oliver Sulky Plow, 2 Oliver Walking Plows, Single and double Shovel Plows, Disc Cultivator, Champion Wheat Drill and Binder, Mower, Hoosier Corn Planter, Hay Rake, new Patent Hay Loader; Wood Harrow, Iron Harrow, both practically good as new; good farm wagon, buggy, 2 sets Work Harness, Set of Buggy Harness, Cream Separator, Garden Tools, etc., 400 doz.. Sheaf Oats; 2 fields of Growing Corn; about four dozen Leghorn Hens. Indiana Silo complete, with galvanized Top; one Five Passenger Overland Touring Car, a good family car; one Continental Truck, in good mechanical condition; good Army Saddle. Household Goods consisting of Upright Mahogany Piano, Stove, Heating Stove, Sideboard, Tables, Chairs, Cupboard, Singer Sewing Machine, and Various other articles too numerous to mention.

Terms of Sale

All Sums Under Five Dollars, Cash in Hand On amounts of Five Dollars and Upwards, a credit of Nine Months will be given, purchaser giving bankable note with approved security. Notes to draw eight per cent interest from date if not paid at maturity. Five per cent discount for cash on Sums over Five Dollars.

No Property to be removed until terms of sale are complied with.

Dinner will be served by the Missionary Society.

Refreshments on the ground.

Anton Sohn

J.P. Ahl, Auctioneer Fred Mitchel, clerk

(8) Betty divorced Donald Hooker and moved to Orlando, Fla.

Anton Peter Sohn's Manhattan Theater on W. Washington Street west of Ill. Street, 1911

The Fulton family, about 1918.

Front Row: Martha Charlie, William Everett, Madonna, Jennie Caroline, Mabel.

Back row: Helen Raymond, Ernie, William, Robert, Ruth. (Courtesy of W. R. Fulton)

Anton P. Sohn, Jackson Co. Farm (1913-20) George P. Sohn, Mary Eliz Sohn, 1877

Anton Peter Sohn, Jackson County Farm (1913-20)

Dad, First Communion, 1897

Dad, 1903

Roy Shepard, Betty Sohn Hooker, Dad, 1922

IX— Ruth Marie (Fulton) Sohn (My Mom, 1903-1986)

Raised on the Prairie

Ruth Marie Fulton grew up in Hindsboro, Illinois, with four sisters and five brothers. She, Martha, and William had artistic abilities; her talents were utilized to provide illustrations for the first annual of the Hindsboro Community High School, *The Question Mark,* published in 1921, the year Mom graduated. In addition to being the class treasurer she was the class poet, however according to her notes she had been writing poems since grade school. The first dated poem, *The Poney of the Sophies,* was 1919. The original 1972 Edition of *The Straight and Narrow* contained 36 poems that Ruth M. Fulton Sohn wrote, I have eliminated all but twelve. All of her poems are in *The Straight and Narrow.* 1992.

Dad, Mae Smith Sohn, 1727 NW Ave. Store, 1907

2402 E. Washington Ave. Store, Dad on the right, 1920

THE PONEY OF THE SOPHIES

Here's to the poney in Caesar I know,
Make him go fast, don't let him go slow,
Or the gay little Soph will weary and stew,
And know not exactly what next to do.
Ride him along at a good gate
Or the other sophies will surely be late.
If he is mean and in his pouts
Open the High School door and let him out.

ONLY A TRAMP

He sleeps beneath the sod today,
By the green grass and flowers over the way
No one sobbed or sang over his bier.
Not one eye dropped a tear.

Only a tramp but some mother's son,
Who sees him not coming when the day is done,
With weary eyes she looks from the door
And in the night weeps more and more.

His weary feet shall go no more
Or beg for a cookie from our door
He has gone to his rest under the sod below,
To be covered with the ice and snow.

SPRING

It is come, It is come
With the flowers, Birds, and busy bees' hum,
The sun in its glory looked down on the earth,
And to insects and animals gives birth,
The world again is young,
No more shall snow glimmer with sun,
The sun comes forth a brilliant hue,
And now the grass is fringed with due,

Nature comes out in a coat of green,
The cold dead boughs are ashamed to to be seen,
Robin is singing high up in a tree,
Everywhere we see,
Spring has come.

(WORLD WIDE WAR) WHEN THEY RETURN HOME

Prelude
They are coming home from across the sea.
We'll welcome them, both you and me,
They have won for freedom and for land,
With no thought of greatness grand.

Our Bill went away in February so soon
But as he went out of the door he whistled a tune,
He told us not he was going away,
At the last said he'd return some day.

For a few weeks he stayed at Camp with a sigh
But over in France he heard the baby's cry.
The ship he was on, soon left this shore,
From our beautiful land of ever more.

The next we heard he had landed there,
Mid flowers of France and its cities so rare,
Gladly he went from our happy land
For was he not serving good old Uncle Sam.

Then one day the war was won
There was shouting, singing and sound of drum,
Gladness was in the air,
And brightened the sadness everywhere,
For did we not know it was coming soon
And now they'll return from over the sea,
We'll welcome them, both you and me.

OUR FLAG

Hang that banner in the sky
So it may be seen by Human eye,
Not a foot shall dare to tread it
Furled and fluttered in the sky.

Every patriot has his dream,
Tho sometimes in the mind unseen,
For his country and the Rest
And the great American Flag.

When the nation comes to tears,
Human's longs and Human fears
But when our flag is on high
We shall rejoice from sky to sky.

LILACS

Three lilac bushes stood by the street,
And people hurrying by,
Would often stop and repeat,
Why they stood without scoff, or cry.

Their sweetness floated along
And soothed the tired man's pain,
Filling the air with song
Like suffering plants greet the rain.

A stylish woman hurried past,
And looked at their nodding heads,
For well they remembered her to the last
Of a grey mother calm and dead.

When life's sweet dream is o'er
And Lilacs bloom and last,
In that beautiful land of evermore
Sweet memories of the past.

FRANCE (THE GREAT WORLDWIDE WAR)

Over there they are crying for bread
Sights for the wounded, mourning for the dead
One wee little girl sat on my knee
And told of her father dead over the lea.

We lived in Laonne, father, mother, and me,
As happy as French citizens we could be
Then one day father went
And to his country, his duty he spent.

He never returned but he's over there,
Amid cannons call and war-stricken air,
Mother died soon after and I left alone
With no bread and no home.

The Germans came and took it one day,
Our neighbors were all killed for in heaps they lay.

EVENING

All day long had been a happy one,
From the Dawn of morn to the setting sun
And far to the west was a rosy glow
That lived reflected in the stream below
The evening star came out in the clouds over head,
Like a wee child sleeping in her cozy bed,
And twinkling its eye in the evening dim,
So its sisters and brothers would come out and join him
Silently the sun went down
With its dancing sunbeams and gleam of fun.
The violets closed up and moon flower came out,
And the wind in the trees seemed to sing and shout.
The milkmaid came on the milky way
And so closed the end of a pleasant day.

THE WEDDING OF THE FLOWERS

As I came along the flowers white and red,
Looked to the sun and bowed each lovely head,
The blue bells rang loud and clear,
To unite the lovers to each other so dear
Under a tall tree by the brook
In a nice cool shady nook
Bridals wreath and Dogtooth violet stood up along the way.
So Jack could talk in the pulpit to-day
This great event had come to pass
And no one should arrive the last
The tall stately lily in dress of pure white
The rose and Buttercup in red, yellow so bright
Violet and morning glory had waken up now,
So they should be first to smile and bow.
The Bleeding heart hung so droopy and sad
While all the others were bright and glad
The Honeysuckle furnished food and drink,
Till the moonflower came out to wonder and blink
The happy pair departed on their life
A wondering husband and a peaceful wife.

ON ACCOUNT OF THIS WAR

I think I'm fat, but am thin,
On account of this war we are trying to win
The days get weaker each day
But if I had my say,
This war would end.

Tonight as I sit and write
I begin to think the Germans do fite
Our meat and flour today,
Are beginning to melt away,
On account of this war.

The Ferns and Flowers gay
Are beginning to Dwindle away.
My grandpa has lost his front teeth
Sol he cannot eat beef,
Because of this war.

A DISAPPOINTED LOVER

I am a disappointed lover, I am disappointed too,
I am so much disappointed I don't know what to do
For I've lost my Susy May, I've lost her for good
Because of a coal black cat of ours wouldn't act as it should
Many the time I went courtin my darlin by the sea
Many the time her and I would sit content and see,
Until one day, Oh, sad to say,
The lovin went the other way.

One night when all was still and quiet, glory shone around,
Says I, "I'll go to Susy's house when no one makes a sound."
I waited till the moon went up and stars bumped the sky
Till I could almost see my darlin laugh and hear the snails sigh
I straight way clattered to Susy's house, my knees tremblin along
Until my steps kept hard step to the doggies simple song,
And then our black cat crossed my path, and my heart could hear,
But I tried to get my sudden hope, and loose my awakening fear.

With my head held high I knocked at the door
And the sounds reechoed through the floor,
But my hopes clattered to the ground as her pa stood there.
Says he "What's this would you have?" "Well ahem," I declared,
"Susy May, is she at home?" says I as faint as I would halter,
Says he, "Susy Mays with Jacob Bean in the Parlor."
I took my heels and left as fast as I could run.

AND FELT LIKE SHOOTIN THAT BLACK CAT WITH POPPERS RIFLE GUN?????????????

The next time anywhere I see that Jacob Bean
I'll run him, and bum him till never more he'll be seen.
I'll wring his neck, I'll bite him on the nose,
I'll turn them wrong side out—his clothes.
I'll up and take his feet and throw them high
And grab off his shoes and throw them to the sky.
I'll turn his lights off so that he will say,
He wish that he was going along some other way.

But when I think perhaps it might not be right,
Perhaps it was our black cat, with him I'd better fight.
I'll let him swim in buttermilk, til he turns white or pink,
To let him die or let him cry, in the milky way he sinks
And them if that doesn't work, I'll sim douse him some more
Until for mercy, land, and sakes my pardon he'll implore
And then perhaps he'll be white and not black again.
I'll put him in some sawdust and cage him in a pen.

Then maybe when that is o'er I'll go to Susy and deplore
If she resists I'll capture her and take her off to San Salvador.
We'll live on honey, cake, cream, and pie
For dear poor Susy May I'll live and die.
If Jacob Bean should to us come and roam
I bet I'll pack his boots and send him home
And then perhaps I can see why dear Susy May Mcknig
Wears false teeth and someone else's hair for a wig.

OH GOD HEAR MY PRAYER

Oh God Hear My prayer
Oh God have you forgotten a sinner
Oh God help me down below
Oh God I've tried to do my duty
But yet the North wind blows

Oh God fill my soul with greatness
Oh God send showers from above
Oh God it's hard to do my duty
Without one little speck of love

Oh God my soul is calling
Oh God from this city of pain
Oh God please lift up my being
And make me rejoice again
Oh God you're my only salvation
Oh God though tempest I trust
No matter whatever the cost
A–men "Never say quit"

By the time Ruth graduated from high school, a brother, William, and two sisters, Helen, and Mabelle were living in the Indianapolis area. Also the orientation of people living in Hindsboro was toward the Hoosier capital. Therefore, it was only natural that she apply to the Protestant Deaconess Hospital, a Christian Church institution, located at the corner of Ohio Street and Senate Avenue in Indianapolis.

The first Protestant Deaconess Hospital was established in Kaiserwerth, Germany, in 1836 as an asylum for discharged women prisoners. Florence Nightingale (1823–1910) trained there and her fame for her humanitarian efforts during the Crimean War is well known. The hospitals quickly spread to America, and the Indianapolis hospital was built in 1898. It had 135 beds, including 52 single rooms. The class size was about ten and the course lasted three years, including three months' probation. The 1923 yearbook states, "Young women of good character, health, refinement, and superior education are selected…receive a reasonable monthly salary and uniform cloth, but purchase the textbooks from the hospital. Nurses are allowed six weeks' vacation and are cared for when sick, but such time is made up."

RUTH FULTON LETTER OF ACCEPTANCE CAME JUNE 26,1921:

"Dear Madam—

"Your application for admission to this training school and letters of reference were received—and your application is accepted—The exact date of entry will be given later.

I shall be very glad to answer any questions which arise or if you are in Indianapolis at any time—to have you come to see me—

"If you know of any other young women who are interested in nursing—I shall be glad to send them literature.

"Very truly yours"

LIZZIE L GOEPPINGER R.N.

Supt. of Nurses—

Ruth Fulton recalled when she arrived in town:

I arrived in Indianapolis Aug. 28, 1921, by way of train which broke down...West edge of city and we had to take bus to...Union Station where my sister and brother-in-law were waiting. It was very hot weather. A few weeks later a parade in honor of W. War I was held. The nurses marched in it...on the circle it rained, and we got very wet. A neighbor from my hometown was standing on curb in front of circle and waved at me. Later, I was put on public health nursing and we began walking all over town. I especially remember the old open air street cars where we had to hurry and step up before it went on. Those that run out West Washington went to the ballpark located there before a new one was built on West [16 Street].

A large women's apparel store called Whitman's (My sister, Helen worked here in 1921) was on North Illinois....

Ruth Fulton recounted the long hours, hard work—the mop and pail was part of the training—and hazing that took place. Sometime during the three years the following poem of despondency was written, but the friends she made lasted a lifetime.

Note: On the back of "Oh God Hear My Prayer" she wrote: "My how lonesome I am in this old hospital and yet I wouldn't say quit for anything. I always did say I could do anything anyone else could. I'm going through or die in the attempt."

Ruth Fulton graduated and worked several years for the Marion County Public Health Department and then, did "private duty nursing." This was the usual career path for a graduate nurse in the 1920s. Most hospital were not interested in hiring nurses since they were expensive, and students were easier to control.

In order to provide the most authentic copy of these poems and the journals quoted in this document minimal editing was done. The grammar is essentially as printed. Some of the spelling errors have been corrected. In some instances it was impossible to determine a word or punctuation. I have tried to make this obvious to the reader by the use of brackets. It is also obvious that the original author did not edit the original document. I have not undertaken the task of trying to make the intent of original author clear which may cause some confusion.

Note: While in nursing **Ruth** Fulton took the first of several trips she made before she married my father. Her companions included 16 individuals; two were nursing school friends, Hazel Vandyke, and Mary Whipple.

MY TOUR OUT WEST, AUG. 2, 1930

Miss Hazel Vandyke, Mary Whipple and I left Indianapolis Saturday about noon on the Monon and arrived in Chicago about 4 p.m. The train stopped at Frankfort, and Rossville on the way. Many fields of corn were very nice, but the grass was burnt up. I noticed a huge bunch of purple flowers under a bridge, and a small stone man on a lawn at Delphi. After a hurried luncheon in the station at Chicago we made inquiries and found our excursion booth in the Depot. We were soon on our train with the rest of our party.

1. Marion Lashway	Milwaukee	Bell Telephone
2. Jim Hicks	Elmhurst	Illinois guide
3. Beulah Perry	Detroit	office girl
4. Ruth Fulton	Indianapolis	Nurse
5. Helen Redules	Westville	?
6. Francis Freitick	Chicago, Illinois	Nurse
7. Adeline Lashway	Milwaukee	Bell Telephone
8. Mrs. Lizzie Lashway	Bourbon, Ind	Bell Telephone
9. Mrs. Sarah Lyndell	Detroit	Bell Telephone
10. Miss Camille Kelly	Davenport. Iowa	Office
11. Hazel Vandyke	Indianapolis	Nurse
12. Elsie Schultz	Chicago Hghts.	office
13. Miss Antonia Reimer	Des Moines, Iowa	office
14. Anna Brietwisch	Milwaukee	Bell Telephone
15. Erna Rideout	Hortonville, Wis.	High School teacher
16. Lizzie Zarling	Milwaukee	Bell Telephone
17. Marry Whipple	Indianapolis	Nurse

Another member of our party Emerson Blackburn of Finley, Ohio became tired of so many ladies and left us. We had christened him "The Admiral" because of his superior egotistical airs. He was continuously telling us Yellowstone Park would disappoint us. I don't know why because, on being questioned he had never been there. After leaving Chicago we passed through Elgin, Illinois, where they make such wonderful watches. Evidently they had had lots of rain because everything was green. A jolly little river ran through the town. Dinner in Dinning car.

My first night on the train. I didn't sleep. Aug. 3. Sunday. 6.48. arrived Excelsior Springs, and walked to the Elms Hotel for breakfast. Francis & Helen attended Catholic church afterwards. We walked through the hotel grounds, and I took a drink at the radio–active springs. It had a salty sweet taste. Afterwards we took an interurban to Kansas City. Everything hot and dry. I saw a man washing clothes on the front porch at Independence.

Housing conditions very poor. At the edge of the city we took a bus. At 10 40 we left on the train for Denver. This was a terrible day. Everybody suffered from the heat. Many placed ice-cold towels on their necks. A few played bridge. The observation car had been taken off at Kansas, so we had no place to go. We stopped at Salinas Kansas, went across to a drug store and got ice cream. At 9 pm we stopped at Ellis a small time. Hazel and I took off our hose, and ate ice on the platform by the train. Went to bed at 9 30 and slept fine. During the night we crossed the line into Colorado.

Aug. 4th. Had rained during night; so cool and damp. Wide stretches of country, probably ranches. Small houses, but widely scattered. arrived 7 am. Denver. Headquarters at Cosmopolitan Hotel.

Denver does not contain any frame houses. It would be an ideal place to live. Our hotel was a wonderful place. Hazel, Mary, and I went together. Our room was high up in the rear of the bldg. on the eleventh floor. The food was good. We had a lot of fun over canapes and consomnes. We didn't know what they were so, we always tried the new ones. They generally turned out some kind of funny fish for canape and soup for consommé. The waiters addressed us as Ma–Dam. After breakfast we took a bus trip over the city to Cheesman Park. Here we saw the home of the Mayer, and a millionaire who owns a gold mine. A memorial in honor of Cheesman's wife, is a large indicator of the mountains. It is like a sun dial. Move the indicator and it will point to any peak you want to know. This park comprising 600 acres was given to the city in 1859.

We saw a beautiful lily pond, a museum of Buffalo, birds, elephants and bears etc. Also a duck pond. The flowers were beautiful. Other things of interest were a Presbyterian and St Joseph's Hospital and two Scottish Rite temples.

At 1 pm we took buses to Lookout Mountain 7400 ft. up. This was a very winding narrow trail to Col. Cody (Buffalo Bills) tomb. The school of Mines is located here. There are many fir trees but little vegetation. We looked through our field glasses across many states. Over the grave is a wire netting in which people have thrown small pieces of money. The museum contains many relics of Col. Codys past. Returned to the hotel, and had dinner. We had time to do a little shopping. We couldn't resist the Sears & Roebuck a few blocks away. How we did luxury in baths that night.

Aug. 5th. After breakfast trip to Colorado Springs. Many white, pink, and red flowers, black eyed Susans. The green Country shows either rain or irrigation. Many snow fences large frames 10–12 ft. high and 10 ft. wide in certain places. We saw Palmer Lake. (in honor of senator) 7000 ft. elevation. The railroad gets to 10,000 ft. Saw the elephant rock, Conoco Oil station and U.S. Post office 10,242 ft. Arrived Colorado Springs 10:50, and took a bus trip to 7 Falls, climbed up and tried to find grave of Helen Hunt Jackson. We went through Cheyenne, Wy.

At 2 pm. sight-seeing trip to Pikes Peak. Many kinds of wonderful flowers, Red Indian Paint Brush and blue forget me nots. Copper deposits on rocks and moss growth. Millions of trees are planted here yearly to replace those destroyed. We bought for get me nots at Glencove to be delivered when we came down. This is a stopping place to refill cars etc. Our Bus driver had burned his hand from the steam from the radiator, so he had this attended to. It was 46 Degrees on the Peak and threatening to storm. We saw the mists coming up. A ford truck ahead of us coming down slipped off the road and broke off two wheels. It rained terribly. Sight-seeing trip to Cave of Winds. This is 19 rooms discovered in 1880 by two brothers who crawled into the original opening. Several couples have been married in the bridal room. The old maids kitchen has a large wire netting at one end. It is a common belief if an unmarried woman will place a hairpin on this she will be married within the year. Needless to say we added ours to the fifty billions already there. All the caves were hung with thousands of beautiful crystals. Drank some more mineral water from a huge stone Indian with a Pot in his hand. Our bus took us to Garden of Gods through a hard rain. Easter services are held here every year at sun rise on the table rock. We saw the kissing camels, petrified man, and huge rocks in old kinds of shapes. I bought mamma a daisy necklace made at the Indian school close by.

Aug. 6. Arrived canon city entrance to Royal Gorge with motor trip to top of canyon after breakfast. Many varieties of cactus and much quartz rock. I think I got my biggest thrill here. Three other girls and I climbed a hill above the bridge to an observation tower and looked through a telescope. I saw a farm 120 miles away, a windmill 125 miles and read the cash register across the canyon at a filling station. It said 2¢. The road downward was very bad. How we scringed when the bus backed up over a precipice to go around a corner. Different portions of the mountain were different colors. We saw many caves along the cliffs. The meals at our hotel were not as good as the others. 1 33 pm left Canyon city. The people in this section raise lots of goats. The train stopped at the swinging bridge 10 min. when I took the two top pictures. The other was the train as it rounded curves ahead of us. The river is the Arkansas. Telephone lines were high on the mountains. The men who helped put them there were surely heroes. A wagon road passed along with us thru picturesque natural rock tunnels. Here the train took on another engine to climb a 66 mile incline up Tennessee Pass. We crossed the great Divide during the night. Pikes Peak Highway was made entirely by convict labor.

Buena Vista, Yale, Princeton, and Yale peaks were pointed out to us. We passed a gold mine which produced $100 an hour in 1872. Leadville is the world's highest incorporated city in the world. It contains the highest peak in the Rockies. There were many gardens of beautiful flowers gardens. The mountains were all capped with snow. Redcliffe, Gen Fremonts Fort is the oldest mining town. During the war it produced $20,000,000 of metal a week at Eagle Canyon. The Black iron mask is another mine. I talked with a man and woman who had a summer camp in the mountains who told me many things The people in this section raise lots of lettuce. We caught a glimpse of Utah Lake 22 miles long. It empties into the Jordan River. The Yellow Sego [Sago] Lily is the Utah state flower. Grain fields were found at the foot of the mountains. Passed large dam.

Aug. 7. Arrive Salt Lake City. Sight-seeing drive and visit to Mormon temple. The streets all run 7 blocks to the mile, and all N & S or E & W. The first 160 families divided the lots into 10 acres apiece. The Bishops Bldgs. use 1/10 of income for education and charity. No collection is taken up. Anybody can go to the Latter-Day Saints college or 16 schools. The wall built around the main buildings 13 ft. by 13 ft. of adobe brick then cemented. The temple is 222 ft to spire which is 12 ft high and made of Gold leaf. In one bldg. only good Mormons may go who observe the rites. It is built with cement or mortar at a cost of $4,000,000 from 1846 to 1886. Some of the blocks were hauled 27 miles. An annex with the other bldgs. is a 100 ft tunnel. The Temple does not have a central support and was put together with wooden pegs. We attended the organ recital at 12:00 This organ contains 9000 pipes and was made from native white pine. Three recitals are held daily. An assembly hall annex with radio connections holds the left-over audiences. Centrally located is a monument to Brigham Young, and another to Jim Bridger and Indian Chief Ute. The Beehive house (House of Many Gables) where B.Y. lived is now a boarding schools for girls. The Eagle Gate entrance is near the school where B.Y's 54 children went to school. Brigham Young had 19 wives, 18 Mother-in-law, 3 adopted children and 51 children. He is buried with 3 wives, 1 Mother-in-law and 3 children in a private cemetery. The government refused to allow the rest of them to be buried here.

The State of Utah capitol built in 1913 returned $215,000 of the $3,000,000 put aside for its use. Ensign Peak is near here where the first settlers settled 3 days after entering valley in 1847 and placed the American flag. The capitol has many designs on the wall in natural marble of butterflies, Persian Rug etc.

Governor Room—Rug from Scotland $6000, curtains from France $500 a pair. Table from Russia inlaid with gold $65,000. The museum contained all kinds of minerals and fruits. They raise the world's largest sugar beets because "you can often find 3 policemen on one beat." Maud Adams cradle is here as well as B.Y.'s furniture and some of his wives clothing. A memory grove has been started on the grounds. This is to have a tree with name plate of all Utah's soldiers who fell in the world war, tree for each soldier. Here is Anderson's Folly tower. A man named Anderson that he would build a tower and charge admission for people to go up and see the surrounding country. But after he started it he found out people could go up in the capitol and see it for nothing. The Episcopal church has a girls school here in which no male except the U. S is allowed. The masonic home has been enlarged 3 times. Jack Dempsey's mother lives here in a large brick house. Five leading Denominations have hospitals here. The city has reducing reservoirs for reducing the water force as it come from the mountains. The Univ. of Utah has 18 bldgs. One is being built entirely by students (The bus co. employees students to drive tourists because they are one armed and love to caress the loudspeaker.) School is compulsory 5–18. 80% of taxers are used for education. 150,000 pop of city. 45% of city Mormons, 65% of state. Yale Ave. has good homes. Bankers and Lawyers row is a little crooked and somewhat shady. The Dollar curve is hard to make. B.Y. gave his private estate of 100 acres for a park. This park contains all kinds of trees but fruit, but you may find a green pair under a tree, pick a peach, and get a lemon, pick a date, or find a Jewish pine with little cones on it. The school children of Salt Lake once bought a female elephant which had a little one. But he died because they forgot to put "moth balls in his trunk." Here is an old settlers log cabin and flour mill built in 1847 which was the country home of B. Y. The mill pond was once natural but is now watered by the weeping willows. One tree planted by Jim Bridger is called "The Tourist's Tree" because it is so well trimmed. When the state passed the law against bigamy they built a home for the left-over wives, but only one applied, a widow. To have more than one wife each man must have the consent of the first wife and show he is able to support them. This is the 2nd most beautiful city in the world (of course your hometown is the first). The sea gull was held in great reverence by the settlers. It is said the first crops were threatened to be destroyed by grasshoppers. B,Y, prayed for deliverance and the sea gulls came down and ate up the insects.

2 p.m. Trip to Salt Lake Beach Very desert like with small green headed ducks, small shrubby growth, irrigation ditches. Royal Crystal Salt co. Island like Mt. in center of lake. The lake is 75 miles long, 50 miles wide, 50 ft deep and 22% salt. The bathing pavilion built in 1893 was destroyed by fire 1925. Six of us girls bathed in Salt Lake. Got a bathing suit too small at first. 8 pm. Left Salt Lake via U.P. Ry. At Bear Lake water is stored for 3 years if necessary if water supply from mountains is limited. Lumber camp at Trude.

Aug 8th 7 a.m. arrive West Yellowstone. We had breakfast at the Lodge owned by the railroad. Hazel and I walked around, and I took her picture by the stagecoach. Here we caught our first glimpse of Park souvenirs and real Indians. I took a pansy off of the breakfast table. On assembling our baggage we found Mary's had been thrown so hard the locks were broken. Here the "Admiral" left us. He had decided to go the Hatch way.

The Yellowstone Park established March 1, 1872 by act of congress is the largest and one of the first national parks established. It has been stated that 100 ft from any road one finds wilderness in the same virgin state in which the early settlers found it. The boundaries embrace 3 states. 426 sq. miles of great terraces which eclipse those of New Zealand, more and greater geysers than are found in Iceland, and canyons whose volcanic sides by decomposition of their minerals have taken on the most brilliant and beautiful colored blends. In this area are found great numbers of wild animals which free from molestation have become comparatively fearless.

Probably the first time anyone ever saw its hot springs or geysers was John Colter who left the Lewis Clark Expedition on its return to St. Louis, 1806, and started for the headwaters of the Yellowstone River to trap and hunt. He continued through a country of hot springs and geysers phenomena, down the Yellowstone River and out of a Northeastern corner of what is now the Park. After four years of peril among the Indians he returned in 1810 to St. Louis. His wonderful tales were hard to believe and the place he describe (which was thought to be the product of his imagination) was termed Colters Hell." Jim Bridger. 1823–24. discovered Great Salt Lake. Just when he explored Yellowstone is not known, probably about 1830, but he discovered Two Ocean Pass where Pacific and Atlantic Creeks flow in such a way that water from both passes into both oceans.

TOUR OF YELLOWSTONE PARK

West Yellowstone, Montana to Madison junction 13.5 miles. Christmas Tree Park 2 miles. We passed the Fountain Paint Pots, a mud caldron of boiling fluid in different colors. They have cones that bubble and whisper "plop plop." We stopped here 10 minutes and arrived at Old Faithful 11:15 am.. A geyser is due to water from Lakes or rivers flowing under ground to a low volcanic area, becoming heated in a narrow-twisted vent and erupting when the tube cannot hold the rapidly boiling water. If this twisted vent becomes removed a hot spring results. In the afternoon we took a walking trip with a Ranger to Greater Geysers I would advise others to have rubbers on these trips. I didn't. These small geysers & hot springs are so frequent one must be careful not to walk in one.

Last year a newspaper correspondent (foreign) listening to a guide stepped into one. Of course he was killed instantly, the water being so hot. I believe I was most impressed with the Riverside geyser and the Morning Glory pool. The Riverside is on the east side of the Firehole river, erupts every 6 to 7 hours 100 ft high. It lasts 8 minutes. It is sometimes called The Musical Geyser because it plays "Over the Waves." The Morning Glory Pool is a symmetrical funnel–like crater whose walls and water is beautiful transparent blue. Diameter 23 ft. temp 170 degrees and depth 29 feet. The Grotto is extraordinary on account of its shape. The guide let us all walk close to it and look in the old handkerchief pool in which older tourists washed so lavishly does not function anymore, having become stopped up. Soap caused a film which makes the steam collect and erupt suddenly. There are many other pools and geysers too numerous to mention.

LECTURE ON BEARS AND ANIMALS

That evening at 7 p.m. we went down to the bear feeding grounds to hear a lecture by US Ranger. Noblest among the animals is the Grizzly. He is high shouldered, long limbed, hair brownish or black with a mantle of black and white. There are about 100 of these in the park, and 275 more timid tree climbing black and browns. Large California sea gulls encircled the bears stealing a bite now and then. The rangers live two together in the mountain vastness during the winter to protect the animals. They live 6 months on skies and cover 1500 miles per man, buying their own equipment except skies. This consists partly of 1 steer, 1 hog, and one case of eggs. When they leave their cabin they must know the landmarks for it may be showed 14 ft under when they return. The skies 81/2 ft long, made of Elk hair strips cover 2 miles per hour. In March the patrol is started in the night. 175 miles to count the buffalo and other animals. Its springtime in the Rockies when the blue bird comes to the 6000 ft level. The Elk come to the 3–4000 ft level and the bulls separate from the herd. The young do not follow for 7 days. They are covered with small spots which blends with the scenery. There are 3 antler shedding animals in the park, the Elk, Deer, and Moose. They grow in 31/2 mo. with profuse bleeding. 641 antelope Prong horn are found. Their horns are hollow and shed in the fall. The coyote is a good scavenger. His fur has gone from $5 to $26 in 25 yrs. There are 213 kinds of birds in the park. The osprey or fish hawk is mated for life. In April it builds its nest or repairs its old one. (30 in across) in the top of a pine or on a pinnacle. The female comes 5–6 days after the male. The male sits on the eggs (as big as your wrist) for hrs. They are generally 4 in number. The male always cleans the fish before presenting it to the female. The grizzly is not friendly. When he came running down all the others bears ran away. The black bear is a climber as a cub, the female always going up the tree first. The female has 1–4 cubs who may be black, brown, or tan. They usually hibernate at the 7000 ft level for 5 1/2 mo., pine leaves are eaten with bark before and in summer they come out and eat herbs & berries. The mother bear becomes pregnant in June or July and the cubs are born Jan or February in hibernation. They are blind with no hair and weigh 8–10 ounces. The black lives 14–15 years and the grizzly 20–25 years. One old grizzly Scarface is 25 years old, weighs 1100 lb. His claw is 36 in across, and can break the back of a bull with a slight tap. One took a 700 lb. chest of food from a ranger cabin and broke it to pieces. Yet he is a simple eater of grass, ants, and mice. His seeing is very poor. The Mother carefully teaches the cubs all of the tricks. Scarface does not have any ears. The cubs are weaned at 2 years, the black bear reaches maturity at 3 years, the grizzly at 8 yrs. There are 200 hold up bears in the Park. 8 15 p.m. Listened to Lecture on History of Park at museum.

Aug 9. Saturday. Took another hike much like geyser trip day before in am. My that ranger could walk fast but yours truly and Mary kept up with him. Nature Trail 3 p.m. 1. geyser Daisy–yellow like Dandelion 2. golden Rod white & yellow. 3. Yarrow like Wild Tannsey 4. wild purple aster. Algae causes discharge of Firehole river to be highly colored. Hot water causes dark color and cold light color. 5. Edible Thistle (Everetts a man lost in the mountains once lived on this. 6. Latest Tressics 7. wild Onions (a purple b. Red c white. 8. Rocky Mt Fringed Gention white. 9 Moon Wort Fern 10 Hare or Blue Bell of Scotland 11. Wild Geranium (a white b Red.) 12. Lodge Pole Pine (hangs onto cones 25–30 yrs, female cones pollinated by Sulphur showers 13. Balsam Fir. (Red, Blue berry, flat leaf) 14. Monk Hood 15. Indian Paint Brush 16. Hilo Mint 17. Lichens—algae, fungus a) Thin crust crutose b) Leaf Faloice c) upright Fructose 18. mush room 200 kinds out of 1000 Edible. White Amanita is poisonous Good ones a) color of spores—white, pink and black b) Gills lose to stem c) Ring around stem & cup structure valva 19. buffalo berries 20. Oregon Grape 21. Barberry 22. Lupin Plant Texas Bluebonnet 23. Wolf Plant (fertilizer) 24. Pearly Everlasting–white clusters 25. Ragwort–witches broom caused by Mistletoe or fungus 26. Siberian juniper 27. Fireweed 28. Early Prime Rose. yellow pollinated by moths 29. Dog Bain 5% rubber 30 Wild currents 31.Wild Buckwheat—Yellow, white. It showered in the woods, and we were to wet to live, no fire nothing, couldn't even find our cabin. But we finally did and built a fire. Watched the searchlight play on Old Faithful erupting. Later dancing and singing by girls & boys. I danced once with Mr Hicks Ha! Ha!

Aug. 10 Sunday. Breakfast and church services after wards 1 50 pm Left Old Faithful 2d Trip to West Thumb of Yellowstone Lake. 39.3 mile arrive Lake 5 50 p.m. usual scenery Main feature of Lake many wildflowers. Listened to usual Park history by Ranger that evening. Did not like matron of Dining Room. Balled Lizzie Z out. Camp entertainment good Little southern girl leader very cute. We liked her very much.

Aug 11th Monday. Very quiet place. Hazel and I walked down around Lake (and got a few specimens of wildflower) 11 am Left Yellowstone Lake. We saw the wonderful mud volcanoes on this trip. The mud volcano is 30 ft deep, filled with a lead-colored mass in violent agitation. In 1898 it erupted very violently. The Dragons Mouth spring belches hot clear water and steam As we neared the canyon the buses stopped awhile, and the sun shone for the first and only time. arrived Mammoth 440 p.m. Took hike to top of Mammoth Hot springs. This was my favorite camp. You have probably heard of that song "Rock Candy Mt." I think they must of had this in mind. It was very slick to the top as it had rained during the night, and it took all the breath you had. Contrary to the name "Hot springs" Mammoth is not hot. It just appears that way. In reality the steam is gas from pure calcium carbonate. The algae again is responsible for most of the coloring. More Entertainment that evening.

Aug 12. Another hike to Devils kitchen, a cave lift by an extinct hot spring, Angel Terrace Jupiter Terrace Pulpit Terrace and many other. The superintendent's office is located here. The Buffalo herd is located here. I bought some crystal Beads and again a tourist was well trimmed. We left at 12 30 pm for Canyon Owing to a washed-out bridge much our way was retraced. Frying pan of simmering mud, Twin Lakes Obsidian cliff is a huge place of rocks with tiny pieces of obsidian or volcanic glass Our bus driver gave me a piece. We stopped at Apollinans spring, and I took a drink again. Passed Golden & Lilver gate and the Hoodoos. These are huge boulders of grey and white scattered for miles. Arriving at Canyon stopped near edge and look way down into space from artists Point It is now 3 03 p.m.

Aug. 13 Wednesday. Took Uncle Tom's Trail in morning a gorgeous dangerous spectacle. The steps go down to the bottom of the canyon. It was nice there were places to rest occasionally. A little tiny geyser about the size of a pencil on the very bottom played constantly So many beautiful rocks I wish I could carry up a bushel, but not the way you lose your breath. In the afternoon we took a hike to Inspiration and Artists point. It was very dangerous. There must have been 200 people following the guide, and everybody anxious to get as near the edge as possible. You know people are like that. A little boy did fall over this year, but fortunately in a tree. We saw a cave where the bears hibernated An ospreys nest, and the old boy himself sailing and circling in the air with a fish in his claws The guide said they always did that. Our cabin was on the very edge of the canyon. You could look out and see the bears. Adeline and I followed one around through the camps. He was turning over all of the ash cans. There were quite a few at this camp. How people did love to feed them. But it is dangerous work. They are so apt to forget their claws tare us humans very easily. A mother and her two cubs was very cute. But we could never snap them together. But old Mr Woodchuck and chip monk were not very much afraid. More entertainment in camp. I wonder if their throats don't get tired. Mt. Washburn highest point reached by auto is here 10,346 feet. On 14. Thursday Left Canyon. 9 15 am. for Cody Wyo. 82.2 miles. Forest of Twin trees, Fishing Bridge, Chimney Rock, Elephant Head, Mutilated Hand, Henry Ford Rock, Holy City–Goose, Thousand-foot cliff and many other. The scenery was gorgeous, so many high cliffs and mountains. We made a stop at a little station, and I bought a piece of petrified tree. Frost and Richard ranch, Hollisters Ranch. Top of Shoshone dam. This was a wonderful sight. We got out of the buses and walked down across it. If it weren't for this marvelous storage of water crops could not be used in this part of country I wish to say here that none of the marvelous colors on postal cards is exaggeration. We passed an abandoned Sulphur mine just outside of Cody. The soil all around is yellow and the smell is very distinctly in the air. At the edge of Cody is a marvelous statue of Buffalo Bill with a museum, a replica of his ranch. We did not have time to stop here. Cody Wyo is a very small town. The inhabitants will not allow payment, as they do not want to be modern. The railroad station was quite a little way from town. We ate our dinner here Left. Cody at 7 15 pm.

Aug 15th Enroute homeward through Montana, South Dakota, and Minnesota. The return trip was very uneventful. Once we stopped at little place. The Indians from the reservation were down at the depot, and to collect a little by the way. The old squaws grabbed some of old men and started dancing. The Mississippi River flowed adjacent to our train for hundreds of miles. I saw many water lilies. Beulah Perry told our fortunes I don't see how mine can come true especially part of it. But part did. But that's nothing new. It would be a funny fortune that didn't.

Aug 16. arrived St Paul 8:30 am. Part of our crowd left us. We had been good friends. We stayed here 11/2 hours. Arrived Chicago 8 p.m. and left everybody. Had 4 hrs wait. For passing away time made certain enquiries and result as expected. Train home, tried to sleep bad results. So ends a delightful trip. I only wish everybody who sees this book could take it also.

EDUCATION TOUR, WASHINGTON D.C./ANNAPOLIS

Monday, June 13th [1932]

I left Indianapolis 430 pm with a party of about 44, most of whom came from Points west, consisting of all women except 4 young men. One, Donald Turney a Freshman from

Decatur was a very unusual lad. He wore various metals on his coat. We came through Connersville and ate supper 630 pm. Martha became acquainted with a lady, whose husband works in the Senate Office Bldg. in Washington. She was very well[... and anxious to inform us. We sat for a few moments with her in her pullman. Stopped in Cincinnati 40 min. Martha brought apricots and plums. Slept very little as train stopped often and people in car talked.

Tuesday, June 14th

Breakfast in dinning car. One girl Mrs. Louise Brown of Decatur became very ill, and was put to bed in pullman. West through Chillicothe, Columbus, Parkersburg W. Virg. Clarksburg and Grafton. We saw the Picturesque Harpers Ferry but only a glimpse as we hurried by. The Potomac valley is very fertile with many fruit trees.

We arrived at Washington about ...30 a.m., met by buses and taken to U.S. Capitol Bldg. Cameras were checked at the door. Pictures cannot be taken of government Bldgs.). The interior is decorated on walls and ceilings with beautiful paintings recording the history of the U.S.

One of the painters aged 70 yrs fell from a scaffolding and died a short time later from the results. A statue of Lincoln carved by an 18 yr. old girl stands near the entrance, as well as two busts gifts from France. The House of Senate was in session, and we were privileged to listen about 8 minutes. Norris of Nebraska was the main speaker Also Borah. They were discussing the tariff on cotton. We passed by and had a glimpse of the House of Representatives.

We next entered the hall of fame, formerly the old Senate chamber. Each state is allowed two representatives Illinois has Francis Willard, and James Shields. Indiana had James P Morton and Robert La follete. La folletes statue was so natural it looked as if it could speak. In one spot in the building the acoustics are so good you can hear a whispered word anywhere in the room. In one portion of the Capitol all of the walls, ceiling all painted all over.

We were returned to the buses, and were driven to our Hotel Martinque. We were assigned to a nice room on the second floor with Gayle Heath from Russville, Indiana. A mad rush to get the train dirt off then to lunch.

At 2 pm. we left the Hotel for a 35-mile ride to Annapolis. It was at one time, the Nation's Capital and is one of our oldest cities. Our first stop was made to the Old Capitol Building where Washington resigned his commission as Commander in Chief. I stood in the exact spot where he did it. This painting is also in the Capitol at Washington. Washingtons wife and stepchildren are standing in the balcony. In the building are also found old signatures of old settlers, also samples of coal and ore.

I was very much surprised to see so many colored people everywhere. On inquiring I was told that one third of the population of Washington is colored.

Our next visit was to The U.S. Naval Academy. first entering the crypt of John Paul Jones under the chapel. Coming out of the sunlight into a dark place the tomb was hazy, and you thought you saw a Specter, but this turned out to be only the guardian of the tomb, and old colored man, who looked to be 70 yrs of age. He told us something about it. The tomb ss enclosed by a golden rope as large as your wrist. This is of gold costing $7000 was made by Tiffany in New York. We registered here and were next allowed to inspect the chapel.

The Academy is situated on beautiful Chesapeake Bay. The grounds are beautiful. As you can see in the picture the tennis courts were screened by thousands of lovely roses. We went to a large gym where dozens of "Gobs" were exercising in every way imaginable on bars, trapeze, wooden horses, and ropes. I guess they were used to visitors as they hardly looked up. We were allowed to board a large boat and saw a submarine in the Bay. Martha was much interested in Chesapeake Bay where the Oysters come from. Long ride home. Saw a large hole like a cave inside of hill.

After supper we made a short visit to the Congressional Library. I looked forward to this and was sorry we couldn't stay longer. If I could have seen this as a child my dream of...would be true. The walls were decorated with wonderful paintings. Here is where you inquire about your ancestry, so we went down but obtained very little information as the people in charge didn't care whether they help you or not. It seems like you have to get a paid worker to help you.

We were able to get a glimpse of the Original Declaration of Independence, also the first Bible. There were many other things in the library, but we didn't have time to stay any longer. Home to the Hotel and to bed.

Wednesday, June. 15

8 o clock Breakfast. Jeannette, Martha, and I walked several blocks to a drug store but were afraid of getting lost so hurried back. The buses were waiting for us. Our first stop was the National Academy of Science, a very beautiful place. The first room is nearly vacant of anything except the Foucault Pendulum. This is a large ball suspended from the ceiling over a compass. You can start this ball moving at a certain angle and in so many hours the ball will be moving along a different angle and yet the position of the ball on the dial has been moved. His proves that the earth has moved since the pendulum was first started. The National Research Council holds their meetings here. We also saw a Violet Ray Machine. When the room was darkened our teeth stood out prominent and red in our dresses blazed like gold.

We passed many famous buildings, site of Dolly Madison's home, daughters of the American Revolution and finally stopped at the Pan American Building. The entrance is a Spanish Courtyard or Patio. Here grows a Tapioca tree, alligator pear, banana, and rubber tree. Here also stands the Peace tree dedicated 4–26–10. The balcony contains the flag of every nation whose representative occupies this building when a session is held. One room is for this purpose as well as an elaborate board room nearby with a marvelous oak table and chairs. Other rooms contain products of different countries: Hat industry of Ecuador, Guatemalan textiles, Colombia cigars, an animal (the Secretariat from Guatemala Honduras. A marvelous picture of Washington 1877 by Cadena is on one wall. It has been loaned temporarily from the Red room of the White House. In the rear of the building is a beautiful garden.

Back to our buses. Our next destination was The Washington Monument. Im sorry to say this did not impress me very much, probably because we did not have time to go to the top of it. It arises 555 ft into the air, and is far more the unusual work of masonry than is commonly adjudged.

I'm sure we were all eager to see the Bureau of Printing. Before we could go in Miss Hostetler our lady guide had to have her fingerprints taken because she was responsible for us. Here is made 40–$80,000,000 of bills every day and $60,000,000 of Postage stamps. The money is made from a special paper mfg. in Mass. The backs are made first, requiring 30 days to one bill. going through 52 hands in 15 different processes. Girls sort the sheets (containing 1000 each) with both hands. Any sheet with a slight defect is taken out. The stamps are printed 1/2¢ to 5¢ 100 stamps to sheet 100 to pack. The Olympiad stamp was being printed to go on sale in California tomorrow, the U.S. later.

We passed the Tidal basin and saw the wonderful cherry blossoms of Japan. They bloom in April but never bear fruit. It is a beautiful sight to see them bloom around the water.

The White House does not stand out nearly as much as the other buildings. This may be due to the fact it is an older building started in 1792. Washington died 3 weeks before it was completed. We passed Equestrian square where Jackson is the main figure. We first entered the famous East room where all presidents who die in office must lie in state. Alice Roosevelt's $15,000 Gold leaf piano is here. We were also admitted by special permission to the upper parlors, the Red Room. Blue Room, State Parlor (Purple) Green Room. A life size picture of Grace Coolidge in a red gown on an entrance wall. Leaving the White House we passed up Pennsylvania Ave. 165 ft wide. 98 soldiers can march abreast down this avenue. Left of the White House is Municipal Hall. Washington citizens have no part the government, neither do they vote. We saw the office of Internal Revenue. the Post office,

Harvey's Cafe famous for the first steamed oyster, a statue of Franklin, 10th St. where Booth escaped, the Ford Theatre on N.W. F S Franklin Institute, and the Masonic temple.

12:30 pm, Luncheon was served at this hotel.

At 2 30 pm. The buses took us to the wharf where we were to take the Steamer Charles Macalester for Mt Vernon. I took this picture of a sister ship as we were leaving the dock. On the journey we passed the war college, Tidal basin, and the U.S. Air station, also a tow boat. In due time we came in view of majestic Mt Vernon. A long winding climb of steps leads us to the private cemetery of the Washingtons and the tomb of our country's father. Gen Washington left instructions for the building of his own tomb in his will that it should be built of brick "On the ground which is marked out! His body was moved from a grave in the cemetery to this. Martha's tomb is by his. There are quite a few buried here of that famous family, but we didn't have time to examine them. One of them read, "Jane Charlotte Washington wife of John–Aug 23–1786—Sept 6,1855. We hastened up the path to the house passing first the coach house. The coach inside was built by Peter Mohr. York Pa in 1764, the wash house, smoke house, old kitchen, Butlers house, Gardener's house and into the mansion itself. Here I must say Mt Vernon far surpassed my ideas of what it would be. In turn we viewed the Library, music room, spinning room, family dining room, West Parlor, Banquet Hall, The Master and Mistress bedroom, Mrs. Washingtons sitting room, Nellis Custis room The Lafayette room. One quilt displayed was made by Martha herself. In the museum I saw the Key to the Bastelle. Washingtons Cane, Model of Bastelle, Worsted flowers made by Martha and Nellie Custis dress as a bride. In the house are the fire dogs presented to Washington by Lafayette, Carpet by Louis XVI that looks just like one of ours to–day. Marble Mantel 1785 by Mr Samuel Vaughn of London. We also viewed the servants quarters. They surely didn't think much of birth control because each room had several cradles.

Somewhat reluctantly we left the spacious gardens and mansions back to the bus for a 21 mile drive down the Potomac to Washington. This boulevard recently built was the scene of a strange happening when it first opened. Three tramps stretched a line across the road and charged everybody a toll. As the local authorities could not control a U.S. highway they had to send to Washington for help. By that time the fortune hunters had vanished with many quarters. Our next top was historic Alexandria. Here was the birth of the "First Public School" still standing and used every day. Washington gave 100 lbs for its upkeep. Others of importance are the Old Jefferson Davis Home, Marshall House, Home of Kate Wallen, Old Presbyterian House, Tomb of unknown soldier of Revolution Methodist church 1791 and John Caroyles Home. Here are the homes of Washingtons physicians, Dr. J. Craig Brown and Dr. Dix who bled him at his illness and really caused his death. Here is the home where the tax was put on tea, the birthplace of the "Constitution," a yellow brick the home of Annie Lee daughter of Gen Lee and the Masonic lodge 1783 where Gen Washington was worshfull master. Mary Washington Lewis' home has windows you can see out of, but no one can see in, the home of Lord Fairfax and the father of Gen Lee.

Most important was historic little Christ church. 159 yrs old where Gen Washington and Lee had pews. As there was no stove each family furnished their own heat. Gen Robert E Lee was confirmed here 7–17–53. The church has always had only one light. Washingtons pew was over in the corner next to a window. In the cemetery opposite many people are buried. One reads "Dorothy Harper Uxor departed this life Sept 3, 1800 after an indisposition of 3 yrs 5 mo. and 8 days, aged 70 yrs and 8 mo. More famous homes are Henry Clay, Alexander Hamilton, Robert E. Lee. The Old Alexander Prison still stands with one of its dummies at the windows keeping sentinel through the ages. If you remember your history you know the garrison so enfeebled by loss of soldiers put dummies in the window to make people think they had many left. Here is the Old Howard school for private pupils and a gaunt old brewery now vacant and deserted.

Back to Washington, a beautiful Rose Garden which blooms 8–10 months in year. Farragut's statue made from metal of a ship. The Y.M.C.A. and a very expensive hotel. A storm was coming up. I was glade our boat trip was over. It was just beginning to rain when we got to the hotel.

That night two senators one from Indiana and one from Illinois came to have dinner with our party. Afterwards Martha, Jeannett and I went to the Earle theater and saw Carole Lombard play in "Sinners in the Sun," a pretty good play. There is a good joke on me and my blue dress.

Thursday, June 16th, 8 am. Breakfast at Hotel

9 am Buses called for us and took us for a drive over the residential district. Homes of Daniel & Scott Webster, Mrs. Hausen of Missouri. The French Embassy, Marshall Field's home. We took a trip to the Zoological Gardens, but were unable to see them as they were closed on account of moving. We passed over Rock Creek where Robert Fulton first launched his small boat. Here are found waterfowls of every kind. known to man, also a $1,000,000 Taft memorial. Senator Borah's home, the Siam Legation, Home of Taft, Hoovers old home now occupied by Kien of New jersey, Home of Woodrow Wilson, Legation road, Sheridan Circle, Bridge of Buffaloes (Bumbartons), Georgetown, Home of Dolly Madison, John Howard Payne who wrote Home sweet Home, Robert Todd Lincoln with red brick walls, Washingtons Headquarters where plans for White House were made. Francis Scot Keys $3,000,000 bridge whose house now makes walls for a store, the

observatory where earthquakes are recorded from all over the U. S. Down Military Road where all funerals pass on their way to Arlington, General MacArthur's sunset view Ft Meyer Gen Coats Home, Bachelor's Headquarters An officer in the army is allowed 3 graves for himself, wife and one child in Arlington Cemetery. A common soldier gets one grave, but his wife may be buried on top of his grave. Round graves are known and square unknown soldiers.

Robert E. Lees Home stands in Arlington Cemetery. It is very similar to Mt Vernon. Downstairs are the spinning room, Drawing room, Family Parlor, 2 dining rooms and upstairs Mrs. Lees Room, Lee Boy, Lafayette room later Miss Mary Lee's, Lee girls playroom and extra bed room, In the basement are the wine cellars, wash room. Outside well, summer kitchen, servant quarters and smoke house. Two thousand one hundred and eleven soldiers were buried in Arlington from the battle of Bull Run Sept 1866. Here is the tomb of John Rodgers commander of U.S. Navy who's airplane fell in the war, also a very remarkable man He was born Aug 12–1861 started with quartermaster of navy and passed every rank.

Next was our greatest thrill of all, "The Tomb of the Unknown Soldier." A marvelous Mass of marble and stone costing over $1,000,000. First we passed into the wonderful amphitheater where each year the president of the U.S. give his memorial day address. (Hoover failed to give one this year) Each foreign country is given seats, and every soldier is in full dress uniform. 1600 soldiers are still buried in France in 4 different cemeteries. It is very interesting to know how the body of the unknown soldier was selected. Gen Pershing appointed Lieut. Younger who was cited 27 times for bravery for [t]his honor. Six bodies were taken and studied by a group of men for marks of identification and all but two eliminated. These two were placed in a room, Lieut. Younger was blind–folded and selected the body. Anyone who lost a relative in the war, but was never found is at liberty to think the unknown soldier might be he. The tomb weighs 55 tons, and is built of Vermont Marble buried very deep in French soil. On the stone is this inscription "Here rests in honored Glory an American Soldier known but to god." A soldier is continually on duty here during visiting hrs. He is on 2 hrs. with 4 hrs. relief. He must continually march back and forth 120 steps to the minute. On the front of the tomb is Love, Victory, and Peace. In the world war section of the cemetery a stone is not placed on the grave until 2 years. Robert Todd Lincoln is buried here. Taft is the only president.

We had a brief stop at Lincoln Memorial. They say if you view him from one way he appears to be smiling but I tried it and failed to see anything but his stern countenance as he appears in all our pictures. Beneath his statue is plain statement "In this temple for whom he saved the union, the memory of A Lincoln is enshrined forever."

Luncheon 12: p.m. at Hotel Martinque.

Motor coaches conveyed our party to the Old National Museum or "Smithsonian Institute" where we first spied Colonel Lindberg's famous plane "The Spirit of St Louis Gowns worn by mistress of the White House (Martha Washington, Mary Todd Lincoln purple, Dolly Madison, Edith Roosevelt blue, Mrs. Wilson black, Mrs. Harding white, Grace Cooleridge red,) A gown of pink brocade, worn by Mrs. James Duane at Washingtons inaugural 1789, a large lump of glass, a plate glass melting pot, The Martin glider 1808. Canton Ohio, the Hawks plane which flew across the continent in 1930 in 8 days. We had a glimpse of a model coke plant, and coal mine. also a colliery model. One room contained all kinds of dress material, another sewing machines, a busy beehive, the vacuum pan used by Gail Bordeu in 1853, Different kinds of autos, especially the gas auto 1893–94 built by Elwood Harper at Kokomo, Ind ran 6 or 7 miles. Victoria 1905, Red River boat, Langley Fly, Model of Clarmont 1807 built by Robert Fulton, Wright Aeroplane 1909–10. One room of all kinds of guns, the statue of Freedom Arquittelles worn by Loyall Farrauet 1809 "Cast of Lincolns hands, China fruit Dish of Washington, silver punch set given Lieut. Armestead by city of Baltimore for defense of Ft McHenry Sept 14, 1814. North sea mine used in war (the U. S. had 56,611 mines planted and last the most wonderful of all "The Original Star-Spangled Banner" taken from Ft McHenry Sept. 13–14, 1814 by Lieut. Armestead. It contained 15 stars, 5 red stripes and 4 white. These articles were in the Arts and Industries Building. We also saw the Colonial Pipe Organ of Christ Church.

We next visited the Natural History Building where the skeletons of Extinct monsters are (The Glyptodian 1846, Family Group of Zulu. Kaffiers, Collection of Pianos. Our visit here was so hurried there were many things we did not see, as our buses were to leave at 12o clock for the train. I would like to say a word here as to the history of Smithsonian Institute. James Smithson, an Englishman who had never been in the United States, died June 27, 1829, bequeathing his fortune of $550,000 to this country, to fund an establishment for the increase and diffusion of Knowledge among men and himself chose the title "The Smithsonian Institution." It is private foundation under government guardianship. Other gifts have increased it to $1,600,000. Smithson died at Genoa, Italy June 27, 1829 but his remains were removed on Jan 25, 1904 in crypt to the left of the entrance. If I ever get back to Washington I hope to spend many days in this marvelous place.

Our buses speedily drove us away to the station. The guide pointed out a statue of Mead, China town, Soldier and Sailor monument US. Census bureau and Masonic Life Insurance Building.

And so Fairwell to Washington. I think every citizen if he has a chance should visit this wonderful city so teeming with things of interest. The last glimpse we had was the Baud A. Union station. Left on Fort Pitt Limited.

The country was beautiful. We passed through many tunnels one 3/4 mile on top of the Allegheny mountains and followed the picturesque Youghioghen River 1:46 pm. Martinsburg W. Virg. 3:59 Cumberland, Maryland. 4:50 Sand Patch–top of Mountains–elevation 2249 ft. 6.30 pm Connellsville Pa (got off train a few minutes) West Newton. 8.10 pm arrive in Pittsburgh, Penn. We were able to get off the train here and stay 45 minutes. Walked downtown and everybody hastened to buy souvenirs. and don't think we forgot to get any in Washington at the big 5 and 10¢ just like we do at home. Only I bought a picture in a Drug store in Pittsburgh.

Left on train for Cincinnati. I slept very little that night but was more comfortable with the pillows we had bought. I read a magazine part of the time. Arrived Little Washington Pa at 10 15 pm. talked to a Porter who said he had worked on this train 18 yrs. He gets every 5th night off. Another Washington but this time in Ohio.

Friday June 17th

7.40 a.m. arrive in Cincinnati. Breakfast at Grand Hotel and such wonderful service for breakfast, even if we did have to climb a lot of stars, 9:15 am Left city 11:40 a.m. arrived Indianapolis Indiana after all a pretty good-looking town.

Fairwell to all the nice people we just now are beginning to get acquainted with especially funny little Donald Turney who has enough ambition to go far in this world if he has a chance.

X—GROWING UP IN IRVINGTON

The members of our family were close and our loyalties to the Sohn and Fulton relatives were strong. Our family's problems were not discussed outside of the home, "We solved our own problems." We may disagree with each other but, we always supported each other. When I was growing up, our weekends, our vacations, our holidays, and our going to church, were family activities.

After Mom and Dad were married, Louise, Bill and, I were born in succeeding years. I am sure that three small children, ages 2, 3, and 4 years, was a good enough reason for them to plan a trip to Florida with Louise, Aunt Martha, and Uncle Elmer Cook to relax away from home.

Trip to Florida Through Ky., Tenn., Georgia

Note: The following is from Ruth Marie Sohn's 1939 diary.

First Day, Feb. 14. Left Indianapolis at 620 am after buying 8 gal of gas at filling station corner Ritter and Brookville road. The speedometer said (mile 18451). 910 am at Louisville (mile 18600). Elmer began to drive. We paid 25¢ bridge toll. At Hidden River Ky 1 pm, we ate dinner which we had brought with us. Annalouise became sick with nausea when we stopped to buy gas at Elizabeth, Ky. (mile 18652) Andy took wheel. We stopped at Manchester, Ky. (mile 18828) Elmer drove. At foot of Mt. Eagle near Chattanooga. (mile 18862) Thus far along our journey we had seen baskets along road for sale. And rain all of the way. At (mile 18905) came into Chattanooga a distance of 454 miles. We ate supper at Chattanooga. We saw evidence of cotton fields from Nashville to Chattanooga

Second Day, Feb. 15. (mile 19073) Elmer began to Drive. Sun began to shine, and we felt better. Annalouise still sick with fever at night but felt better today. Stopped at Forsythe Georgia in front of courthouse and ate dinner. Along the way we were surprised to see houses built on stilts and much red ground. Began to see flowers blooming at Atlanta Georgia. (mile 19193) Andy drove. Rain started. We saw peach orchards and plums in bloom. Also pecan trees and turpentine belt. (mile 19284) In Valdosta, Georgia where we stayed all night at the Valdosta House.

Feb. 16, 1939. (mile 19407) Elmer drove. At 830 am came to Florida line. We were surprised at the bleakness of the landscape and lack of vegetation. Andy and Elmer got out of car and examined a turpentine tree. At 11:45 we stopped at Rainbow Falls and took a ride in a glass bottom boat. The day was sunny and clear. We wrapped Louise in a blanket on the boat. It was a beautiful trip. The guide gave us bits of bread which we fed to fish that came up to the boat. They took bread from our hands. We left the falls and arrived in Hancock County. Near Brookville, Florida, we stopped and were thrilled at our first orange grove. The owner, Tom Hancock, came out and obligingly showed us through. He gave us some fruit, and we took several pictures. We left and stopped at our first cabin at Camp Comfort on Nebraska St. We bought groceries for supper and enjoyed ourselves very much.

Feb. 17, 1939. We left our cabin at 745 am and arrived at Tampa. As the state fair was going on we decide to go at 900 am. We were a little disappointed as the fair didn't seem to cover as much acreage as our own fair back home. As this was the last day many exhibits were gone. Dad bought ice cream and a monkey for Annalouise. We left the fair at 1230 and drove around Tampa, down to bay, and started to drive across to Clear Water, but turned around and came back because we didn't want to pay the high Toll. We saw many beautiful flowers. Tampa was first visited by white men in 1528 by Nararez and De Sota in 1539. Tampa Bay was the rendezvous of many pirates. Taking route 79 we left Tampa. At 2 pm we stopped across from a filling station and ate dinner. This road across to Lake Wales was a much deserted one, no houses or filling stations. A ditch or stream followed the road part way. Coming into strawberry country we stopped and bought a qt. for 10¢ from a little girl standing by the road. We ask her name. She said it was Willie. At 430 pm we came to Lake Wales, where the singing Tower is located. It is a very beautiful place, the gigantic tower makes a beautiful pink shadow in the water below. Edward William Bok gave this Singing Tower to the people as a memorial to his beauty loving grandparents. The 60 bells weigh 123,164 lbs. This is the highest point in Florida. That night we stayed at Camp Tower.

Feb. 18, 1939. (mile 19764) We left the Camp at 745 Saturday morning and journeyed on to Melbourne Florida. We read about the Jungle gardens at Vera Beach having Banana trees and so much of interest to see so decided to go there at 930 am. It was interesting, but not quite as magnificent as we expected Perhaps the $1 we paid was a little too much. We ate dinner which we purchased at nearby grocery store. It seemed hard to buy lunch meat which was really fresh. We stayed all night in Melbourne at a really nice cabin with 2 bedrooms, kitchenette and combination dining and living room. Our neighbor in the next cabin gave us a big ocean fish which the men cleaned, and we cooked. Martha has a bad cold now. We drove across the I river on the bridge to get to the ocean. The men took off their shoes and waded into the ocean. They weren't expecting the big waves to wash up so high and got their pants wet. Men were picking up periwinkles which are good to make soup. The man explained to I how these things seem to know where the water is coming in. That night we went downtown to Melbourne and shopped. The stores are scarce and carry little stock. I bought I a doll and Martha looked for a hat.

Feb. 19, 1939. Sunday, 930 am. (mile 19856) Elmer drove. I had heard so much about southern food. I said lets go to a really good place and get dinner We stopped at Port Orange Inn, and did we get stung. One piece chicken, biscuit potatoes unseasoned squash for $2.60–desert and drink separate. I'll never forget that meal. (mile 19863) Stopped at Marine Gardens, a gigantic aquarium of ocean fish. It was worth the $1 apiece we paid to see all kinds of deep-sea fish. We stopped at Posts Camp in St Augustine, the oldest city in U.S.A. I'll never forget Daytona beach we saw this day. Here is a gigantic hard beach where the historic races are held, and cars are tested. You can drive along it for miles. It is a good solid road.

Anton Peter & Ruth Marie Sohn Married at 378 S. Downey Ave. 2/13/33 at 3 pm

Feb. 20, 1939. (mile 20028) Left Posts Camp for journey of town. We would have liked to ride with the Negro driver on his hack, but time was short. We saw bridge of Lion, Oldest House & School in U.S.A. Old Fort San Marco, old city gates, slave market and also Fountain of Youth. Of course we had to take a drink, take a picture of Indian, and saw the old Indian burial ground. Little Andy saw their picture when we came back. He says, "Daddy did the Flies eat all the meat off of them things." It was a most interesting place with its little narrow streets and early settler ruins. At Jacksonville we went to Docks and went through a ship also shopping. We had lunch at Capitol Camp, 30 miles from Jacksonville and stopped at Lumbertown, Georgia for night. A colored boy aerated our cabin. A train ran behind cabins. Not such a good one as we had had earlier but comfortable. It was raining hard, but we went into the little town for supper and a very good one. Martha forgot her aversion to negro cooks. We had corn bread, buttermilk, peas, hominy, potatoes with roast beef, choc. pie; a very good meal. We went into several groceries, and found one named Cook. Andy bought some Georgia Casses (?) and sweet potatoes.

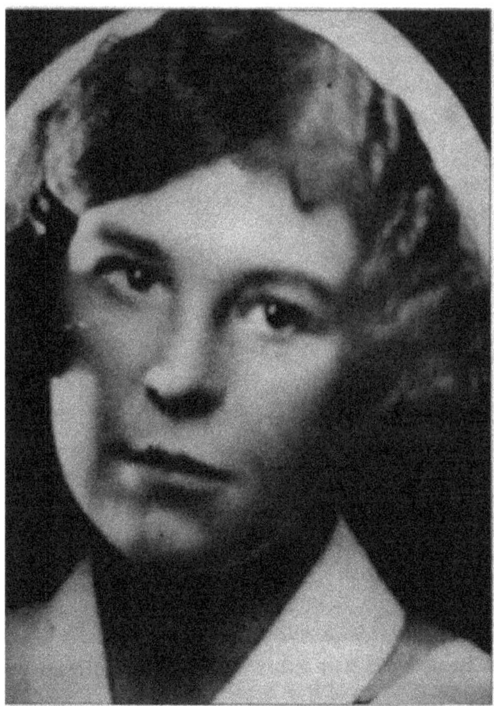

(Left) Ruth Marie Fulton graduated in 1924. *(Courtesy of W. P. Sohn)* *(Below)* 1035 Fletcher Avenue in about 1926. *(Left to right)* --, Anton, Betty, Robert Shepard. *(Courtesy of Betty Hooker)*

Feb. 21, 1939 (mile 20725) We left Lumbertown at 8 am. We stopped at Pecan factory in Helena, Georgia, after passing through Turpentine belts. More rain. The Factory was a nice clean place, but they charged us too much for some pecans. Also bought some pralines. (mile 2039) Elmer drove. We ate dinner at Hampton, Ga., a most sumptuous meal. It consisted of veg. soup, buttermilk, corn bread and crackers, green beans, lima beans, blackeye peas, hash, tomato sauce, slaw, choc. cake and scalloped Potatoes for 50¢. We stayed at Fords Cottage, kept by an old lady who also sold & made bedspreads. We bought 2. We bought groceries and had supper.

(Above) Nurses at Deaconess Hospital, with Ruth Fulton on the left. *(Below)* Deaconess Hospital at Ohio and Capital Streets. (Courtesy of W. P. Sohn)

Feb. 22, 1939. Left Fords cottage. (mile 20450) 630 am. Martha and I bought baby bedspreads. At 10 am back in Chattanooga. We took a guide at Lookout Mountain. It is very interesting because of the battles fought here in Civil war. Scott Trobasco, wealthiest man in town, lived here. There are many unusual rocks, caves, and caverns here. A large expensive hotel is located here. Built for $1,250,000 it sold for $125,000 and finally $65,000.

Charges were $10 a day and no meals. The view is magnificent from the top of Mountain. On clear days you can see 3 states. Lookout Mountain City is here, has its own laws, schools. Back at 1230 pm we had a good dinner at the market house. People have furs for sale along the road. We stopped at Stump, Ky., at Shell Camp a very nice place with bath. We ate at Camp lunchroom.

Mom and APS, Dec. 1935.

APS, Oct. 1936.

Grandma Fulton and APS, 1937.

Left: APS, Louise, Bill, and Dad at 378 S. Downey, 1937.

Feb. 23, 1939. Left Stump, Ky. It had been snowing and we were high in Mountains, some places were a little dizzy. 550 am left. (mile 20744) At Burnside, Ky. (mile 20780) Ate breakfast at combination store and lunchroom ran by a woman. We had a monstrous breakfast of ham, eggs, gravy, biscuits—all we could eat and more. Deliberated whether to go through Blue Grass country. We went to Frankfort, Ky. through museums, and old & new court houses. At 1205. (mile 20945) Going out of Madison, snowing all the time. Upon high places. Home at mile 21041, a total distance of 2590 miles.

XI—SOHN HOME LIFE

In our home, we were encouraged to read. One of my most cherished memories was *Uncle Tom Andy Bill, a Story of Bears and Indian Treasure,* by Charles Major, an Indiana author, read to us by Dad. This story sparked my interest in the outdoors and nature. I lived in the shoes of the frontiersmen, survived the winters and explored the unknown. I was born one hundred years too late to know the American frontier, but I have experienced some of the American wilderness. Today, the outdoors and the study of nature are a favorite activity.

When I was growing up I played in the hills along the Baltimore and Ohio (B&O) Railroad, explored the frozen ponds at three trestles, east of Irvington, where the Pennsylvania RR and B&O crossed, played along Pleasant Run Creek and was drawn to the woods of Indiana. In the summer the outdoors is exciting, but in the winter camping is more challenging. Christmas brings family activities.

Our family celebrated Christmas at home and at church. Santa Claus would come during the night and leave the toys under the tree, erected some days before. During World War II, popcorn on a thread, along with lights and ornaments, decorated the tree that after New Year's, was placed outside for the birds. Dad sold Christmas trees at the store; therefore, we always got the perfect tree. Another tradition, popular at the time, was a wreath with a candle–light bulb placed in the window.

Early Christmas morning my brothers and I would try to sneak pass our parents bed (through their room was the only way to the living room). Dad's arm was always in the way until the whole family could join the excitement. The milk and cookies left for Santa was always gone. He ate the home–made molasses candy we left out. At church, on Christmas, we got oranges and hard candy.

For Christmas and birthdays I received books about Tarzan, the Lone Rider, and other cowboy heroes. Most of my childhood books were destroyed when our home was partially burned in 1959. Mother read extensively and we followed her example. After dinner it was family custom to retire to the living room where Mom and Dad would read the paper, the Bible, or a book.

We also received educational toys as gifts for Christmas, Easter, and our birthdays. Bill was interested in tools and mechanical devices. One Easter, he got a crystal radio to build. I received a chemistry set for Christmas. After bedtime, in the darkness of our room, I mixed zinc and sulfur, lit a match, and luckily only suffered the loss of hair and my eyebrows.

During the cold damp Indiana winter, many a time the "Sunday Car," a Nash, wouldn't start, but the "Dirty Car," Mom's 1920s Ford, always started; a crank never failed to start the Ford. (If one didn't know how to use a crank a broken thumb could result.) We would pile in the back seat under a heavy, blue, velvet "rug" and head to church to celebrate Christ's Birth.

Easter was another special time for our family. Dad always closed the store at noon for two hours on Good Friday for prayer and meditation, but the Easter bunny usually came after church on Easter Sunday. Sometimes, Dad would take us up to the fire station (#25) in Irvington—where a neighbor was a fireman—so Mom could hide the eggs. One time we got a bunny; and it bit Dad's hand resulting in blood poisoning. When the rabbit died we buried it between two walnut trees in the back. Another time we got a small chicken. Usually, we got colored eggs, candy, and small toys.

Birthdays were another family event; friends usually were not included until we were teenagers. When I was about ten years old, a tradition of giving a dime for each year of age was started. We saved the dimes and deposited them in the savings and loan bank in Irvington.

Holidays such as Memorial Day and the Fourth of July were celebrated in New Albany, Indiana, with Dad's relatives or in Arcola, Illinois, with Mom's relatives. Uncle Elmer (Cook) had several farms in Arcola, the prime corn and soybean area of Illinois. His farm animals—sheep, cattle, pigs, horses, and chickens—were an experience. He also had a slaughterhouse where we saw pigs killed with a sledgehammer and cattle slaughtered with a "22"–caliber rifle.

I can vividly recall while lying in bed at Uncle Elmer's, the trains coming across the Illinois prairie during the night. One could hear them for—what seemed like—hours coming to and leaving town. Then, whistling into the night the stillness of the prairie lingered.

When we visited Aunt Amelia in New Albany, we always begged Dad to drive across the bridge high above the Ohio river. We also enjoyed driving past the house in which Dad was born. Also in New Albany, the Kaiser Tobacco Store on the hill above the river presented forbidden habits. I still have the small pipe given to me with Dad's reluctant O.K.

Before Memorial Day, the "500" qualifications were in the news. The time trials were as much fun as going to the race. In our neighborhood—at Jack Master's at the corner of Ritter and Downey—we built a 3′ x 5′ dirt track and raced our small hand-size cars. At one time we placed a bolt in the center of our cement basketball court, behind our house, and raced small carbon dioxide propelled cars on a wire. On Memorial Day we always listened to the race on the radio. Today, we observe this tradition in Reno. Since action is infrequent the race doesn't interrupt other activities.

Family reunions were an event where we got together with our cousins and ate potato salad, baked beans, Cole slaw, soda pop, hot dogs, and watermelon. These "get-togethers" usually took place at Christian Park where there was a wading pool with a fountain. Once or twice we went to Brookside Park.

On Thanksgiving, we traveled to the country, either to Aunt Mabel's at Homeplace, a community she named, near Carmel, Indiana, or to Aunt Helen's in Westfield, Indiana. Her house was small, and it had a big basement that was used as an underground station during the Civil War. Her drive was narrow and went up a hill. At one family reunion Bill and I released the hand brake and took an exciting backwards ride across the highway in the "Sunday Car."

Labor Day meant Dad's store was closed. If we stayed in town we usually went to the Indiana State Fair. The Western States have their rodeos, but they are minor events compared to the crowds of the Indiana State Fair. Dad always enjoyed the animal shows and harness racing. The Indiana pacing or trotting races were the largest in the nation.

In the Midwest, family meals are special and ours were no exception. We didn't eat until everyone was seated. Then, a simple prayer was said, usually by Dad, but sometimes we were asked to say the blessing. We always had something to be thankful for. During the war we had a variety and plenty of food and meat. Hamburger and French fries were becoming a popular meal. We—my brothers and sister—complained because we had steak when our friends were eating hamburger. Pan fried steak—now known as chicken fried steak—cooked by Dad, was the usual Sunday noon meal. It was usually served with mashed potatoes and gravy or fried potatoes. Dad made fun of us kids when we put lots of catsup on our fried potatoes. He used only pepper on his potatoes. Other than at Dad's store, this was the only time Dad cooked. For Sunday morning breakfast, fried apples with biscuits and gravy was a favorite.

Mom was a strong proponent of three "square" meals a day. Usually, before school we had a hot meal consisting of either eggs, oatmeal, cream of wheat, pancakes, or bacon. School was five blocks from our house, and we came home for lunch. Again, a hot item—soup…—was served with sandwiches.

The big meal was the evening meal since Dad was home from his store. The food we sometimes ate was unusual: calf brains, many pork dishes, liver, sauerkraut, and spareribs, but we always had potatoes and meat with the evening meal. Food was never scarce in the Sohn household. During the War the only vegetable I can remember that was scarce was potatoes. Mom tried to convince us that cooked turnips tasted like potatoes. None of us kids agreed with this, and I'm not even sure Dad liked cooked turnips. On the other hand, the only thing he stated a dislike for was fresh tomatoes.

When the war was over, the United Mine Workers of America led by John L. Lewis decided the time was ripe to demand $100 a month for pensions. Negotiations broke down and the miners went out on strike. Coal became scarce therefore, public agencies, schools, and some private industries had to shut down for lack of coal for heat. Dad and Mom made the decision to get a friend to run the store and we took a family vacation to Florida.

In March of 1948 we packed our family into the car and headed south. We stopped in Murphysboro, Tennessee, to visit a friend of Dad's who use to have a grocery in Indianapolis. Breakfast with all the trimmings: steak, gravy, potatoes, biscuits, bacon was the big meal in the South.... One morning, **Dad** went squirrel hunting, so **Bill** and I went with the local boys to a cave where we smoked cigarettes. Our new friends also chewed tobacco, but we were not so adventurous.

Traveling south across the Smokey Mountains, after we left Kentucky, we passed the site of an army bomber crash. Military police were patrolling the highway in the rain and dense fog. Further up the mountain we stopped to see the bears. Bob, who was about four years old, ran between a mother bear and her cubs while we helplessly watched. Luckily, she did not feel threatened. The countryside was in full peach blossom when we travelled through Georgia.

When we got to Melbourne, Florida, we visited Uncle Elmer Cook and Uncle Ernie Fulton, who had winter homes next to each other. Besides being on the East Coast the town had other interesting attractions; nearby, was the training site for a major league baseball team and a field house where the Florida State high school basketball tournament was held. Bill, Cousin John Kibler, and I climbed on the roof to watch the game through the clearstory windows. In the 1940s the Florida tournament was like grade school when compared to Hoosier Hysteria.

After a few days in Melbourne and fishing in the Indian River, we headed south to Key West, Harry Truman's Winter White House. Here, military police were guarding American prisoners when we tried to walk through the ranks. When crossing the Keys, Dad got sick, and Mom had to drive across the seemingly endless bridges. This trip was a rare one–week vacation.

On one other occasion, before I started grade school, we took a vacation to Lake Michigan in 1940. We stayed in a small cabin in the woods. The smell of heating and cooking with kerosene permeated the cabin. The windblown lake and the Northwoods furthered my interest in nature.

XII—Our Neighborhood, Center of our World

The center of our neighborhood was 378 South Downey Avenue. Our home was situated on a large lot—really two lots—(Lot 21 and the East Half of Lot 22 in Ohmer's Subdivision of Lot 36 and 37 in Downey and Ohmer's Woodland Park Addition to Irvington, now a part of Indianapolis, as per plat thereof recorded in Plat Book 14, page 6 in the Office of the Recorder of Marion County, Indiana) which extended from Downey to Burgess Avenue. On the eastside is a one–lane, unpaved, alley.

First recorded as "one- and one-half acre ground" on 22 December 1831 the land had several owners including John and Hester Mary Downey on 7 January 1871 and Nicholas and Jennie Ohmer, 27 May 1871. It was later owned by Rhoda Cunningham 2 August 1906, Harry and Kate Ohmer 15 January 1906, John W. Stroh 12 February 1907, Wellington Downing 26 January 1907, and Lillian Lance Jackson 29 September 1910. Elizabeth Olsen purchased several lots—including 36 and 37—on 23 December 1906. She owned the property until she died 20 April 1929. Some of these names are still associated with the neighborhood as names of streets.

South Bend, Indiana: Anton Paul, Anton Peter, Annlouise, Carrie Rupe and William Peter Sohn. Taken in 1941. *(Courtesy of Mary E. Grantz)*

A mortgage for a sidewalk was recorded 22 May 1914 and for a sanitary sewer 4 March 1929. The house was built with a mortgage for $3,000 in 1915. Four days before Elizabeth died another mortgage for $3,000 was recorded. Dad bought the house and lots for $4,000 from her estate.

The style of our house was common and represented middle–class America. It was one- and one-half stories high with an unfinished basement and front and back porches. During the early years there was a handpump on the back porch to pump gutter run–off out of the cistern. The "soft water" was used to wash hair. In 1959, after the fire, the back porch was incorporated into the kitchen and the cistern was filled with dirt.

The ground floor was about 1,200 square feet and consisted of six rooms, not including the bath, pantry, and porches. Oak hardwood floors were throughout the house and the walls were papered. When Bill and I were older, part of the upstairs was finished with a bedroom and a full bathroom. We slept in a double bed which created an interesting situation when Bill and I had one of our frequent disagreements.

There was a coal chute under the kitchen window, but it was sealed when a gas furnace was installed after WW II. Before then, Dad would let the coal fire burn out during the night. In the morning, we lit the oven and congregated in the kitchen until the furnace heated the house. There was a small wood stove in the basement to burn paper trash. In about 1950 a shower was added in the basement.

The one car garage had a shack—an old chicken coop—added on the rear, so it could accommodate two cars. It became so decrepit that after Dad died Bill had it replaced with a two–car garage.

Mom had a "green thumb" and planted flowers—tulips, roses, lilies, peonies, irises…in the yard, but there were many wildflowers, including, lily of the valley (*Convallaria majalis*)—during the humid Indiana spring the fragrance carried like incense—that grew on the Westside of the house. Violets (*Violaceae* …) were in the back with wild strawberries and blackberries. Behind the playhouse was a large lilac bush where a family of rabbits lived. Honeysuckle (*Lonicera*…) grew on the fence behind the garage; its fragrance became dominate when the lily of the valley receded.

We had a Victory Garden during the War and, after retirement Dad planted a few vegetables, including tomatoes. There was an apricot tree in our backyard. I don't think it ever had fruit before it died.

Our neighbors were typical middle-class: they had great pride in their homes and were either buying or were owners. On the west lived the Kirkhoffs. Mr. Henry Kirkhoff worked for the post office. His son, John, was my age and we were best friends until high school when we formed different friends. Their widowed grandmother, Ida Reid, lived with them. I believe her husband had been a doctor in New Palestine, Indiana. After high school, John tried premed for a year or two; then, he dropped out of college.

Across the alley, on the East, lived the Wickliffes. Mr. Wickliffe drove a tanker truck for a bulk liquid supply company. They moved about the time I started high school. Next to them lived a carpenter-contractor, Luther Hinds. Ms. Martha McBride, an unmarried lady who taught at Washington High School, lived across the street. Her neighbor was Mrs. Emma Flanagan. She was a grouchy person; as a result, the neighborhood kids made life interesting for her at Halloween. Later, after her husband died of Huntington's Chorea, she mellowed and became one of Mom's best friends. Next to her was the Taylor residence, a large two–story house owned by the Christian Church. Frequently, visiting missionaries roomed with the Taylor family. David Taylor was a year younger than me, but we were in the same grade, and we were friends through grade school and high school.

Across the alley, behind the Wickliffes, in a house that fronted on Ritter, lived the Walkers. Mr. Arlie Walker was a shop supervisor at the International Harvester (Now, Navistar). My sister, Louise dated their son, Robert, and they were married on 19 December 1959.

Another neighbor, Sue Amos, Louise's best friend, married Jack Masters. Jack was a good friend although he was a couple of years older. I was an usher in their wedding. They lived in Cincinnati before moving to South Carolina.

Up the street the houses were more spacious, older, and more elegant. They were built before the turn of the century, and some were Victorian. Several had stables and hay lofts, and many were associated with faculty of Butler University. Irvington was a college community with its own culture.

The anatomy of our neighborhood deserves further attention. There was a railroad—the B&O; Downey Avenue where we lived was a curved street, that runs both north and south then, east and west; a major street, Ritter Avenue; the National Highway, Washington Street or U.S. Highway 40; and Brookville Road, U.S. Highway 52. The importance of these roads in the '40s and '50s, was not that they were paths to travel, but they framed the woods, the parks, the natural environment, the buildings, and the schools of the physical world where I grew up.

The B&O Railroad was one of the first nationwide rail system. The track behind our house was a freight line. The only exception to this was during the War when it sometimes carried troops. When this happened, the cry would go out and we would run to wave to the soldiers. Not only were soldiers riding the rails during those years but, tramps were passing through. Several times they would come to our back door and ask for food. They always got something.

Regularly, the switch train brought coal to the Irvington Ice and Coal Company—Judith Cummings' (a school friend) father worked there—across the tracks behind our house. During the summers, the clang of the coal on the powered chutes was a daily rhythm.

The rail approach to the ice company behind our house was up a valley between two hills. This area known, simply, as "The Hills," was a favorite place to play soldiers and wait in ambush. Sometimes, it was necessary to dig "rifle pits" so the engineer couldn't see us.

We became acquainted with the conductors and sometimes, we rode in the caboose, but if we were shooed away, we were not above hoping a car, up the way from the workmen. The inside of the caboose was stark: all wood, with wooden pallets for beds, a wooden booth for eating, and a wood stove. A favorite place was the watch tower where the whole train could be observed.

Across Ritter from the icehouse was the "putty car" house where the two-men hand-propelled railcar was stored. The operators repaired the tracks. On a clear day one could see—down the tracks—all the way downtown. The distance was approximately three miles and we were level with tops of the 300 feet high downtown buildings. Next to "The Hills" was an orchard with three green (Transparent) apple trees and a sour cherry (Montmorency) tree. I spent many hours sitting on a branch tempting—but I never got—the well-known "belly ache" associated with eating too many green apples. Between the trees, the older boys had built a "club house" in which my brother and I, on rare occasion, were permitted.

Further down the rail was the wide-open expanse where Butler University was situated before it moved to North Indianapolis in 1928. Northwestern Christian University moved to Irvington in 1875 after a donation of $50,000 and twenty-five acres from the residents.(1) Two years later the name was changed to Butler in honor of Ovid Butler, the prime benefactor. In the 1940s the campus was in ruins: there were two buildings, twenty–five acres of hills and ruble, and a caved-in well. In one of the brick three story classroom buildings was a small apartment—the rest of the structure was in shambles—where a caretaker and his family lived. They shared the building with hundreds of pigeons. The building was easily accessible, but challenging since the caretaker could be lurking around the corner.

"Egg fights" with pigeon eggs in the attic of the old classroom building, where the dust was a health hazard, were not fun to lose.(2) Most of the time the winner also lost. Tract homes, built on the campus at the end of WW II replaced the brick buildings. The construction sites with the "steam shovels" were almost as much fun as the old ruins. Today, the only remaining building from the Butler days is the Bona Thompson Memorial Library (built in 1902) on the corner of Downey and University Avenues; later, this building became the Mission Building when it was converted into the international headquarters for the missions of the Christian Church.(3)

Lyle Hannah, Dick Wickliff, Ralph Williams, Leo Schiblehut, APS
Shack at 378 S. Downey Ave., 1940

APS, Bill, Uncle Harry Stanley at his Home on English Ave., 1940

Bill. Mom, Bob, Louise, Dad, APS, 1945 (Back Cover)

John Kirkhoff (next-door neighbor), Louise, APS, 378 S. Downey Ave., 1941

We, frequently, played around—and in—the Mission building, a classic Greek, pillared, turn of the century Indiana limestone building. It was especially fun to sneak in the annex and ride the elevator. Two of my supposed friends—named Terhune broke into the building and stole some Chinese or East Indian artifacts. In custody, they had the audacity to claim I was with them. This was one time that I was saved by religion; we were in church the Sunday night of the break-in.

One block from the Mission building—and three blocks from our house—at 5432 University Avenue is the David C. Stephenson mansion, a large, white, Greek–columned house that would have been more appropriate on a plantation in the South. In the 1920s Stephenson was the Grand Dragon of the Indiana Ku Klux Klan, but in addition to "white supremacy," he was interested in life in the fast lane with booze and women. Madge Oberholtzer, an attractive young lady, testified that Stephenson assaulted and raped her in train on the evening of 15 March 1925; then, he held her captive for two days. She took poison and died, but not before giving testimony that sent Stephenson away for a life sentence. He served 25 years in prison and pulled down the governor, Edward L. Jackson, as the result of a disclosed bribe.(4)

During my school years several families lived in the mansion that was divided into apartments. One spacious living quarter was above the garage. We, and most of the neighbors, knew of the sordid history of the Stephenson mansion.

Jack Master's father, Mr. Otis Masters, was a neighborhood hero because he operated the "monster" crane on the Pennsylvania Railroad. In those days, a train wreck was big news, and he would be gone for days lifting engines and cars back on the track. Uncle Harry Stanley also worked for a railroad, the New York Central. On one occasion the Union Station had an open house to show off one of their new locomotives. Uncle Harry was the office in charge of security, and he allowed us to climb up in the cabin of the engine while the other kids marveled.

In the Masters's basement, Jack would show pictures—*The Three Stooges* was popular—on their 32 mm movie projector. He, also, had a hand powered electric magnet from an old telephone. We would stand in a circle holding hands while someone turned the crank to start the electricity. The first one to let go was "chicken."

Jack also had a pair of wood, 8 feet long skis that dated from the war. I think they were army surplus. We would take them to the Hilton U. Brown home at the corner of Emerson and Washington which had one of the longest hills, outside of the golf course, in Irvington.(5) Two or three of us would climb on the skis and head straight down the hill, just stopping on a little rise before busy Washington Street.

When summer rolled around we would head out east, along the B&O Railroad, about one mile, to Speedrome, a midget racetrack. During those years, midget auto racing was almost as big in Indiana as basketball. Certainly, the "500 Mile" Race was always popular, but it only came once a year while the midgets raced every Friday and Saturday night. All of the well-known and successful drivers traveled and raced on the midget circuit. Contrary to what one might think, the night before the "500" most of the name drivers were not relaxing in their rooms, but were "down the road" in a midget race.

In the spring, we, eagerly, awaited the opening of the track and would walk or ride our bikes out to Speedrome midget track. Because the races were in the evening we seldom were permitted to go to a race, but if we were lucky we got in the pits, the afternoon before the race. At the time, the midget cars were the elite, but in later years they were replaced by stock cars and racing wrecks. The last car running was the winner. Out at the track, the smell of the castor oil and fuel was poignant.

Late in the night
    The whine of the engine,
The cheer of the crowd
    The victor took the flag,
Was heard at our house;
    Then,
The rev of the engine died.

Another dangerous business is the brakemen's job of switching railroad cars. Many brakemen have been injured and killed between two boxcars. We also had our near miss with the railroad. One evening after dark, when Dad and I were coming home from the store a switch train pulled out on the main line at Ritter Avenue without tripping the signal. The train pushed us about forty feet—sideways—before it could stop. The cowcatcher hit the passenger side of the "Dirty Car" where I was sitting. The car came to rest against a horizontal rail placed in the ground alongside of the track. No injuries occurred, but there was excitement when I ran the two blocks home and informed Mom. Dad repaired the car and Bill and I drove it until we graduated from high school.

Besides the railroads, the woods in our neighborhood were an integral part of our environment. I have never met a woods or forest I didn't like or one that I wasn't tempted to explore. The natural make-up and beauty of Irvington—and Indiana for that matter—is due to the presence of many native hardwood trees. In front of our house were four magnificent silver maples (*Acer saccharinum*). The largest was about three feet in diameter and the others were about eighteen inches in diameter, just right for a young boy to shinny up.

At the side of our house, directly—20 feet—in front of the garage, was a flowering crabapple tree (*Malus...*). The light pink blossoms were a welcomed harbinger of spring. The location of the tree was a hindrance to basketball and Mom had trouble missing it when backing out of the garage. As a result, the axe was its fate.

There were many black walnut (*Juglans nigra*) trees in our area and in our yard, but we did not use the nuts. They stained the hands and were hard to crack, but the fruit is well–worth the effort. Some years back, I saw that similar trees to those in our yard, two to three feet in diameter, sold for $50,000 a tree.

In the back yard were two catalpa (*Catalpa bignonioides*) trees. They were over three feet in diameter and hard to climb until we drove in railroad spikes, for steps. The branch structure is perfect for building tree houses and suspending chains or ropes for swings. "Indian cigars" up to ten inches in length grow from the branches. (Don't bother to try and smoke them.)

Of all the trees in our area the white oaks (*Quercus…*) were the largest and the most magnificent. One, by our basketball court, was about four feet in diameter. One of the largest and oldest Bur oaks *(Quercus macrocarpa)* in America is on a dedicated public site about four blocks from our house. Estimated to be between 300–400 years–old, the tree, today, is five feet in diameter and it has a crown spread of 123 feet.

We had a weeping willow tree (*Salix alba tristis*), on our property line. Its trunk was easily four feet in diameter. (Extract of the bark of willow trees was used during the Civil War by the South as a substitute for aspirin. (6) It shaded the entire rear of our house, but its roots invaded the basement and the cistern. In addition, falling limbs were a danger to our house and it was finally cut down.

Also, on the property line with the Kirkhoff's were three American elm trees (*Ulmus americana*). Each was about 18 inches in diameter and over 30 feet high. Dutch Elm disease was their fate, and they were removed.

In our neighborhood were two small virgin woods worthy of comment: the largest—about 300 x 300 feet—was on the east side of Ritter Avenue and extended north from the railroad to Burgess Street. In the summer, when the vegetation was full grown, one could see only three feet into the woods from the street. Many small birds and animals lived there, but the only threat to humans—and particularly me—was poison ivy (*Rhus toxicodendron*). There was one well-worn path, used for a short-cut, through the woods and heavy undergrowth. Man cannot let nature alone and, the trees were cut to make room for a housing development.

The other woods—about 125 x 250 feet—was across from our house and belonged to the Stultz Family, who lived in a large house on the property. (The woods has been replaced with a nursing home.) A family of opossums (*Didelphis virginiana*) lived there for a short while; the mother with her babies tried to cross Ritter Avenue and became a casualty of progress—the automobile.

South on Ritter from Downey (approximately four blocks) was State Road #52 known as Brookville Road. Its eventual destination was Cincinnati, but to the southwest was the route to our store and Calvary Tabernacle. On the south of Brookville Road, blocking Ritter, was the International Harvester Company, now known as Navistar. Proceeding west on Brookville Road, one passed the Speedrome midget racetrack and came to Arlington Avenue, out in the country. We rode our bikes south on Arlington to Minnesota Street and the Silver Hills riding stable where for $1 one could ride for an hour.

North on Ritter five blocks was Washington Street and the George W. Julian (#57) grade school. George W. Julian was a prominent Hoosier Republican and radical abolitionist in the mid-nineteenth century when he was elected to the U.S. congress.(7)

He was a proponent of women's rights and later, a Free-Soil candidate for vice-president of the United States.(8)

Although #57 was the most prominent building in the center of Irvington the shopping area along Washington Street was the vital nerve center of the community. Included was Wolman's Drugs, Haag's Drugstore, Woolworth's 5 and 10¢ Store, Danner's Dime Store, the Irving Theater where Jack Masters worked, the Fletcher Trust Bank, the Masonic Lodge, a barber shop, a shoe repair shop, Mr. Bromley's Music Store, Eisenhut's Drugstore, fire–station #25 and the Eastside Chevrolet dealership. In these store we bought our model airplanes, music instruments, sundaes, and other necessary things. The merchants also started a Halloween competition and the contestants painted cartoons in showcard paint on the windows.

All four of us started and finished all eight grades at the corner of Ritter and Washington. Five blocks north was Ellenberger Park where I learned to swim. The tennis courts were clay, like most courts in Indianapolis at that time. Pleasant Run Creek ran through the park; it was the site of hockey in the winter and exploration during the summer.

At the coroner of Ritter and Washington, Uncle William's dentist office—above the Fletcher Trust bank building—was located. He shared a waiting room with Dr. Walter F. Kelly, our family physician. Louise, Bill, Bob, and I were delivered by Dr. Kelly at Saint Francis Hospital in Beech Grove. When we were too sick to go to the office, Dr. Kelly always came to our house, laid on hands, gave a shot, and we got well. When he retired Dr. Frances Shennan bought his practice and treated all of us except Dad who went to "Ole Doc Lewis" whose office was in the Pine Apartments near the store on fletcher Ave.

Since Mom was a Registered Nurse she saw to most of our health needs. Home remedies were utilized in our home and cough syrup was made from onions marinated in sugar on top of the refrigerator. Cod liver oil—constipation was the cause of many ailments—was given in liberal doses. The use of cathartics, "tonics," were used in the spring and fall to help the body adjust to seasonal variation. When the tonics didn't work a wool cloth impregnated with Vick's salve was applied to the chest to treat colds and respiratory infections. When Bill and I had "growing" muscle pains during the night, cloths—with loving kindness—and a little salve were tied around arms and legs.

Uncle William treated all of our dental problems. Each visit meant a lecture on education, pride, or building character; always when he was working in my mouth, and I couldn't reply. Since then, I have observed that all dentists like to talk when they are working in your mouth.

REFERENCES:

(1) Emma Lou Thornbrough, *Indiana in the Civil War Era 1850-1880* (Indiana Historical Society Indianapolis 1989), p. 519.
(2) Histoplasmosis is a fungus disease associated with birds and is indigenous in the middle–west. In medical school I had a positive skin test showing I had been exposed to the fungus.
(3) There is no cornerstone or record of construction. The date was postulated by Steve Busey, head of buildings and grounds when I visited with him in July, 1991.
(4) Madison, *Indiana Through Tradition and Change,* (Indiana Historical Society Indianapolis 1962) p. 68.
(5) Hilton U. Brown was a famous graduate of Butler University, a Phi Delt, and the manager of the Indianapolis News.
(6) F. Terry Hambrecht, *A Medical Purveyor in the Army of the Confederate States of America,* (American Association For The History Of Medicine 1991)
(7) Clifton J. Phillips, *Indiana in Transition 1880-1920,* (Indiana Historical Society Indianapolis 1968), p. 10.
(8) Thornbrough, *Indiana in the Civil War I,* pp. 28, 34, 54, 241.

Bill, APS, 1941

Bill, APS, 1941

1941, Left Anton, Louise, Bill. Bob in cradle used by Governor James Whitcomb, Indiana Governor 1843-1848 (Relative of mother, Ruth Fulton Sohn)

XIII—Dad's Grocery Store

Economic Center of our World

Our lives revolved around the Anton Sohn Grocery at 1035 Fletcher Avenue and our church two blocks up the street on Fletcher Ave. The store was in a nineteenth century frame building without central heating or indoor toilet facilities; a toilet was installed after the war. The store was approximately 25 x 75 feet and comprised one half of the building's ground floor. The other half was a barber shop and a small two–room apartment behind the barber shop. The basement, accessible through the barber shop, was dark and cave–like. Its only purpose was to contain the compressor for the meat cooler. There were two apartments upstairs. One was occupied by a middle–age couple, the Sanders. Mr. Sanders was 90 percent blind, but he got religion and his sight was restored. Behind the building was a shed where the coal for the potbelly stove was stored. It contained other links to early America—the two–hole outdoor toilet—was one. The interior of the building was distinctly pre-twentieth century.

The ceiling of the store was nineteenth century pressed metal. The old gas fixtures were still present—and worked. The well–worn floor was tongue and groove hardwood. In one area were the burlap sacks of dried beans and, in another area were the 100 pounds sacks of sugar waiting to be shoveled into one-, five-, and ten-pound paper sacks. Near the front door were the 100 pounds sacks of potatoes waiting for me to place in paper sacks to sell. Eggs came in crates; pickled pig's feet and pickles were in bulk. Frozen food and ice cream were a thing of the future when a newly purchased used freezer necessitated relocation of the dried beans.

Dad's workday started at 5:00 A.M. when he took the Dirty Car—a 1929 Model A Ford bought by Mom when she was a public health nurse—to the farmer's market. He removed the back seat, and the right front passenger seat was folded up to accommodate the bushels and pecks of vegetables and fruit; the 100 pounds sacks of potatoes were carried on the front fenders.

He would get to the store at 6:00 a.m. During World War II customers would already be waiting to buy lunch meat and other items for their lunch pail. When I helped, my first chore was to unlock the big bread box out front and carry in the fresh doughnuts and bread. The bread box was also a favorite place to play, in the summer, when I was small and not much help in the store.

In the winter, the first chore of the day was to build a fire in the potbelly stove. Since it was located in the back room and there was never enough heat to warm all the way to the front, but it did break the chill and prevent freezing. Several times, the stove got red hot; as a result, the walls were scorched. On really cold Sundays it was necessary to stop and build a fire on the way home from church. During working hours, a sweater or two was necessary.

The back room (18 x 25 feet), in addition to the stove, contained a sink, a built–in table under the window, a stool, and a two–burner gas grill. Above, on the shelf was the blackjack, unloaded pistol and a five–cent box of matches. Dad's big reclining chair, a favorite place to nap was in front of the stove. Boxes of canned goods were also stored in the corner near an old cooler once used to ice meat. Later, an enclosed toilet was mandated by the health department. It was located in the backroom.

When we went home at night the last thing to do was to lock and bar the back door to prevent a "break–in." This didn't always work, but the most that was ever taken was a few cartons of cigarettes and loose change. The cash register was left open during the night to minimize damage during a robbery. Little did the thieves know that there were rolls of coins in a can beneath a brick under the meat block.

Our store was one of a dying breed of neighborhood groceries; supermarkets, mass buying, and advertising would force them out of business. Unions and social security tax would also add economic pressure. Dad did join the butcher's union and social security was a boon; he only paid FICA for a couple of months before retirement at 65. He received benefits until he died at 71. After he died, Mom and Bob, as an underage college student, received benefits for several years. Today, when I complain about my payroll deductions I remember how we were ahead in the early years.

To supply our customers, quarters of meat were delivered from Kingan's, Rath's, and other local slaughterhouses. I learned to butcher and the proper caring and sharpening of knives. To slaughter fowl was another thing. One time, Dad brought home a live chicken for Thanksgiving and killed it by decapitation in the back yard. My phobia for chickens dates to my childhood when a headless chicken chased me in our back yard on Downey Avenue.

In the neighborhood of the store were several old, elegant homes that bespoke of an earlier more affluent community. One such home owned by two retired schoolteacher sisters, named Forsyth, was up the street across from the store on Fletcher. They traded with Dad, and I frequently delivered groceries to them on my bike. Their brother, William Forsyth, was a portrait painter and offered to paint the Sohn children. Unfortunately, Dad did not take him up on the offer. He was a member of the famous Hoosier group of painters, which included J. Ottis Adams, Otto Stark, and Theodore C. Steele. When the sisters died, Dad was instrumental in purchasing the property for Calvary Tabernacle. The house was demolished and replaced with a parking lot.

Toward the end of WW II the public health department was clamping down on owners of old boarding homes in South Indianapolis. One such owner was, Mr. Saunders, a vendor of homemade jelly. His wife sang in the opera. Dad bought two houses from him—for $2,000 to $4,000—that were condemned because the wiring was defective. The most important was at 616 Lexington Avenue—a full two–story, three bath, mid–nineteen century house divided into six apartments that Dad rented out to itinerant workers from Kentucky. After the rewiring, Bill and I spent many hours painting and papering the rooms. On one occasion, I came out of the rooming house to find Dad sitting on the running board of the car where he apparently had blacked out. His heart disease was becoming more obvious. Although Bill and I didn't appreciate working at 616, the income paid for our education. Later, the building was torn down and the property was given to Calvary Tabernacle.

My role, at the store, was to work during the summer and sporadically until the sixth grade. Then, I started working every other day after school. For a while I worked Monday, Wednesday, Friday, and Saturday. Bill worked Tuesday and Thursday. We received, the princely sum of $1 a day and $5 on Saturday. In retrospect, I can see that our help was necessary. Dad's health was not good. His heart disease was sapping his strength. During the 28 years he owned "1035" he did not miss more than a couple of days of work because of health. In about 1950, tonsillitis and a heart murmur were diagnosed; as a result, his tonsils were removed by Dr. Lewis. He would spend more time in the back, in the big chair, with his feet up on the stove or a box to prevent pedal edema.

In the evenings when Dad got home from the store he honked, "whogha!" then we ran out to open the garage. After he was in the house he went to his favorite chair, and we helped pull off the elastic stocking that minimized pedal edema. His varicose veins were the worst I have ever seen. Heart failure was also present; digitalis was prescribed. When I was in medical school I sometimes studied at home. Dad would come up the stairs to talk. It was several minutes before he could get his breath. A chest x–ray revealed that his heart was enlarged—it comprised one half of his chest—and congestive heart failure due to valvular insufficiency was a reality.

In the building next to the store was the Fred Hildewein Bakery where German items were a specialty. My favorite was springerle cookies at Christmas, but more memorable was when Fred would walk out behind the bakery and with a loud voice say, "I have to do all of the worrying. Nobody helps me worry." The Smart sisters bought the bakery and established a beauty shoppe. Next to their shoppe was Joe Krammer drug store and soda fountain. When we bought ice cream treats Dad advised us to buy ice cream rather than popsicles because we got more value for our money. "Popsicles are just frozen water with flavoring."

Ben, the barber next to the store, had a peg leg and for a while lived behind his shop with his wife, Hattie, and son, Jim, who was blind. When we were small we went up to Jim and placed our hands into his; he could tell who we were. They moved out to Speedway and Ben was killed by an auto one night when he stepped off the bus on the way home. Ben, Hattie, and Jim were missed. The next barber was only in business for a short while. We were not surprised when he was sent to prison for robbery. The type of people that visited him raised suspicion.

The Fountain Square was near the store and every Saturday Mom went there to the Fletcher Avenue Bank with the store profits and shopped at the five–and–ten–cent store. As children we looked forward to shopping at the Fountain Square with a real running water fountain where horses were watered in early times. When I was in college, Dad sold the store and took a deserved retirement. The store formed our lives, shaped our values, and helped pay for our education.

XIV—Calvary Tabernacle

Spiritual CENTER of our World

In 1932 my parents converted to the Apostolic faith in a small church on Pleasant street. The following record by my father is his only historic account other than letters and it is fitting that it record religious material. It reads:

"Anton Sohn, and Ruth M. Fulton, were baptized at the Pleasant Street Pentecost Church in December 1932. The assembly then moved in a store building on Prospect St. They married in February of 1933. In the spring of 1934, they bought the Holy Angel Church from the Episcopalians on the corner of Fletcher and Cedar St. which had been vacant. The large house in the rear then rented for $6.00 monthly which was included in the sale. It was painted and services were held that summer. Bro Oscar Hughes was the pastor and lived in the big house. A Brother Duncan held the first revival.

"I had a grocery store at 1035 Fletcher Avenue, and invited many of the customers to come. The first lady to be baptized wept and repented when we talked to her about her soul, in the store. Brother Hughes said, "You must come and be baptized tonight." But she could not come that night. So they baptized her at one o'clock that day, and she received the Holy Ghost in the water.

"Brother Adars was the next person baptized. Brother **Frank Watson** was the Sunday School Superintendent, and Delphan Whitson was Secretary of the Sunday School. Brother Whitson was deacon. Frank Watson was tragically gored to death by a bull on his farm in Brownsburg, Indiana, on Thanksgiving Day, 23 November 1950. At his funeral we learned that he had been a CIA agent during WW II.

"The church voted on the name and became The Fletcher Avenue Pentecost Church. It was dedicated on Labor Day, 1934. Sister Sohn was in the hospital with Annelouise and spoke in tongues at her birth.

"Brother Curts of Cincinnati was to dedicate the new church, but came an hour late."(1)

—Anton Peter Sohn

Later, the congregation moved to 902 Fletcher Avenue. Dad was a founder and charter member. Calvary Tabernacle grew to be one of the largest of the denomination in the country and had as many as 1,200 members. For as long as I can remember he was a deacon and trustee "In these important capacities he was a 'balance wheel' and able advisor on the...official board. His good business judgment was invaluable. For many years he used his grocery business…to express his personal and real convictions about the Lord."(2) Dad said, "The board would spend all of the money, and then spend money they didn't have." He was the conservative vote that stopped excessive spending.

I frequently heard Dad talk to customers in the store about religion. He never deviated from his convictions. Paying tithes—ten percent—was a weekly responsibility. Only once did I hear him swear when he said, "Damn." During my lifetime he never touched alcohol.

Mom was equally fervent in her Pentecostal beliefs. She was in charge of the children's church until she voluntarily retired shortly before she died. The following poem was written by her in 1969 to commemorate Pastor and Mrs. Urshan's twentieth anniversary.

In 1954 I (APS) abandoned the teachings of Calvary Tabernacle as teachings of man and not God.

The Trail of Memories (3)

Twenty years ago from God's throne
There came a Heavenly voice.
Our pastor and his wife heard the call,
And made Calvary Tabernacle their choice.

They preached the gospel around the world.
And sang God's praises far and wide.
Living the life, praying for the sick,
Bro. and Sis. Urshan served side by side.

My Jesus, the steps of their lives
Are ordered by your Holy will.
They are a witness of thy love
Your hands support them still.

The Lord delights to see their ways.
Their virtues are like the doves.
He showers them with his grace
God protects the Urshans whom he loves.

A Heavenly heritage is their life,
Their portion and their fame.
He cares for them, makes them His heirs,
His blessings long forever claim.

And when God's holiest work is done,
These are the ones His face shall see.
As man's soul depends on grace along
They will dwell forever Lord with thee.
—Ruth Sohn

We went to church on Tuesday night, Thursday night, Sunday morning, and Sunday Night—the main service. Since all of the Sohn kids played in the orchestra, another night at church was frequently committed to practice. Revivals were a big thing and our family's attendance stepped up. In high school we could frequently stay home during the week, using homework as an excuse.

During the summer, tent meeting revivals and Bible School were command performances. In the summer of 1951, for one week, Louise and I attended the Illinois District Youth Camp and School of the United Pentecostal Church at Murphysboro, Illinois. Friends were made and we had the best times at the lake. Another summer we attended Bible camp at Buckeye Lake in Ohio. The best times, at this camp, involved sneaking out at night. We hitch–hiked to the local amusement park. In spite of our activities, I was, at that time, really interested in Old Testament, Doctrine, Evangelism, and Christian Conduct, but I was also interested in having a good time.

One summer, the family attended a camp meeting near Lafayette, Indiana, at the Tippecanoe Battleground Memorial on the Wabash River. Without permission, Bob took the "Sunday car" out late during church and rolled it off the road in a ditch. Dad drove the car home with the roof caved in. I also got in trouble because I climbed on one of the monuments at the battleground and was caught by the caretaker.

As a result of my religious upbringing, I had never tasted alcohol until midway through college, but experimenting with smoking was another thing. On one occasion, Dad, realizing my lack of interest in church, made a plea, "Whatever you do, go to some church." He further emphasized, "The Catholic faith was acceptable." The Apostolic church was strict, its members weren't allowed to attend movies, go to dances, or do other disapproved things. Our parents were more liberal. We did go to dances and had many nonchurch friends.

Many a time, I heard Dad say that there are good and bad people, both in and out of the church. Religion was personal to him, but he didn't have blinders on and believe everything that was said in God's name

REFERENCES:

(1) The Voice of Calvary Tabernacle, Vol. 21, Nov.'69, No.11.
(2) The Voice of Calvary Tabernacle, Vol. 16, Nov.'61, No.11.
(3) *Ibid*

XV—World War II, Threat to our World

World War II was in full swing when I started the first grade. Air raid alerts were routine. When the alarm sounded, we went to the school basement and gathered under the tables in the lunchroom. We were too young to go to war, but we had three relatives in the war: Uncle Charlie (Fulton) and two cousins fought in the European Theater. Two came home; a cousin—by marriage to Jenette Cook—John Kibler, lost 8 July 1943 during a bombing mission over Austria, didn't. Mom received tissue paper thin, censored, "air mail" letters from her brother and nephew. Military service was a continuation of a family tradition started in the 1700s: "right or wrong, when our country calls, we respond." We may question, but we respond.

Food and gasoline rationing brought the war closer to home. We were allowed more gas than some families because the grocery business was considered vital. A sticker with three by four-inch letters was affixed to the car windshield to indicate our allotted amount of gas. One evening a week we glued the food coupons, collected at the store, in books for the Office of Price Administration (OPA). Meat and certain canned foods were scarce. Tobacco was prized and sometimes hard to get. Food rationing of some items used in the war was necessary. We did our part in the war effort by buying war bonds. A $25 bond cost $18.75. Mom and Dad helped all of us buy bonds that we cashed in after they reached maturity. It was a sign of our maturity to take the cash to bank and sign on the dotted line.

For me, the greatest World War II events were the parades. The Man who drove the Yum-Yum Bread Truck to the store, was a fireman in the Indiana National Guard. He steered the rear wheels of the gigantic fire–engine in the parade. Stout Field, the National Guard home base was near our farm on West Raymond. Whenever Dad drove out to check up on the farm, we always begged to go by Stout Field to watch the military planes take off and land. Those days were exciting. Once, Bob wondered off, during a parade in downtown Indianapolis and ended up in the police station.

Life was good to the Sohn family during the War. We, including Mom, worked long hours, but profits at the store were strong. Dad said that he made money "hand over fist" because customers would buy everything. It became necessary to hire a girl to "live in" and babysit. Several girls came and went before Carrie Rupe was hired.

Jenette, "Carrie" Rupe was fresh out of Kentucky when she came to stay at the Sohns. Life was tough in the foothills of the Smokey Mountains. Shoes were foreign and the use of tobacco was a habit even for children. Life had to be better in the North. Dad recalled,

"We took Carrie home to visit her family, the cabin was up a hollow without roads." Carrie married Joseph Rupe (in our home), converted to the Pentecostal faith, divorced Joe, had a kidney removed with tuberculosis, and still called me "Bubbie" after I graduated from medical school. Carrie was part of the family. She entertained us with songs such as, *"When The Hearse Comes To Take You Away."*

All of the Sohn children helped with the chores. I hated doing the dishes, wash one night, dry the next. Another dreaded activity was to be sent to Saturday daycare school, located near the store, in the basement of a grade school on State Street so Mom could work at the store. (My military service in Vietnam was more fun.) Bill and I were about the same size. Some thought we were twins because Mom dressed us alike. The worst experience involved the wool army uniforms—including wool shirt—we had to wear. I still itch when I think about it. We managed to survive by wearing our pajamas under our fighting clothes.

The most exciting thing to come during the war was a new baby brother, Robert Fulton, born 1941. We met him for the first time on the front (living) room couch. He was different. He had brown eyes, a Fulton inheritance. Bill and I loved to let Bob know, years later (in jest) that he was a Fulton. In stature, he was a Sohn, the only one in our immediate family over six feet tall. When Mom was in labor in the hospital, Louise and Bill were farmed out to relatives, but I stayed with Dad and went to the store every day. This was the first time I ate out. Every night, we ate at the Big Four Grill on Shelby Street by the Big Four roundhouse.(1)

REFERENCE:

(1) The Big Four Railroad is the New York Central Railroad

XVI—Annlouise Sohn (In Her Words, 1992)

"I was born on Wednesday, August 29, 1934, at 3:00 p.m. at St. Francis Hospital attended by Dr. Kelly. My mother said I was a beautiful baby, although I think she was influenced by my father to whom I was always close. I was named Annlouise Coral Sohn and there still is a lot of discussion about whom I was named after. My mother and father took me to the Pleasant Street Pentecost Church and all the people would turn around and look when we arrived. The Sunday school teacher would stop and tell everyone to look at the baby so they could get back to the lesson.

"My first memories were about kindergarten when I was five years old. The school was in at a two-story yellow house at the corner of Arlington and Washington Streets. Many of the friends there were, also, my classmates in grade school and in high school. The attic was a scary place and we thought it was haunted. We went to kindergarten in a carpool although it wasn't called that then.

"A surprise party was given for my sixth birthday. Friends were invited from my Sunday School class at Calvary Tabernacle and from the neighborhood. The party was in the attic and balloons and suckers were hung from the ceiling with a teepee in the corner of the room. We played Pin the Tail on the Donkey and fished for prizes which were tied on a fishing pole.

"In about the first grade, at Grade School #57, my good friend, Sue Amos, lived across the alley and walked to school with me. Our route was straight down Ritter in the morning, home at noon, back after lunch, and home at 3:00 p.m. It was one half mile each way and was a 15-minute walk. One time after school, Sue and I decided to go home around Downey with another friend. I was late getting home, and mother was very upset. The next day I had to stand in the front of the room and the first-grade teacher, Miss Kantz, talked to me quite severely. Needless to say, I went straight home after that.

"We went home during the lunch hour and usually ate sandwiches and soup. Mother listened to *My Girl Sunday* or *Stella Dallas* on the radio. Billy and Bubby teased Bobby and picked fights with each other. Monday was wash day and Mother did the washing in the machine with the wringer. She did the ironing on the mangle on Tuesday, and it was fun to see her do the shirts—a skill I never managed.

"Bobby was born when I was 7 years old. I called him Uggie and was especially close to him. Until he was about 5 years old, he loved to come into my bedroom and get in bed with me. I don't remember too much when he was a baby, but I probably helped take care of him. I remember Billy constantly teasing him.

“Other school memories include going to the Brown Library which was in a two-story house next to the school. The children's section was upstairs, and I would get books every week. The first book I read was about a cat. I always looked forward to the summer reading club and my special friends were Nancy Drew and Polly Anna, among others.

“During World War II the War Bond drives were a part of school memories. We went to the school auditorium and bought stamps to put in books. When the book was full, were received a bond. We collected newspapers for paper sales and tin cans although I don't remember the particulars. I was an office messenger during my junior high days and rang the chimes for class breaks. I sang in a girls ensemble, and we went to Miss Winder's house after school to practice. We sang for clubs and church functions that she arranged.

“I was a brownie and girl scout and sold girl scout cookies and worked for badges although I dropped out after junior scouts. I took piano lessons at a house on Ritter Avenue and would stop there on my way home from school.

“Social activities were lots of fun during my junior high days. We had parties at different friend's houses and played Spin the Milk Bottle and Post Office. I had the usual crushes on many of my classmates and it seems many of them were named David. My social group was the "in group” so junior high was fun. Stephen Shirley was a member of our group, and his family owned the Shirley Brother’s Funeral Home in Irvington. One friend who had a heart condition died in sixth grade which was a shock to all of us. When we went to the viewing Steve took us on a tour of the funeral home, an experience I haven't forgotten.

“My childhood was happy and filled with memories playing with Sue. Dad bought a playhouse where we played dolls and had tea parties. The furnishings included a table, chairs, a doll bed, and curtains at the windows. We had a swing set in the back yard, and it was fun for me to hang by my feet and do summersaults. We made mud pies and swung on a tire tied to a tree by the blackberry bushes. Games such as kick the can, red light and green light and hide and seek were played with Bubby and Billy and our neighborhood friends. We rode our bicycles and skated on the sidewalks up and down Downey Avenue. On Saturday's we went to Jack Master's house and watched movies in his basement. You always had to have a ticket.

“I had another friend, Justine Collins who went to a Catholic school. She lived a block away in a big house. We played dolls at her house and games in her back yard. Her parents were older, and she had older brothers and a sister which was different.

Church was an important part of our lives, and we went to Sunday School and church plus Bible study on Thursday night. Dad was the church treasurer so many of our friends were church friends. On Sunday mornings we always had a big breakfast of eggs and fried potatoes or fried apples, bacon, and bread. We went to church in the Sunday car, a Lafayette Nash, which Dad seemed to favor. Sunday dinner was usually steak and mashed potatoes or sometimes fried chicken. Dad would bring home produce that didn't sell for Mother to can. Sometimes I got to help. I learned how to weigh produce, sack sugar and dry beans to mention a few. There were always shelves to stock and orders to fill.

During the war, we helped count and sort the rationing stamps on Saturday nights. There were rationing chips to sort and count, too.

My high school days at Howe included taking college preparatory classes combined with a business course. My friends and I were in a sub deb club called the Dots. We went to the usual parties, wiener roasts, and slumber parties. Basketball and football games made up much of our social calendar and the Basketball Sectionals were the highlight of the year. There also were social activities in the youth group at church so I had a busy life although not being able to go to movies or dances restricted my social activities somewhat; I dated very little.

Music was a part of my studies. I played violin in grade school but dropped all music in high school as there wasn't room because I took college preparatory courses. I did take accordion lessons and played in the church orchestra. I also took baritone horn lessons for a period of time, but I don't remember why.

I chose to go to Earlham College because it didn't have sororities as I had enough of the sub deb clubs at Howe. My college years were happy, and I made many friends. I also decided to be called Louise at this time. During my sophomore year, I decided I wanted to become a missionary and would like to go to Bible school, Apostolic Bible Institute, (ABI) at St. Paul, Minnesota. Dad said that would be fine, but I had to take college courses at Macalester College, so I went to ABI in the mornings and Macalester in the afternoons. I was very happy and had an active social life. I dated one of the sophomores and when we broke up, I decided to return to Earlham for my senior year. My senior year was filled with student teaching and many happy memories.

After graduation from Earlham College in June of 1956, I applied for a job with the Indianapolis Public Schools. I taught second and third grades at School #72 for 5 years while living at home. During this time I met Bob Walker and after a courtship of a year and a half, we were married and thus ended my sojourn as Annlouise Sohn.

Bill, APS, Louise, Dad, Uncle Emer's in Tuscola, Ill., 1941

Left: Louise, APS, Dad, Bill1; B&O train wreck ¼ mile from our house, 1940

Baltimore & Ohio Wreck In Irvington Ties Up Line

Wreckage of nine empty stock cars and one coal gondola on the Baltimore & Ohio Railroad, Cincinnati to Indianapolis route, in Irvington near Spencer street, which piled up yesterday afternoon, is shown. The wreck was caused when a drawbar on the gondola pulled loose from the car ahead, causing the stock cars to crash together and overturn.

Louise, 1943

XVII—WILLIAM PETER SOHN (IN HIS WORDS, 1992)

"I was born on December 2, 1936, and named William Peter Sohn, probably the William after my grandfather Fulton and Peter was my grandfather and father's middle name. I was the second born son and was always considered by my father to be his look alike. Hanging on a door at our home, 378 Downey, was a picture of Dad when he was three or four, dressed in a skirt, with his dog. (I have the original picture.) Dad would hold his hand over the bottom half of the picture and ask friends to identify the baby. There was, also, a picture of me at the same age, in a pink dress, in my Dad's arms and most everyone would say that's Billy. I guess parents always want their offspring to look like them.

"Our hired girl, Carrie, took a liking to me. Mom and Dad said that she was the only one who could understand everything I said. Lucky me, did I learn my English from my teachers and parents, or did I learn grammar from an uneducated, Kentucky–speaking native.

"I guess I tried to be like my dad in that I always wanted to be in business like him. When I was around 12 years old I tried to sell a talking Bible for profit to members of our church. Dad had a Bennett Brothers Catalog, a blue book, where we could buy merchandize, including talking Bibles, wholesale. I printed up a postcard advertising the Bible and mailed it to members of the church, hoping to make a profit. It didn't sell. Next, I brought eggs from Dad in wooden cases, 30 dozen to the case and then, I sacked and peddled them to the neighbors, door to door. This venture was more profitable.

"My early life wasn't all work as I played right along with the rest of the kids in the neighborhood. When I was about 12, I buddied around with my older cousin, Bill Fulton. One time, we mixed baking soda and vinegar in a jar and shook it up. It blew up and I was lucky that the flying glass didn't put out my eye. He shared my interest in radios and we built all kinds of electronic gadgets, There was a radio repair shop on Spencer Avenue across the railroad tracks. I went there and the man would give me all kinds of radio parts. Another early passion was keys. Mom fixed me a ring of old key that I just loved having.

"We were in the cub scouts and the boy scouts. We camped out overnight many times and cooked over open fires. It was fun and I still like camping. Andy was always interested in science and the arts while I was interested in mechanical things and tools, Dad said that whenever he would give me a tool I would see how fast I could make it go and then break it.

"We walked to school and came home for lunch. When it rained we would float sticks along the gutter on Ritter Avenue playing like they were boats.

"During World War II, we stood in line at school #57 to buy 25¢ stamps for war bond books. When we had $18.75 worth the book was turned in for a $25.00 bond. During that period there were few metal toys available, and many Christmas presents were made of cardboard. I saved tin cans, taking the labels off and smashing them flat. They were picked up at the curb and recycled for the war effort.

"Dad closed the store on Labor Day and we, usually, went to the Indiana State Fair. We parked next to a building that had a covered area, sort of like an open patio. Dad would take us to the animal barns when in reality we wanted to go the midway.

"In high school I worked after school at Dad's store. I would walk from Howe High School over to the streetcar tracks where I would board the street car for five cents. It ran on tracks with steel wheels and a trolley overhead to provide the electricity. I would get off at Shelby Street and walk to the store, a distance of about two miles.

"Dad paid Andy (APS) and I, each, 50¢ an hour. We didn't realize it at the time, but we were getting an education that one couldn't get anyplace else. Whenever I rode down to the store with Dad in the dirty car, he would put his hand on my knee and pray out loud all of the way to the store.

"When I was 12 he went over to the bank at Fountain Square and left me to run the store. I, also, delivered groceries on my bicycle. One time, a hired hand, Jimmy Mickel, took me—I was probably nine or ten—with him on a delivery and ran off and left me. I was lost and crying, but someone took me and called Dad. Needless to say, Jimmy got fired.

"We went to church on Sunday morning, Sunday night, Tuesday night and Thursday night. Mom and Dad believed that religious education was important for us. If you ask me who my hero is—I only have one, my dad. He was the most decent man I have ever knew. He practiced what he preached every single day. This included Mom, also.

"In high school, Andy socialized more than me. I was always working and earning money. At age 15, I started at the Standard Grocery, in Irvington, working for the union wage of 74¢ per hour. After school, I went to work at 4:00 p.m. and worked until midnight. Working 40 hours a week, I saved $1,800 and bought a new two-tone green convertible 1952 Chevrolet when I was 16. Needless to say, I never had much time for other activities. All work and no play makes Jack a dull boy. Well, I think that all work and no play makes Jack.

"Louise was older and moved in different circles. I listened to *Curtain Time* on Saturday nights with her when she was babysitting me. One time she took a pair of scissors and cut the cord on my headphones. They were ruined since I could not repair them. In the afternoon, all of us kids ate cereal while listening on the radio to *Tom Mix* and *The Lone Ranger* who were cowboy heroes. Other popular programs were *Captain Midnight* and *Hop Harrigan,* a bomber pilot in World War II. On Sunday afternoons, we listened to *The Shadow,* a person who could make himself invisible while he solved crimes.

"Bob being five years younger was involved in totally different things than me. Mother got angry because she said I picked on him. Once, she hit me with a broom and the plastic cover scratched my arm resulting in a three-inch scar.

"In school, I ran around with a group of guys that considered getting good grades as being sissy. It just wasn't the thing to do. Only the sissy guys got good grades. I never really tried, and my teachers wrote on my report card that I was not working up to my capability.

"During my freshman year a I.U. I stayed in the Men's Quadrangle. The cost was $675 per year. For the first time, I drank beer bought by an older roommate in the dorm. I worked at the I.U. Cold Storage Plant which prepared all of the meat for the dorms. I, also, carried mail for the I.U. Postal Department. On weekends I came home and worked at Holliday Park Realty Corporation as a salesman. In between jobs I studied. At Christmas I carried mail for the U.S. Postal Department.

"Andy came to I.U. at the start of my second year and we roomed in an old house on East Ninth Street. We did all of our cooking in the basement. There were several other students living in the house. Manuel Piakas nicknamed "Buns," and Frank Carr were athletes and not serious students. Paulie Poff, a fifth–year basketball player from New Albany frequently visited. Frank would bring a town girl named Libby up to his room. Jim Bales, a predental student, lived in one of the rooms. We studied and had fun. One time, Andy had a blind date and we agreed that if he didn't like her he would stop by and then I would come down and take his place. We looked a lot alike in those days and I think we pulled it off.

"During my second year, I pledged Phi Delta Theta where I lived my last two years in college. Dad paid for everything and gave us $5 a week spending money. I broke my foot playing basketball on the basketball court at the Phi Delt house. Andy ran around with "responsible" premedical students. I ran around and 'raised hell' with 'irresponsible' business students.

"In my senior year I tried really hard and got my best grades. I was appointed head judge of the Phi Delt Judicial Committee which heard appeals of members who had been fined. President Bill Snapp appointed me. Andy was house manager.

"The Sohn family had a good life. Mom and Dad loved and cared for us. Dad was acknowledged by everyone to be financially astute. He hardly ever spent money, but whenever we needed anything we got it. He always paid cash for everything. He never had life or health insurance. I guess one could say he saved all of this money. Mom was just like him."

XVIII—Robert Fulton Sohn (Edited by Him, 2022)

"I grew up in Irvington on the east side of Indianapolis. It was a nice neighborhood with friendly people. We really didn't socialize with any of the neighbors because Dad worked from dawn to dusk, six days a week, and Sunday was devoted to church.

"We had a big yard that was about 300 feet deep and maybe 60 feet wide. The house was old, but in good shape. The garage, however, was literally falling down. It had a dirt floor, and a chicken coop on the back. There was no light to speak of, so the contents hadn't seen the light of day in years. I always wondered what was really in there. It was always sort of a mystery to me. The yard was weeds farther back. Sometime in later years we started cutting it. We had a basketball court in the back. I remember it was first made out of cinders. If you fell, you were scraped up. The next one was made out of concrete, but it was too thin and crumbled apart. The next one was also concrete and is probably still there today. It was made to last. We put lights on it so we could play at night. I remember playing in the rain and snow, after dark, all night, by myself, and often with others. I used to fantasize about being in a big game and going up for big shots. Sometimes they fell, sometimes they didn't. Even if it's fantasy, they don't always fall!

"Our house was pretty old, but I think Dad may have bought it when it was fairly new. I always found the basement interesting. There were lots of things down there. I remember an old chest that contained the stone masons tools of Grandfather Sohn. There was an old workbench, built by Uncle Harry. It was rarely used except by Bill. In one corner was a crude shelf arrangement where Mom put up canned food. But I don't think she was really into it too much since we had a grocery. I can remember when our coal furnace was replaced with a gas furnace. The coal furnace had some sort of a chain control to the damper that was sort of like a toy. The basement had a stove where we burned our trash. In another corner of the basement was a pile of coal that never got any smaller since we no longer burned coal. The basement also contained the washer and dryer, and a wash tub made out of metal with two sides with drains in the bottoms. Under the rest of the house was a crawl space where Dad reportedly buried money in Mason jars. If you ever got locked out of the house, you could always push open a basement window and crawl in.

"I slept in a small sunroom off my parent's bedroom. In junior high and in high school when I came home late I would have to crawl past my parent's bed to get to my room. Sometimes, Dad would just reach out his hand and catch me as I went by. When I was small I would also crawl past their bed to sneak into my sister's room where I would get in bed with her. My brothers, Andy, and Bill, slept in a room upstairs that was, I think, a finished–off attic. Louise had a room in the front of the house that wasn't very private, but then neither was my room. My room didn't even have a door. We had one bathroom that was located down a long hallway in the middle of the house.

"There were maple trees in the front yard that were fun to climb. We had an alley that ran alongside our house. A couple of walnut trees always made the alley smell of walnuts after cars ran over them. In the back yard there was a playhouse that no one ever seemed to use. There was a huge willow tree that eventually fell down. I also remember a catalpa tree that had a platform up in it. You got to it by climbing up railroad spikes that had been driven into the tree by my brothers. Another big tree, maybe a catalpa, had a tire swing. We also had a big lilac bush, raspberry bushes, a crabapple tree, and more walnut trees.

"The neighborhood seemed OK to me, but as a family we did not socialize with anyone that lived there. Up the street was a family named Cougill that had lots of boys just a few years younger than me. I played with them a lot. They lived next door to the house where the former president of Butler University lived. It is now called the Benton House and is open for tours conducted by the historical society.

"I remember Dad always seemed to be working when I was young. He retired from the store when I was ten years old. He would get up early, maybe 4-5 a.m., leave and not get home till 6-8 in the evening. He had terrible varicose veins from being on his feet all of his life. When he came home, I pulled off his elastic stockings. His legs were a wreck. Sometimes I had to go with him to the store in the morning. I hated it. On the way to the store he would then place his hand on my knee and pray the all way there. I hated the whole trip. Sometimes, he took his handkerchief out of his pocket and wet it with his tongue to wipe dirt off of my face.

"He never really spent any recreational time with me. There was no father-son relationship like I have with my boys. He didn't seem athletic at all. I remember being really surprised that he could not throw a ball very well. In all the years that I played sports, he only attended one game and he apparently walked out because it was too noisy. While I was at Purdue, I learned that he died. My car needed a fuel pump, so I went and got one and hurriedly put it on, working under the car the entire time with tears in my eyes.

"Mom was always at home except on Saturdays when she worked at the Sohn grocery. When I came home from school for lunch she was always there with lunch ready. She lived a pretty simple life around our family. Monday or Tuesday was her shopping day, and she would ride the bus downtown every week.

"I went to the George Julian Grade School. It was Public School #57! I remember big rooms with big glass windows that opened. The first-grade teacher was Mrs. Gantz. She was very old. I think she was the first-grade teacher for everyone in our family. I remember the principal. Her name was Mrs. Wallace Montague. I do sort of remember the 6th grade teacher because he made something of an impression on me and was my first male teacher. I also remember the coach, Mr. Sullivan. He coached all sports. I was sort of a natural athlete. The school had a field day every year, and I always did something well. I was never the fastest runner, but I usually had something I excelled in. I found I could shotput better than anyone, so I got into it and won some ribbons. My best event was the football far throw. In the eighth grade I could throw the football farther than fifty yards. I always won the event. In the regional there was a boy named Bill Mitchell that I had beaten in the sectional, but he beat me with a really long toss.

"I wanted to play football and the coach wanted me to play because of how well I could throw the ball. My mother wouldn't let me because she was afraid I would get hurt. So one year I forged her signature so I could play. But fate was working against me, and I got caught. I ended up being the assistant to the coach, but I had the best arm in the school. There was another assistant named Bill Warren. Since there was no football for me, my best sport became basketball. I practiced every day and made the team, easily. I remember playing organized basketball for the first time in the 6th grade, and playing every year thereafter. I was usually a starter unless the coach was mad at me. I played really hard and was probably best on defense. I was a good shooter, but didn't shoot very much. When I was in the 6th grade I would go to practice after school, and then I would have to go to the store to help Dad. I would catch the bus right behind school. Then, I would ride it to about Rural and English, where I transferred to another bus that took me to within 2-3 blocks of the store, and then I walked the rest of the way.

"The store was in a really old building. Dad had been there more than 30 years. There was no toilet until the very end, so we used an outhouse toilet behind the store that I did not like. The toilet was in a dirty old building that had a dirt floor. The building was sort of a mystery to a little kid, because it was crammed with lots of indescribable junk. The store had a back room that had a coal burning stove for heat, and a funny smelling sink with a single cold-water faucet. The back room was always stacked full of boxes and junk. The neat part was behind the meat counter where there were two butcher blocks that had to be brushed down with wire brushes every day, and knives that Dad sharpened every time he used them. They had been sharpened so often that a good part of the blade was missing. The old cash register had 4-5 drawers and lots of buttons and a crank that operated the drawers. I always marveled at this thing. The candy selection was kept off to the side. I remember it well.

"Out front there was a counter where people collected the things they bought. Dad added up the groceries in his head at a phenomenal rate. There was an ice cream freezer that he added in the later years. I also remember a gripper, used to get things on shelves that were too high to reach. A scale was near the front door, and we used it to weigh potatoes in 5-10 lb. bags. The potatoes were sometimes rotten and smelled terrible. There were cockroaches that Dad would kill with his hand. There was a scale for bagging sugar, and lots of miscellaneous drawers that didn't seem to contain anything in particular, but did have interesting things in them to keep a little guy going. There was a Colonial bread box out front where bread was delivered and locked before Dad got to the store in the morning. It was orange and fun to play in.

"Next door there was a barber shop where we all got our hair cut and there was a drug store on the corner. I delivered some groceries, but not often. Dad retired when I was ten.

"We went to church all the time and that meant twice on Sundays, sometimes on Tuesdays, and usually on Thursdays. I remember Dad would get up Sunday morning and wash the car before we went to church. Now, I wash my car on Sunday, if I can, but I don't go to church. We would get dressed in our Sunday finest. I wore hand-me-down clothes. There was a wool suit, in particular, that was *so scratchy* that I had to wear my pajamas under it. Church seemed to last forever, usually till about 1:00 p.m. on Sunday. After church we would go to the store to pick up some groceries. I think we were really just checking on things. Sometimes other people from church would go and buy groceries. I can remember that on more than one occasion we found someone had broken into the store. I don't think they ever got much.

"Church dominated our lives. There were lots of rules—no makeup for women, no dancing, no movies, no drinking or swearing, and women couldn't cut their hair. Nothing "worldly" was allowed and that covered everything! I played the drums in the orchestra and thought I got pretty good. I never liked it because I had to sit through the services in my wool suit. Dad was a deacon. He was respected and we were always the last to leave, because he usually counted the money in the donation box. He prayed a lot, and seemed to be involved, but neither he nor Mom ever seemed to be really deep into it. I never saw either one of them speak in tongues, which was supposed to be the sign that you were "saved."

"I used to walk about a mile to Howe High School. In high school was the first time I ate at school; in grade school I always walked home for lunch. I remember that in physical education, my first year, they tested all the new boys. I scored very high in a variety of skill-dexterity tests. I was in the top 10 of my freshman class, as I remember. I was thrilled because I could climb a rope better than most of the guys.

"I ran cross country my freshman year. They made me do it in order to play basketball. I was really a pretty good runner, but I thought of it as below me, so I didn't put too much effort into it. Most of my friends did not have to run because they were playing football. I did place 11th in the city meet without much training. The coach was really surprised. I know now I should have pursued distance running a little more because I enjoy it a lot and seem to have a natural ability for it.

"I made the basketball team easily, my freshman year, although I was afraid I wouldn't. I made it every year thereafter, and was a starter most of the time. I was sort of a defensive specialist and never scored too many points. I think my highest point output was 14. I was a real scraper, and you would always find me diving for loose balls.

"I also ran track every year if you could call shot putting running track. I was quick and coordinated and could get across the ring fast. I practiced even at home and got to where I would always place and sometimes win.

"I won a varsity letter as a sophomore, which was a little unusual for sophomores. Most of my friends did not win a letter. I ran with most of the jocks. I also belonged to a club called the Treys, which Andy had started. We didn't do anything except hang out together.

"While in high school, and I don't remember what year, the pastor of the church told Dad that my playing basketball was putting me in the public light and that the church didn't support it. My dad refused to make me quit. I think he knew that there was no way to back out and he always supported us. One evening after church, a guy named Frank Cory made the mistake of flipping my tie. I blasted him in the nose, and he was a wreck. His nose was broken and there was lots of blood. He took off around the block and was telling people that he was going to kill me. The pastor told dad that perhaps I should quit the orchestra. We all agreed. It was the best thing that had happened to me in a while. From that point on I was pulling away from that church.

"I used to tell Mom and Dad that I was going to the Irvington Presbyterian church. I would get dressed and leave the house. When they left for church, I came back home. So much for church.

"When I was a senior or even junior, I don't remember exactly when, I went to a careers day program and heard about pharmacy. It really interested me because it was mostly chemistry, and chemistry was really neat because it was all rules and logic. I liked accounting for the same reason. What really got me going in chemistry was that you could take one substance and mix it with something else, and get something altogether different. It was magic! Pharmacy was for me.

"There are only two places to study pharmacy in Indiana, Purdue and Butler. Dad didn't like Purdue. He offered to buy me a new car of my choice if I would go to Butler, and live at home. I could even join a fraternity. He was not high on fraternities because of Andy and Bill's experiences, whatever they were. No way! I wasn't living at home.

"During my high school years, Dad was retired. He had lots of rental properties. I became his handyman-enforcer. If something needed doing, I usually got the nod. The rental places were old and dirty. There were lots of bugs and the people were not any better. He would take me with him for protection when he collected the rent. I wanted out of there!

"Purdue was a new and wonderful experience for me. Very few people from Howe went to Purdue. Those that attended college, and I don't think there were that many, went to Indiana University. I lived in a dormitory my freshman year. My roommate was a nerd named Bill Carney who was also in pharmacy. A nerd and a high school jock didn't mix, and I dumped him after one semester. My second roommate was David Lippens from Michigan City. He was a good guy, but a lousy student. He broke his shoulder and spent most of the time at Lake Schaffer shacked up with someone.

"My grades were OK the first semester. I think they were 4.24 which was just above C. I was rushed hard by the Phi Delts by a guy named Roger Jacobson. It was what I wanted because Andy and Bill were Phi Delts. I pledged, and moved in the fraternity house at the start of my sophomore year. Pledging was hard on my grades, and I almost flunked chemistry and physics. Both of the professors agreed to give me an incomplete and allowed me to take a grade for the year based on my second semesters grade. I got A's and ended up with respectable grades.

"During my first year I took a math class that was required. It turned out to be just a repeat of some math that I had in high school. In that class was a girl that caught my eye--Mimi Hosp. I never really found a way to approach her that year, but that was to come later.

"The Phi Delts and the Chi Omegas put on a show, called V2, (Victory Variety) after a football game. The theme was *Brigadoon*. Mimi was the musical director of the program, and I was one of the guys that danced the Highland Fling. We were getting to know each other. Following the Victory Variety program the Chi Os had a sorority dance where the girls invited a date. Mimi asked me because she knew that I could dance. Our relationship flourished from that point on. We were married between semesters of our senior year.

"We spent our honeymoon, which was just a couple of days, at the Wagon Wheel Resort, which was located on the Illinois-Wisconsin border. It was 35 degrees below zero. We moved into married student housing at Purdue. It wasn't much, but it didn't matter.

On Mimi's twenty–first birthday I had some really severe pain that was diagnosed by the medical staff to be an appendicitis. It was probably later diagnosed correctly by Dr. Healey as a kidney stone. It was surgery for me and some bed type recuperation. My teachers felt sorry for me, I guess, and gave me pretty much a free ride that semester. I didn't buy a book and got reasonable grades.

"It was during that last semester that I interviewed with Lilly and accepted a job in the capsule pilot plant. I was to start in the fall after I did my apprenticeship with Haag drugs. The selective service was, however, still to be dealt with. I was 1-A the whole time I was in school. Fearing the draft, I applied to and was accepted into the navy OCS program. I later turned it down when I decided to take my chances with the draft. This was one of the best decisions I ever made in my life. The navy sent me an innocent looking postcard and asked me to sign and return it. If I had done so I would have been in the navy.

"My life up to this point had been great, and I had reveled in every minute. I wouldn't go back or trade it!" So much more happened in the next 60 years, but I guess that is meant for another book if Andy ever gets around to it.

XIX—Anton Paul Sohn (In My Words, 1992)

Grandma Jennie Fulton's nephew, Albert Edward, was born 18 April 1897 and lived in St. Louis. When I was born, he wrote the following two poems.

My Friend, the clown—To Anton Paul Sohn

When I was born my mother smiled,
My dad just had to grin,
My nurse with laughter nearly died,
And so did all my kin.
The neighbors came to take a peek,
I tell you it was awful.
The way those people laughed and roared,
I wondered if 'twas lawful.
The Doctor laughed so boisterously,
He loosened every rafter.
This child was born, he told my dad,
To bring this old-world laughter.
He'll never be a great man, sir,
But you can mark this down,
In life he will be loved by all,
For folks all love a clown.
Now time has proved that he was right.
I never will be great.
But I have made folks happy with
The non-sense I create.
Let others have great wealth and fame,
They were not meant for me.
It's better if I make folks laugh,
That happy they may be.
—Albert Devita

Long Ago—Anton II

Time was when I was very small,
I couldn't walk, I couldn't crawl.
Could only lie there in my crib,
Play peek a boo behind my bib.
Not much was there that I could do,
All things to me were then so new.
Sometimes for hours I'd wink and blink.
If lonesome sometimes I might be
And wanted folks for company,
I'd make a fuss and folks would say
Although he's small. He gets his way.
Of girls I had a lengthy list,
And by them often I was kissed
Into my mouth I put my feet,
This made them say, "Now isn't that sweet"
They liked to hold me in their arms,
Enchanted by my manly charms.
I liked to have them hold me tight,
Girls were to me a great delight.
Sometimes for help I'd send a call,
I did this with a lusty bawl.
They'd pick me up and look so strange,
Say knowingly, he needs a change.
With furrowed brow I'd frown and scowl,
And like a man I'd loudly growl.
Against their strength I had no chance,
They'd conquer me and change my pants.
—Albert Devita

My Life (1935-1949) An Eighth-grade writing assignment

The First Great Event in My Life

On October 1, [Tuesday] 1935 the first great event took place in my life. I was born. I was named Anton Paul Sohn, after my father. Sohn is a German name which means son. My sister called me "Bubby" because she could not say brother.

I was born in St. Francis Hospital in Beech Grove, Indiana. My sister, my brother, and I were all born in the same room. The week I was born my father bought a new car. A Lafayette Nash, affectionately known as the Sunday Car.

I was not like the other babies in our family because I was baldheaded when I was born. When the doctor showed me to my father he called me "Baldie." I was not unusual because I cried a lot like most babies. I was the second baby in our family and the first boy. When I was a baby I slept in the cradle, the late Governor Whitcomb slept in.

My Early Childhood

When I was about four we got a trapeze for Christmas. Brother Bill, John Kirkhoff, and I would go up and down the street and get kids to play on it and would charge them leaves for money. We made quite a profit. About that time my father put a big rope swing up in our backyard. We lost a little interest in the trapeze. We had fun on the tree that the swing was hung on. We used it for an airplane. Finally, one day, the limb broke off, and that was the end of the airplane and the swing.

My father then bought a playhouse. We used it for a jail house many a time during a cop and robber battle. One time I was locking my cousin in jail, and he shoved me through the window and broke it.

A Week at the Lakes

Before my first day at kindergarten we went to Lake Michigan for a week. It was my first week of adventure at the lakes. The day before we left Mother was ironing and getting ready to go. I came into the kitchen and pulled the iron down on me and got a bad burn on the leg.

We took Carrie Rupe, our hired girl, with us. On the way we stopped and made beds out of the seats and slept in the car. One morning down on the beach I put a big black bug in my mouth.

Looking Toward the Future

I have been looking forward to going to Howe for many years. One thing I have been [looking] forward to is athletics. I plan to try out for it if I am good enough or not. After I graduate from high school I plan to go to Indiana University to become a conservationist or an architect. I plan to live in Irvington.

Grade School Years "The Start of Education"

We walked to our grade school, five blocks down Ritter Avenue crossing the Pennsylvania Railroad. At the RR we encountered the first of several crossings guarded by patrols of sixth, seventh and eighth graders. On the Northeast corner at the RR was an elevated house maned by an employee who controlled the crossing gates. Years before, Dad had a friend, related to his second wife, who worked here and was injured on the job.

I, also, knew of two individuals who were killed on the railroad right–away within several hundred yards of the crossing. One student, Rhinehart, was going to Lady of Lourdes school and was walking along the track, an activity forbidden by our traffic patrols. The Catholic school didn't provide traffic guards. The second person, Phil Padget was in my scout troop. He tried, on his bike, to beat a west–bound train to the crossing at South Audubon Road. He lost.

At George W. Julian Grade School (#57), all of us—Louise, Bill, Bob, and I—took music lessons. A friend of the family was a talented trumpeter and had a scholarship through college. Later, he was in the military band and played "taps" at Arlington Cemetery in Washington, D.C. Dad, somewhat over optimistically, thought that if we couldn't afford college we could get music scholarships. Our initial exposure to music was in the grade school "tonette" band, a summer school activity that was not entirely appreciated when the rest of my friends were enjoying the lazy days of summer. Later, I played the coronet; Louise, the violin (Mom's), piano and accordion; Bill, the trombone; and Bob, the drums.(1) None of us became accomplished musicians, but we played in the church orchestra and in the high school band. I played two years in the University of Cincinnati marching band. Luckily, Dad could afford to pay for college because no music scholarships ever came my way.

My interests in elementary school were math, science, and art. I won several awards for art projects. David Taylor and I tied in an art contest designing wall hangings; I gave mine to Mrs. Montague, #57 principal. In another art project I made a small, maroon, ceramic elephant. My interest and abilities in art became evident in the first grade. In other subjects, I had As and Bs (above average and average). I was not a serious student. My report card consistently said, "Anton needs to be less playful and more business–like." The truth of the matter is that I was always in trouble.

At home, school attendance was stressed. We had to be really sick to miss school. Whooping cough, measles, mumps, and scarlet fever were legitimate reasons to miss school. When we were sick the doctor would come to the house, notify the health department; then, a health officer would come to tack a six inch by eight inch "quarantine" sign on the front porch. In this manner the usual childhood diseases were recognized by the health department, but polio was another more dreaded. During the "high alert" months Mom kept us home from the public swimming pools. Occasionally, the pools were closed to prevent the spread of polio. I did not know of anyone in our area that had polio, but an acquaintance got polio midway through high school.

Gra–Y, a YMCA organization in grade school, was the first club to which I belonged. I learned the rudiments of Robert's Rules of Order and was elected secretary. Our one memorable field trip was to the Butler Stadium to watch a football game. Butler played Indiana Central College, now, known as Indianapolis University.

The friends I formed in grade school—Gene Toole, Harold Brown, Harry Smith, Bob Schram, Bill Ropp, and David Taylor—remained friends in high school (and for life) and some of us still get together, both at class reunions and for other activities.

Some of my teachers stand out: Mrs. Van Zant was a friend in the early grades, but most of her colleagues did not appreciate my sense of humor. Mr. Virgil J. Wise, my eight-grade home room teacher and the second male teacher I had at #57, was stern, but understanding. The other male was Hershel Whitaker who taught wood shop and was in his late '50s. Mrs. Wallace Montague was the principal and had the most understanding for my dry wit.

Miss Martha Barber was a very tolerant art teacher, but I was not very popular with Miss Ruby Winders, our music teacher. In 1962 when I was serving a *locum tenens* for a general practioneer, Dr. Victor Vollrath, in Indianapolis where she was a patient, she told me, "Anton, I always knew you had it in you." Laura Benson, my English teacher was unmarried and liked to talk about how important her family was. Only my art teacher, Miss Barber, inspired me. Mrs. Montague trusted me and taught me to believe in myself.

REFERENCE:

(1) Mom took violin lessons in nursing school and bought the violin from her teacher.

Scouting—Appreciating Nature

Cub Scouts and Boy Scouts had a deep and lasting influence on my life. Dad, the sole proprietor of a neighborhood grocery, didn't take many vacations and my exposure to camping and outdoor skills was through scouting. Bill and I joined Cub Pack 9. Also, my friends from scouting which were my grade school friends remained loyal through high school. The most recent reunion, in the summer of 1990, was a camping trip at Pistol Creek on the Middle Fork of the Salmon River.

As a Cub Scout, I was diligent in my advancements. I worked my way up to Lion Scout with the appropriate bronze, silver and gold arrows. At age 12, I entered scout Troop 19, but my interest waned when I was a sophomore in high school. On 23 February 1950 I was certified as a Star Scout and when I left scouting I had enough merit badges to become a Life Scout.

Several experiences in scouting deserve mentioning. The first overnight camp and summer camping at Chank–Tun–Un–Gi are fond memories. This Boy Scout camp, next to Fort Benjamin Harrison, is on Fall Creek northeast of Indianapolis and comprises several hundred acres. Later, the Central Indiana Council cast aside the Indian chief's name for a local scout leader's name and renamed the wooded area, Camp Belzer.

The first overnight camping trip took place at Chank–Tun–Un–Gi in the Winter of 1947. The War was two years in the past and the scare of escaping German prisoners from Fort Benjamin Harrison, located next to scout camp, was gone. War surplus supplies were on the market, and I bought my first sleeping bag for $2. (For $3 I could have bought a down sleeping bag.) The $2 bag was army wool—like those dreaded army uniforms Bill and I wore—and had a zipper down the front: a mummy sleeping bag which led to disaster.

We hiked one half mile into the forest to a three–sided log cabin with a fire pit in the entrance. The structure was typical of the primitive homes built by early Indiana pioneers. The sleeping lofts contained straw. The weather was stormy, and it snowed during the day, but the night was cold and clear. I was surrounded by my friends and scout leaders, but I was alone when listening to the night sounds.

Sometime after midnight, the heart chilling cry of a "wolf" split the night. A three–sided cabin, dying fire, and a surplus sleeping bag were not nearly enough protection for a frightened boy who did not know the difference between the howl of a wolf and a great horned owl (*Bubo virginianus*). One cannot learn the wilderness until the sounds, the sights, and the fear of being alone in the woods are experienced. Later, nature called, but the zipper was at my back and wet pants resulted. The rest of the night was spent trying to stoke up the fire to produce heat to dry my bag and pants.

During the summer, paper drives and money saved meant a week at Chank–Tun–Un–Gi to swim, canoe, camp in the woods and earn merit badges. The first summer was difficult for a Tenderfoot because of the inevitable initiation and harassment. As I advanced in rank I was the harasser. Sometimes, my cousin, Sonny (Bill Fulton), and I were in trouble because of our monkey business.

My love of the outdoors was kindled at Chank–Tun–Un–Gi. Signing up for bird study meant getting up at 5:00 a.m. and going over to the lagoon where the birds—great blue heron, various hawks, and other wildlife—were seen. The birds in our neighborhood on Downey Avenue were mostly jays, robins, Downey woodpeckers, cardinals, wrens, hummingbirds, and bats in the summer. In the Kirkhoff's backyard we threw rocks in the air to get the bats to swoop and dive.

In the winter, Jamborees at the Indiana State Fairground Coliseum, camping, and activities in the gym at Downey Avenue Church occupied our time. Once, a night sledding event was scheduled at the Pleasant Run golf course. Mom said, "No, it's too dangerous!" Moms are always right—I stayed home. A good friend, Bill Ropp, got a laceration on his forehead requiring a trip to the emergency room and sutures.

A year or two later Calvary Tabernacle formed an Explorer Troop that provided a good excuse to drive. We bought an old dilapidated inboard motorboat with the intent of refinishing it. We bit off more than we could chew, and the venture came to naught.

Sports—Physical Education

Basketball was (is) big in Indiana. I mean really big. We played for hours, indoors or outdoors, winter or summer, in the rain or snow, and day or night. My first home basketball court was gravel with a bushel basket nailed up over the garage door.

The Sohns had the perfect place on the back of our lot for a concrete court. The site was about 250 feet from our house and 100 feet from the neighbor's house. One neighbor, George Harris, who worked for the telephone company provided the telephone pole for the basket and electric wires to light the area. Glenroy Construction Company provided the cement. We had one of the best courts in Irvington. It was about 25 x 30 feet. In the summer we would pitch tents and have tournaments that would last two days.

The Downey Avenue Christian Church had a gym with two baskets. It was a favorite place to play. Sometimes, we had to sneak in, but when I was a boy scout (Troop 19) we played after each meeting. Bill and I were also in the cub scouts (Pack 9) at that church. The Irvington Our Lady of Lourdes Catholic Church had an outdoors court with two baskets. We were always looking for a place to shoot baskets.

By the sixth grade my loyalties to Howe High were developed. We were permitted to miss school—if we had our parent's permit—to attend the sectional basketball tournament at the Butler Fieldhouse. Three or four friends and I would take the bus downtown and transfer for the ride out to Butler. Howe never won the Sectionals during the years I went, but the fact that my parents permitted me to go was a major breakthrough.

Thomas Carr Howe High School

Education and Social Awareness

Education is a learning process, and—we tend to forget—a process that should be creative. As one advances from one level of education to another wider opportunities should occur. Medicine is a good example of advancement and widening of opportunities. It is impossible to know the whole field and there are always new challenges and developments. Our educational system allows one to learn new skills and step up to the next level. ("Let each new temple, nobler than the last.") In many countries educational opportunities are not available to everyone.

Art, drafting, and mathematics remained my interests in high school. As my skills in these areas became developed, architecture became the logical career choice. Although I found the mandatory health course interesting, I never gave medicine or science a second thought for a career. I took physics and got top grades. Biology—making butterfly and leaf collections—took too much extracurricular time and I didn't have enough curricular time to take chemistry.

During my junior and senior years, I was the top drafting student. Mr. Wathen Leasor gave me the responsibility of overseeing the class and lettering the school schedule. As a result, when the Indianapolis Water Company came to recruit, I got the job. The job paid around $1.25 per hour, and I made $424.44 during the Summer of '52. From the earnings of my first job—besides working for Dad—the government withheld $54.60. The second year I moved up from designing and locating water mains on plot plans to working on a surveying crew laying out the new Geist Reservoir. Working in the woods near Noblesville, Indiana,—even during the humid summer—was enjoyable. The second year my earnings were $580.50, and the income tax was $87.50.

My interest in sports continued, but Mom was against football as being too violent and dangerous. "Mothers are always right." It was hard for me to accept her decision that I could not try out for football. Basketball was also denied in order for me to help Dad at the store. Track and cross country were substituted for my two favorite sports. I was an average athlete in these running activities. My junior year Mom signed the mandatory consent form, but she didn't appreciate the significance of "all sports" that I had written in on the form. I went out for the football team, but I was two weeks late and scrimmage was in full swing. As a left halfback carrying the ball on the first play-off tackle I was hit on the inside of my left knee by a helmet. I immediately knew I had serious trouble, but I didn't realize that my athletic career was over. Dr. Frances Shennan diagnosed a sprain, and I used crutches for two weeks. The knee was re–injured several dozen times before I had it repaired after my first year in medical school. The anterior cruciate ligament was severed and the medial meniscus were damaged.

During high school I continued to take music lessons and play the coronet. My progress was not spectacular, but I advanced to the "A" band and enjoyed marching at football games and in parades. Mr. Robert Burford, the band director, was a favorite teacher and knew how to relate to students. Unfortunately, he quit teaching—to make more money—and became a real estate appraiser.

The social structure of high school is important. In Indianapolis most, if not all, schools have subdeb/squire clubs that are somewhat like fraternities and sororities. My friends—David Taylor, Bill Ropp, Harold Brown, Harry Smith, and Gene Toole—from grade school and I organized the Treys, squire club. Bob Schram, John Cordill, and Jim Fleener were our first pledges. Later, Bill Thompson, Jim Ross, Bob Ball, John Mocabee, and juniors Keith Cogan and Norman Thompson were initiated.

We met weekly at a member's home; then usually disbanded to play basketball at the Sohn's or went to a drive–in restaurant. Occasionally, we had a joint meeting with a subdeb club, usually the Sweethearts. We attended high school and social events—mostly basketball and football games. The big event of the year was our annual week at Lake Shaffer. David Taylor's father chaperoned the first year, but the following year we were trusted to go alone. Besides swimming and boating, the nightly dance at the amusement park where the "big bands" played was the place to meet girls. The park was always popular because subded clubs from a number of Indianapolis schools went to the Lake Shaffer.

During one of our summer trips to Lake Schaffer I experienced my first exposure to the so–called "dirty" books since risqué stories were not permitted at home. Bill Ropp acquired a well–worn copy of Mickey Spillane's *I, the Jury,* a story of violence and naked women. During the drive to the lake, we took turns eagerly reading Mike Hammer's adventures. In one scene, in order to promote justice, he drills a neat round hole with a .45 bullet beneath the belly button of a naked blond and indifferently states: "She was a real blond."

Since I was training for cross country I would get up at the crack of dawn and run along the backyards near the lake. One particular morning, I passed a farm and decided to stop and buy a chicken for dinner. (Our meals were simple and sparse.) When I got back everyone was still in bed, so I carried the cement sack with the live chicken into the bedroom of the cabin. Nobody believed me until—I believe it was—Toole stuck his hand into the sack and came up with feathers.

The consensus was that I stole the chicken—to this day I can't convince them I paid $1. We took it out in the woods behind the cabin to kill it. (The county sheriff owned the cabins where we stayed.) The chicken got loose, and we had to retreat to the cabin to get blankets to capture the prey. The next task was to take its life, but we were not experienced at that sort of thing. The solution was to whack its neck with a limb. Nobody could eat the fried chicken—I think we cleaned it improperly—but the girls in the next cabin brought over an apple pie that became the main course of our dinner.

After I reached sixteen, my bicycle was replaced with Mom's Model A Ford. There were restrictions. I was supposed to drive straight to school, but I managed to pick up my friends. During the lunch hour, we would leave school and "cruise." The engine sometimes wouldn't start because teeth were missing in the fly wheel. This required a shove—one person could do it—and we were off. Once, when this happened Harold Brown's foot got in the way of a back wheel, and I ran over his foot. No damage was done as there was no weight in the back. The brakes were also worn, and it was a calculated risk where we stopped. Sometimes, we would hold our breath and make a sharp turn at an intersection or at a railroad crossing. Amazing as it seems, we never had an accident.

In addition to driving, camping was still a favorite activity. Jim Ross' father had cabin on a creek near Greencastle, Indiana. Jim, Frank McCormick, and I went there over a long weekend in the winter of 1952–53. Somehow, Armand Roach, who was a year younger, invited himself and we took off in Jim's family Packard. The water at the cabin was frozen and we had to carry water to drink. The area was remote and heavily wooded. Armond was a little "crazy" and he claimed he shot at a horse in the woods. We played ice hockey on the creek and explored the woods.

Another memorable outdoors trip was when Bill, Jim Grayson, and I took a canoe down White River from Anderson to Indianapolis. Rain poured down the whole trip. We finally had enough and called Dad to pick us up at the Izaak Walton League north of Indianapolis. I will never forget how disgusting it was to see raw sewerage being dumped in the river at towns along the way. Yes, we did accidentally tip our canoe over. According to Bill, we passed around a bottle of Carstairs whiskey while we were standing wet in the river.

Graduation from high school was a time of reflection for me. To know that I would never see most of these friends and, I was moving on to college was sobering. I was sad when the music—*To Howe We're Loyal*—was played. The Senior–Alumni Dance on 10 June 1953 was at the Indiana Roof where Dad's Manhattan Theater had been. The music was provided by the Fred Dale orchestra.

Howe High School Treys Pin

APS, 1952

James Ross,1952

Cincinnati University

Higher Education

During the summer of 1953 I worked as a draftsman for Glenroy Construction Company under Raymond VonSpreckelson, a graduate architect from the University of Illinois. One task assigned to me involved redesigning—for free and I am sure, certain political favors—the bathroom in the mayor's private residence. Drawing a toilet accurately in perspective was no easy task.

Plans for Cincinnati University were under way. Letters from fraternities and the Y.M.C.A orientation camp were arriving. I chose Cincinnati University because of its co–op plan, a schedule whereby after the first year a student would alternate six weeks of work with six weeks of school. On a family trip we visited Iowa State University that had an outstanding art and architecture program, but the out–of–state tuition was high. The University of Illinois also had a good program, but had the same tuition problem. (In 1953 Indiana had no school of architecture.)

ca 1947, Troop 19, Downey Ave. Christian Church, Left, unknown, Anton Sohn, William Fulton, Gene Toole, Jack Silvers, and Scout Master Alexander

Lake Shaffer Cabin, 1950

Harry Smith, Bill Ropp, Lake Shaffer, 1950

Howe High School Freshmen Track,
Front left: Bill Foster, unk, Leroy Thompson, Gene Toole.
Second row: John Kirkhoff, unk, Louis Hoynes, APS.
Third row: Jerry Webb, Mattingly, unk, Bob Pirtle, 1950

I did not register to stay in a dormitory. I decided to go through the fraternity rush. Dad was not particularly happy since he was not too sure about fraternities and advised me, "You can always join a fraternity." When I decided to pledge he advised, "Keep them all guessing." Jim Ashcraft, a WW II veteran, who lived in Irvington and attended U.C. came by our house a couple of times and convinced me to live in the Phi Delta Theta house at the start of rush. Dave Weir was president of Louise's class at Howe and a Phi

Delt. The other person I knew at U.C. from Howe was Ron Dougherty. He tried to get me to rush Acacia, but I didn't fit in with their members. I stayed at the Beta Theta Pi house for a couple of nights, but it was obvious that its reputation wasn't as good as the Phi Delts. The Sigma Chis called and wanted me to visit their house, but my mind was made up.

For the first time in my life I was not directly under parental guidance. As with most college freshmen this was the greatest year of my young life. I was admitted to the College of Applied Arts on 15 September 1953 to start work on a six–year program culminating with a B.S. in architecture. The week before school was an elective Freshmen Orientation Camp sponsored by the campus Y.M.C.A. I adapted to college life and was elected secretary of the freshmen class using the slogan, "Handy Andy."

The Phi Delta Theta Fraternity was the right environment for me because extracurricular activities, including student government, and leadership was encouraged. The seed was planted, for the rest of my life I did more than my job, I was involved. Several experiences stand out during my two years at U.C. I became interested in student government and served two years as the class representative on the Applied Arts Tribunal. As a result of my extracurricular activities I was one of eleven elected to Sophos, honorary for outstanding sophomores.

My interest in outdoor activities was still keen. A pledge brother, Irv Bakemeier, and I took a canoe trip down the Miami River in Southern Ohio. In the spring of 1955 Paul Clayton, my second-year roommate, and I made a canoe trip on a lake near his home in Northern Ohio. We camped on a small island during a rainstorm. The water came up in the tent, so we made our bed on branches and leaves. Little did I know that poison ivy was mixed in the leaves. I quickly became covered from head to foot with a red rash. When we returned to civilization a lotion with an alcohol base, Epidermalot, was given to me by Paul's brother. I never will forget the excruciating burning that occurred when I applied the lotion to my private parts. I held on to the faucet in the bathroom for dear life while my gonads were on fire. However, I was cured for life. I never again got poison ivy.

During my first year at U.C. I maintained a B+ average, but I wasn't getting a well–rounded education. I was proficient in math and art was challenging, however there was no time for elective courses. I did not have time to learn another language. Also, I felt that I was as smart as the premed majors I knew, and medicine was more challenging than architecture. In addition, I had a desire to help others. One event I will never forget was forgetting Mom's birthday. Dad wrote me a letter: "Du bist ein Basé Bupp!" You are bad boy—in German.

In my sophomore year I became more disenchanted with architecture and enrolled in night school to take psychology and public speaking. By Christmas of 1954 I had made up my mind to switch out of architecture. Medical illustration seemed a natural selection since I had skill in art. I visited that department at the U.C. Medical School, but the illustration course was too technical. My mother were cautious and advised against medicine, "Medicine is difficult, long and the hours are not desirable." My mind was made up, I accepted the challenge. The natural decision was to transfer to Indiana University where instate tuition was much lower than U.C. My first-year expenses at U.C., including tuition were $1,484, the second-year cost $1,367 while the first-year expenses at Indiana University were $708.

My co–op job in the summer of 1955 was with the Cincinnati Recreation Department on a survey crew, but I was enrolled in summer school taking two semesters of zoology. This was the baptism of fire to see if I had an aptitude for biology—I did.

Premedical education at Indiana University

(Continuing Higher Education)

In mid–summer of 1955 I hitchhiked to Bloomington to enroll at I.U. I arrived in Bloomington, the campus was deserted, evening was approaching, my funds were limited, and I had no place to stay. I carried my suitcase the two miles out to the Phi Delt house knowing I could stay there, but the door was locked, and the building was uninhabited for the summer. I decided to try all of the windows and doors. Luckily, a basement window was unlocked. Gingerly, I lowered myself into the basement, there was a loud noise as multiple objects met the floor. I groped for a wall and a light switch that was found after several minutes. With light I could see that I was in the chapter room, and I had stumbled on fraternity icons knocking them to the floor. I heard a noise upstairs; I turned the light off and waited—nothing happened. I rearranged the items, locked the window, and ventured out into the hall to find a place to sleep. In the fall, I found out that the houseboy, "Chipper," was asleep upstairs and heard the noise, but he departed in a hurry because he knew the chapter room was locked and the house was vacant.

In the morning, the Associate Dean of the Arts and Sciences College, Byron Doenges, interviewed me and we found a mutual interest in architecture because his wife designed homes. A year later, he got me a $125 academic scholarship.

Since Bill was starting his second year in business school we roomed together. We got a room at 618 East Ninth Street with cooking facilities in the basement. Much of our food came from home since Bill went to Indianapolis, frequently, to visit his girlfriend. He pledged Phi Delt, and we ate some meals at the fraternity house, usually the night of pledge and active meetings.

Premed classes were easy since I was competing with freshmen, but I missed using my artistic skills. When studying was done, I sat on the roof outside our room and sketched. I was involved in art projects—designing sets for activities—at the Phi Delt house and audited an oil painting course. Campus activities were important, I was an officer in the YMCA. Next year, Bill and I moved in the fraternity house; my roommates were Lloyd Lempke and John Records. Phi Delta Theta was one of the oldest fraternities at IU; and it was the first Phi Delt colony (1849) from the Miami University mother chapter in Oxford, Ohio.

When we arrived in Bloomington the chapter house was only a couple of years old. All of the members slept in the third-floor dormitories—one cold, with the windows opened, and one heated. Bill and I always slept in the cold dormitory under a pile of covers. The rooms were designed for dressing and studying.

Lloyd Lempke, Bob Crist, Jerry Cartmel, and I drove to the Phi Delt convention in Colorado Springs, Colorado, the next summer, 1956. Late in the night when crossing the Kansas prairie we ran out of gas. Not a light was in sight. Since there were no other cars on the road we decided to pitch our sleeping bags next to the car. We could solve our problem in the morning. The wind howled across our uncomfortable and tired bodies, emphasizing our isolation. Luckily, when we awoke there was a filling station about a quarter of a mile away. Even more luckily, we didn't have to walk, it was at the foot of the hill where we spent the night. We coasted up to the pump.

Lloyd, John, and I were the serious premed students and were opposed for elected house offices by the less serious "partying" students. Lloyd was elected president and I was pledge trainer. During my second year I was appointed a member of the Student Foundation Committee: "one of the highest honors to be bestowed upon any student at Indiana University."(1)

One of my closest friends was Al Strong who was a first-year law student and live–in chapter adviser. Al was president of the Young Republicans club. Together, we went to the regional meeting at the University of Wisconsin in Madison. In June of 1957 we attended the Junior Republican National Convention in Washington, D.C., where President Eisenhower spoke. Later that summer, we went on a one-week muskie fishing trip at the Lake of the Woods, Ontario. All expenses were covered by the outfitter since Al's father was a yearly customer and represented him at the Chicago Sportsmen Show.

Muskellunge, known as muskie, is the largest member of the pike family and is known for its two outstanding characteristics: it is considered one of the best food fishes, but more importantly, it is prized among fishermen for its fighting ability. Fishermen consider one strike in a week a successful trip. To catch a large muskie thirty–five pounds or more is a once in a lifetime thrill. We fished for a week and did not get a strike. A trophy fish caught by Al's dad was hanging in the Kenora Chamber of Commerce information office.

The fishing camp owned by Keith Hook consisted of eight to ten one–room cabins with porches and a main lodge with dining and lounge facilities. The meals were served in elegant, first-rate style. The fishermen would leave after breakfast in the morning in outboard motorboats with Indian guides. Since the muskie is a territorial fish the guides knew which island and which bay contained a fish. To catch it is another thing.

We arrived at the camp in the late afternoon and were relaxing on our porch before dinner when two men, holding hands, came by on the path in front of our cabin. I looked at Al and voiced my concern about the sexual orientation of our campmates. The next morning as our guide piloted our boat around an island we passed the same two men in a small bay fishing about ten feet from land. The more obese of the two stood up and made a cast of about 30 feet. The only problem was that his cast was toward the island. They forgot to turn him toward the open water. I could almost hear what the guide was thinking when he climbed the tree to retrieve the lure. I learned the man was a successful lawyer in Chicago. Most of the fishermen in camp were from Chicago.

In the fall I started medical school and didn't see much of Al who was busy starting his law practice. He got married and I was in his wedding. Tragically, Al died of Hodgkin's disease when I was an intern in San Francisco.

In addition to forwarding grades and an application, admission to medical school requires three steps: 1. Taking the Medical College Admission Test (MCAT) which I did on 5 May 1956; 2. Getting two letters of recommendation; 3. And having an interview by two faculty. The last is the most dreaded, and horror stories abound. I decided to apply to three schools: Indiana University, Cincinnati University, and the University of Louisville. I wrote to Louisville and was told to not bother, because it was a city–supported school and only took residents.... Although "Cincy" was similar, I had gone there for two plus years and I knew a famous alumnus, Paul "Ram" Hawley, Surgeon General during WW II. I met Ram at the Phi Delt convention in Colorado where he was elected president of the General Council. He wrote on 7 September: "Thank you for your letter. I think I told you that the one aspect of the presidency which pleases me most is that, after 107 years of continuous existence Indiana Alpha finally gets the presidency of the General Council. We have waited too long ....

"I will write to the Dean of the School of Medicine at the University of Cincinnati today recommending you for admission. It will please me very much to have you there since I graduated in Medicine at the University of Cincinnati and was an intern and resident in the Cincinnati General Hospital."

I decided against applying to Cincy. The cost was higher than Indiana and grade requirements were high for nonresidents. I put "all of my eggs into one basket" and applied only to I.U. I asked Ray VonSpreckelson to write a letter of recommendation which was a "stroke of luck." Ernest B. Haswell, a Cincinnati artist, favorite teacher, and advisor also wrote me a letter: "I received and filled out the blank for Medical College. I told them I thought you could saw off a leg as clean as the next man, but seriously I wish you luck.'

My interview was conducted by Dr. Glenn Irwin, internist and later, dean of the school and another physician. The "stroke of luck" was that Irwin was next-door neighbor, friend, and tennis partner of Ray VonSpreckelson. The interview was nothing more than a friendly chat about tennis....

On 19 December 1956 the letter came: "This is to notify you that you have been accepted by the Committee on Admissions as a member of the next freshman class of the Indiana University School of Medicine, September 1957 to June 1958. This acceptance applies to this class only. You are accepted subject to the satisfactory completion of your premedical record in every respect.

"Subject to the satisfactory completion of your record" means that if at the close of any semester there are qualitative or quantitative deficiencies, as a result of the work of that semester, the Committee reserves the right to drop you from the list.

"Indiana University School of Medicine at Bloomington will have microscopes available for rental to students of the freshman medical class.

"Your formal acceptance of this appointment must be received at this office not later than January 15, 1957. If you accept a place in the September 1957 class, it will be necessary for us to have a deposit of fifty ($50.00) dollars by January 15, 1957. Checks should be made payable to J.A. Franklin, Treasurer, Indiana University. You will understand that this deposit will apply to your regular fees when you enter the school. If you are called to military service during this interval, the deposit will be refunded.

"I am very glad to congratulate you on your acceptance to the School of Medicine." Very sincerely yours, J.D. VanNuys, M.D. Dean Medical School (Indiana University)

November 23, 1956, Dear Andy:

"One of the highest honors to be bestowed upon any student at Indiana University is to be appointed to the Student Foundation committee. The list for the 1956–57 Committee has just been named, and it is with great pleasure that I congratulate you on the great honor of your selection.

"It is my pleasure to work very closely with the Committee, and I am looking forward to the experiences we will share, along with the opportunity to know you better. As you know, the number one function is the work done in promoting the "Little 500" Bicycle Race. Great plans are in the making for that gala affair to be held on May 11, and there is a very responsible position for you in connection with this event. The Board of Directors of the Foundation entertain the new members of the Student Committee each year. The annual dinner will be Sunday evening, December 2 at 5:30 p.m. in Alumni Hall. You will see the first showing of last year's "Little 500" movie and hear some of the plans for the coming year. Please notify the Foundation office by November 29 if you will be present for this affair. Again, congratulations and best of everything.

"Yours Very Sincerely, William S. Armstrong"

XX—Ruth Marie Sohn's Diary

April 15, 1956. Mrs. Bauman on the farm west of Raymond at farm called and said our farmhouse had burned down the night before. Cause unknown. Man sleeping awakened to find house full of smoke. Unable to get to phone. Had to go to neighbor's. Woman and children away. Police arrested babysitter and man who came intoxicated to fire. Following week they were held in county court. Woman and man serve short term. Andy started immediately to contact different people to build block house. Completed 3 mo. later. We got $3000 insurance.

Southside of 378 S. Downey after a fire in 1959. Bob on the left and Bill.

Eastside of rebuilt 378 S. Downey after the fire. Dad at the side of the house.

June 3 , 1956. Louise' commencement. Bob, Dad and I went. Stayed all night. College paid for Dad & me, meals and room. We paid $1 for Bob and his meals. Baccalaureate Sun. am was cloudy, very cold. Service was nice and we enjoyed it very much. They served us lunch under trees. Commencement after noon. Was first in building. Then, since it couldn't seat everyone was held outside. It didn't rain and everything finally planned out OK. On Sat night we had seen class play. *Blood Wedding.* Good, but everyone got killed.

The following week Louise and a couple of girls went to St. Paul to the commencement. Billy worked for Lumber Co. Andy worked for Glenroy. Sis worked at Methodist Hospital. Andy went to Boulder, Colorado, to a Phi convention. Dad, Sis, Bob & I went to Washington D.C. Aug. 12 for a week. We were home a week. Then, went to Lafayette Campground. But Sis had a bad cold after we were there 2 nights so Dad stayed & we came home. She went back Fri. night. Slept on Floor. Didn't help cold any. Sat Bill went to Canada with Johnathan [Urshan] to take Priscilla home.

Sept. 2. Sunday. Andy came home from Colorado. Shortly after the boys left him they wrecked their dad's Cadillac at Wash & Audubon.

1956, Sept. 3. Dad, Sis & I went to Elwood to meeting. Bro. Urshan preached. We had dinner at 4 P.M. in church's back yd. Went to see Mae Austin, Dad's cousin. Came home.

Sept. 4. Martha & Elmer came.

Sept. 5. We meet Mabel, Sol, Martha & Elmer at State Fair. Very hot. Louise went to Teacher meetings Tues and wrecked car coming home in front of Uncle Harry's. Dad & Andy went to Dale's auto lot & got Bill's car in which we drove to Fair.

Sept. 6. Thursday. Bill came home from Canada with Urshan well pleased with treatment from Johnathan's sis & family. Louise rode with teacher a couple of days. Then her bro. got killed up in Mich. by train & gone.

Sept. 7. Bill & Dad went to Fair.

Sept. 8. Took Andy to Bloomington, also friend of his, Joe Wahl.

Sept. 13. Billy left to go to school Fell playing Basketball broke his foot.

Sept. 18. Bill came home had cast put on at St. Vincent's Hospital.

Sept. 19. Bill went back.

Sept 27, PM Woman called said bad fire apt house shed burning down.

Oct. 3. Daddy and Bro Kerner went to Muncie conference.

Oct. 4. We went to Muncie. On way home about 11 o clock passed scene where 11 people (colored) were killed 10 in one car.

Oct. 5. Boys came home. I had a chiropractor treatment for my back.

Oct. 18. Louise went to Memphis on airliner. We took her to airport. They were going to celebrate opening of new bldg. that night. Gloomy. We were impressed by many air liners coming in. Around 32, getting off and on. We left when we saw her get on and stopped at farm. We had supper and went to store.

Oct. 20, Sat. Bob, Dad & I went to Illinois. Were much impressed by the oil wells. Uncle Elmer has 2, capped big one because so much explosive gas was escaping. Twins were at Arcola for weekend. We got home Sun. evening.

Monday AM. Daddy went after girls at town. Sis had a wonderful time at convention. Lots of people, so crowded.

Nov. 6, Election day. The world is much disturbed over waring conditions in Austria and Holy Land. Woman murdered at 5400 S. keystone in basement while washing. Murdered by her nephew. New living room rug. The weather his month has been unusually nice.

Xmas. We had such a lovely tree. Sister's pupil's father gave her for her room, so we had it at home. We all got such nice presents, Bob's surf coat he wanted so badly, Shirts, gloves for boys. Sis got 23 presents from her children, perfume and trinkets.

1957, Jan. 7. Got new Wilton rug for dining room. Very beautiful and my back gave me trouble. Dad & Sis went to church. Bought salve for my back. I slept with hot pad all night.

Jan. 11. Back much better, but still very sore. Got new lamp for L. room, Sis is getting it for Dad's birthday.

Feb. 1. Anniversary 24th. Daddy bought me a lovely pink azalea. Daddy went to Ohio and Penn. We got new mattress for boys. Sister gave me money to buy a new dress. I got a purple one.

Feb. 26, 8 AM. Andy & I started to Florida–raining. Got to New Albany about 10:15. Amelia wasn't home. Left. Ate dinner near Bowling Green, Ky. at roadside pk. Got to Birmingham, Ala. near dark but decided to go on thru before getting cabin. Finally got one 50 miles the other side. 2d rate motel on highway near railroad track–clean beds, but outside restroom. More rain

Feb. 27. Got to Orlando 8 PM. Called Betty & Don from filling station. Met at super shopping center. Stayed 2 nights. Visited Betty's church, a lovely park with flowers, sweet peas, also Don' office building.

Mar. 1, 2 PM. Left for Melbourne. Got off road by 10 miles. Had to go back. Got to Melbourne. Alice had finished mopping about 5 PM.

March 2. My birthday. We went to town, and I bought a lamp shade. The boys wired me flowers. Gladiolus cream—3 carnations & others.

March 3. Madonna & Harry came on train 1 hr. late. We went to S. School–28 present. We went down to Ocean and a man gave me a fish he caught. We went fishing and caught several small ones. Ernie was helping a man build a boat. We went out to orchard & picked a bushel of oranges. Bro. Griffin gave us some Mulberries and I made pies, twice. Also a large avocado we saved to take home. I bought 2 coconut heads. Also purse for sister. We went to new church on highway, and I played piano. Bro Miaggo who has building for old peoples home, very nice.

March 11, Monday. We left early before folks were up. Car stalled and I pushed it down the grade. Stopped at Jacksonville, Fla., to see Mary Ann. We stayed at motel 30 miles from Atlanta, Georgia, fairly nice motel, but next morning we discovered window broken.

March 12. We got breakfast, oatmeal, at nice place. Went over high toll bridge, lots of water. Got to Dunn, N.C. late afternoon. Met Theresa coming down lane. Fried chicken and wonderful supper. The Magruders really gave us royal welcome.

1957, March 13. Magruders & all of us went to Dunn. Theresa bought big shad. We went on truck in woods to Pioneer cemetery.

March 14. Left in rain. Theresa gave us ham, bread, preserves. We stopped & I bought remitment of material. Stopped & bought Pecan candy, perfume. We stayed all night 10 miles from Corbin, Ky.

March 15. Left 8 after fixing flat tire. Man bumped us in Louisville at stop lite. Nice man with insurance. Stopped at Amelia's. Not home. Got home about 6 PM.

Last of March we had a family party at Helen's.

May. We went to IU Founders Day. Anton (APS) received honors. Mother's Day dinner at Phi Delta Theta. Church at Bro. Hughes. Anton bought me a Frat. plate. Very nice. Daddy brought home red geranium plant.

June. School out. We took sister to St Paul to YMCA camp. Anton Paul stopped off at Lake Geneva to YMCA camp. Met Al [Strong] first of week and they spent week in Wash. D.C. at Young Republicans' convention. This has been a very hot summer with floods prevailing thru out country. Also several cyclones. We had dinner with Daddy's cousin and son, Tom, a delightful character in St Paul.

July 31. Birthday party for Bob. About 24 inc. our family present. It was very nice and unexpected as people who we thought would come didn't, but several unexpected did. Dad & boys painted the house. Dad & Bob papered hall and dining room. We have a new look. We went to Elwood after Louise on Sat. Made friends with woman across from Sis' friends.

August, Monday. We went to Camp at Lafayette. Saw man dead on road from wreck. We got part of lower half of cottage with Habig's. Bro Dunwoodie went home and left twins in our charge. We made our usual trip to town and Sis. Habig bought Bro. Urshan pajamas. Daddy got Louise a record player. Bob sang with youth choir. It was raining. Later about 8o clock strange man came to side door motioned to Daddy. He brought Bob and Donnie Cunningham. They had taken the car and had a bad wreck on slick place on road. It was a miracle God saved their lives. Daddy went home with Bob & car. I stayed 2 nites & Sis & I came home with Habigs. Fri morning. I told stories at children's church twice a day. 2 women from Richmond in charge.

Sept. Louise is still teaching at school #72. Dad & I went to Fair. Met Mabel, Sol, Martha & Elmer there. Andy entered first year medical school.

Dec. Our car is still at Mooresville. All they do is promise. Daddy calls and makes a trip out there occasionally. We had a very lovely tree, so pretty. We got lots of nice thing. I got electric skillet (sis) shurg (Andy) scarf (Bill). Daddy had Turner Polland make a shelf for my dolls. I sang with choir at Joilletta Mental Hosp YMCA. Very rainy weather.

1958 Jan. I got sinus infection, hard to get over. Daddy had fire in vacant room in Lexington. My violets froze that night. We got car back this month, but Daddy has had to do lots of work on it. We had Habigs and all the Perry sisters for supper. They played scrabble and some of us worked on tablecloth Sis. Habig intended for Nila. Mary & Martha's had a personal shower for Nila at Carolene. We made a poem for her. Sis took us out to Heritage for Daddy's birthday.

Feb. 1. Sis. Miller invited us for buffet supper on our 25th Wedding anniversary. Present were Currys, Habigs, Mars, and Hicks. Lois & her husband came later. Billy bought us a silver bowl for our anniversary.

Feb 14, 1958
To Nila and Hugh Rose

Shower Poem

Dear friend, we have gathered from everywhere,
To show Mister & Miss Music how much we care.
Hugh is a fine choir director we all say,
And Nila, our pianist awaits Valentine's Day.
Our Heavenly Father also knows and cares,
So Brother Jordan, will you please say the prayer.

The Cunningham sisters 1–2–3 will sing us a song very pleasantly.
Brother Kenny is here, to play his horn and bring good cheer.

In beautiful Ohio, Lake Buckeye is found on the map,
Hugh & Nila first met at Pentecostal Youth Camp.
Then Mister Music came to Indiana with his smile so sweet,
Miss Music decided life with him would be very complete.

So together in God's work they go,
They will be very successful we know.,

My tale is complete,
Let peace and quiet abide,
While they open the gifts,
We'll enjoy the mysteries inside.

Dedication Poem

Our church is rejoicing as to heaven we go,
Thanking God for our pastor, as the true way he does show
His sermons and lessons brightening our day,
And fill our hearts with joy when we kneel to pray.

God said, "It is good for man not to be alone,"
So He sent Sister Jean to serve and brighten his home.
God gave them three children to make life complete,
And later little Andy with his smile so sweet.

Together they preach the gospel and sing,
Telling the story of Jesus our King.
They visit the sick, bring comfort and cheer,
Willingly working each day of the year.

Bless our pastor when radiant the evening skies,
Let God watch over his house with a thousand eyes.
As the broad wing of heaven's gate be unfurled,
Bless the welfare of his sleeping world.

Abide with them until the Lord's day is spent,
When over the earth your message is sent,
Jesus' blessed coming will soon be near,
And all of your children know no darkness or fear.

Bless our Pastor

Bless our pastor and his wife,
Angles guard, protect their lives.
Bless them in the hours of night,
In the gloom before the light.
Bless our shepherd, let him win
Saints for thee, lost souls from sin.
Bless their health that they may be
Ever faithful in serving Thee.
2d Verse to be sung with song, *Bless this House*, choir at Dedication of New Building.

May 8, 1958
To Jonathen

I
Jesus, the Savior, can be found everywhere
So he called a man from Jerusalem, a city so fair,
Then he provided a ship from across the sea
To bring our friend to the land of liberty.
II
In the land of New York he first made his home
With kindred dear he was not alone
Then to St. Paul Bible School setting his goal
God begun to work at saving his soul.
III
Jesus has a purpose for every man's life
But often must be overcome much sorrow and strife
So to Indpls. he came for a visit they say
But it was only so Jesus could have his own Holy Way.
IV
Then Uncle Sam begun to figure his own plan
And sent Jonathen out to be a brave soldier man
But finally God has his own righteous way
Our friend is in Evangelistic work saving souls every day.

March 2. My birthday. Sis. Suddith invited us to her house for dinner. Sunday. Billy is fixing the lower part of my kitchen with plastic light blue tile. I went to get my driver's license and because I studied the wrong book I got wrong answers. She gave me another chance and passed me.

March 17. We had a bad fire at 616 Lexington. Burnt out two front rooms upstairs, damaged hall. $857 insurance. Daddy supervised work himself. Saved half of cost. We let my African violets freeze.

April 6, Easter Sunday. We had revival 3 weeks previous with Bro. Jolley. I made dedication poem and verse to Bless this house at request of Bro. Rose. Dedication Apr. 4.

May 4. We went to New Albany. Some little rain. Stop. at Andy's house at Bloomington on way down. Stop at grocery in little town and made sandwiches. We got home Sunday evening about 6:30.

May. Mother's day. Mary and Martha dinner. Shelby St. very nice with program.

May 8, 1958
Patty's Baby Shower

We wish you much Joy
If it's a girl or a boy
Either will be very sweet
For a baby makes life so complete
We think it would be very bad
If Baby arrived unclad
So we made something to add to the rest
Of the clothes in baby's Hope Chest

To Patty Lloyd
Mary and Martha Dinner

May Mother's Day

It's not her beautiful features
Nor the way she wears her hair
Not her step so light and graceful
That makes her seem so fair
But her face aglow with feeling
When her eyes light up with fae
As she prays to hm in Heaven
This is what we most admire.

To Sister Habig

We wish to honor our eldest mother,
One with friendliness in her eyes
At the Back of the church greeting others
Her gestures of giving are tender and wise.

There is none on earth as sweet as you mother
Serving you always your closet friend
In all the land you won't find another
Who will stay with you to the end.

In Heaven beyond this earthly land
When Jesus reigns wise and fair
We know full well her willing hands with Palms of Victory wear.

Here is a Posy for our youngest Mother
Her deeds are many, rewards are few.
In her place can be no other
She only wants Gods to see her children through.

Indianapolis is my hometown
To live anywhere else would make me frown
Policeman, fireman make our life safe and complete
The sanitary department does its part everyday
So we, all work together to keep our city clean this way.

Madelyn's Baby Shower at Urshan's Sept 6

A young Mother works for her baby
Each day she carefully prepares
Doing each duty with patience
Each task is a loving care
None saw the unending effort
None saw her wonderful plan
For the task of loving & giving
are unseen by the eyes of man.

Soon gone is this happy Baby
Adulthood too quick is a must
But always shall look to her mother
For her gentleness love & trust
But the child the mother built
Shall endure while God's ages roll
For the child's life the mother created
Is the child's immortal sold.

1958 June 8. We went to Sonny's (Bill Fulton) Wedding, Sun. Afternoon. That nite went out to Mabel's. Martha & Elmer, Harry, Madonna, Helen, and Clarence there. Stayed until 9 PM.

Monday, June 9th. To boys' commencement. Rained going and during commencement, but sun came out afterwards and we took pictures. Stopped at restaurant and ate dinner. School out on Fri., June 13.

Mon., June 16. Took Louise to Camp Delight where she was to council for summer.

June 23. Andy left for Chicago for his trip to Europe. We did not hear from him for about 12 days. Dad & I were concerned about him. Sis got a card, and we got 3 letters in couple of weeks. Bill got Bob job with furnace crew at Holliday Park.

July 4th. Dad & I spent day with Mabel, Sol & Don.

July 19. Jonny moved off farm. Mr. Owens, wife, & 4 children moved on. This has been a very rainy season, rains every day. Very unusual for sun to shine. Horse show at Camp Delight. Dad & I went. Bob Walker was there. Louise has gone with him a couple of times. She gone out of camp Aug. 15.

Tues. Aug. 19. We prepared to go on our trip to Canada. Imelda Roth and her family called 6 A.M. and came over. We had breakfast for them, and it was 9:30 before we left. Went through Marion and ate picnic dinner in the country North of Ft. Wayne. Got to Toledo, Ohio. Stayed at Motel, $5. Went sight-seeing at nite.

Wed. Arrived at Detroit, M. Went to Greenfield village and Ind. Museum. Farmers cottages of people, Edison etc. Ate dinner at Museum. Stayed at Winsor, Canada, at Blue Bell Motel. Ran by Syrian $6. Toured town.

Thursday. St Catherine, Canada. Mrs. Filbrick's Motel who owned first orchards on place. She gave everyone breakfast.

Friday. Went to Toronto Industrial Fair, beautiful clean bldgs. At evening left. Got in such a terrific traffic jam we thought there had been a terrible accident. Got back to Filbrick's about 10 P.M. where we stayed again. Louise bought a burnt orange skirt in Toronto.

Saturday. Left Filbrick's who directed us to go to Niagara on the Lakes, Canada. Failed to see anything. Beautiful drive back to Niagara, Canada. We saw little car rides across top of Falls. Took picture, on to Falls. Ate dinner and went to town. We bought some dishes & book. Dad bought some teas. Left Canada went to U.S. side. Gate motel at Niagara Falls, U.S. Went to falls all around diff. parts. Night went back to see lights on Falls and oldest museum very interesting, old mummy's and signatures of Lincoln and party. Also others who had visited Falls. M. H motel.

Sunday AM. Ate breakfast and went to town. In shops bought Indian dolls. Rained. Ate dinner. Stayed at Mannings Motel at Salamaca, New York. Tried that night to find a church to go. Finally found Salvation Army Bible School commencement. Also Missionary Alliance B. C. commencement.

Monday. Ate breakfast at Bradford, Penn. Ate dinner at Green Parrott, Cleveland Westlake. Stayed all night at Bellville Motel.

Tues. Breakfast at Carrier. Came thru Cleveland, Ohio. Very big town. Streets went to 300 and more. Got home early afternoon.

Aug. 26th. Got call from New York from Andy saying he was staying with a man in city he came over on ship with, 5 yr. old son.

Labor Day. Louise & Bob went to Fair. He gave her a calf's skin pocketbook he made. Very beautiful. She also got an evening purse. Dad & I went to Elwood to hear Bro. Ben Pemberton. Went to see Cousin Mae, Marilyn has a baby. Andy called Sept. 4 and said meet him at airport at 230 as he was flying home. We met him. He has arranged for his friend to get car.

Sept. 8. Andy's school started.

Sept. 12. Bill & Dad left on TWA plane at 1 PM for New York to bring Andy's car home.

Sept. 13. Andy got a returned letter from Europe, and I found out it is a radio he is bringing. He calls it a High Fi, so I don't know much more what it is. Louise has had a very bad cold with hoarseness for 3 days. Bob bought her over a beautiful corsage and a little dog.

Sept. 14. To S. School. Stanleys & Barkers went to New York in afternoon & came home following Wed.

Sept. 15. Card from boys.

Sept. 16. Dad & Bill came home afternoon. Hi fi, dishes for sis, Wine set.

Sept. 20. Carol Cheek, Andy's girlfriend, came from Bloomington Sat. even. Bob came over & showed Andy's pictures. Party afterward.

Sept. 21. S. School. Dinner. Bob Came over after dishes. We went to Fortville to Alumnae, 24 present. Sis went with Bob to his sis for supper. Grayson stayed all nite & Dad took them to train at 330 bound for St Louis & Ft. Leonard Wood, Missouri.

Sept. 28. We got letters from Billy everyday full of philosophy. He was restricted to base during basic training.

Oct. Madonna operated on for breast tumor. She came through OK. She & Patty went to Florida.

Nov. Sun after Thanksgiving we, Dad & I went out to Aunt Mabel's for dinner. Uncle Wm, Aunt Helen, Uncle Clarence and Anton Paul showed Andy's pictures of Europe.

Dec. 20. Billy came home by bus. We had a nice Christmas, nice tree. Mr. , Principal of Harry E. Wood gave Sis $5 to treat her room to ice cream.

Mon. Dec 29. We had to dinner Bro & Sis G. Perry, Bro & Sis Freeman Wilson. Mercers came late to see pictures Andy showed of Europe. Anton Paul went to Michigan to go skiing. Came back on New Year's Day. Pumps at farm froze up.

1959 New Years. Daddy and I stayed home. Everyone else went out. Pumps froze up at farm.

Jan. Daddy sold the house on 1240 English to Mr. & Mrs. Owens who worked at Burnett Binford Lumber Co. Ted & Pricilla got a new baby girl New Year's Eve.

Jan. 12 Daddy's birthday. Louise got him a new Pr. grey pants. Grayson & Bill had accident going back to Texas.

Feb. 1. Daddy took us to dinner. Sis was feeling bad. Our 26th Wedding Anniversary. Daddy got me a 6-piece set of silver ware from Arsenal Savings & Loan Co.

March. Mabel & Helen come to our house for dinner. Billy came home middle of March.

May. Helen operated on, good results. Donna bad news.

June. Billy had pneumonia 3 weeks after his 2 weeks service at Ft. Ben Harrison. He had back set after getting up & we had to have doctor return. Louise got her diamond ring on way to her girlfriend, Miriam's Wedding. She called us long distance. Aunt Amelia, Mary Edith and family were here to Bill's friend's wedding. Sis. Habig died & I had infected little finger.

July 15. In Am Madonna's death.

July 17. Funeral. We decided to go immediately on our trip so we could overcome our sorrows.

Mon., July 27, 1959. Left center of Indpls. 7 AM. Ate sandwich along road near Decatur–arrived 1005 AM. Field of Shetland ponies near Springfield, Ill. About 10 miles out of Springfield we saw storm gathering so we tried to outrun it. We went thru several hard rainstorms to Jacksonville 2 PM. Ate dinner 1230. 6 PM stayed all nite Seneca, Ka. Nice Motel–Breakfast.

July 28, Tues. Breakfast in front of motel. 930 countryside is more picturesque. 1130 stop for dinner at Hill City. Stop at IGA & bought groceries. Also Sis got a cushion. Got to Colorado Springs. Motel had store and cabinet. Went to 7 Falls at night. Climbed stairs. Saw Indian Dance.

July 29, Wed. Up early, 7 our time, Went out to Garden of Gods. Went up to see Cliff Dweller Indian's abode. Went back to Garden of Gods. Followed trail up mountain. Went so far and only saw 3 cars so finally turned around & came back as we did not know where we were going. Started to Royal Gorge. It was 44 miles, so we turned around & started for Denver. Ate dinner roadside park. Denver 2 P.M. Got motel then down to Capitol Bldg. Thru museum, very educational. Saw outside of Mint. Came home to grocery. Ate supper. Went to town. Got Bob cards and home at 920

July 30, Thursday, 7. Top of Cheyenne Mt. Buffalo Bills Grave. To Loveland Big Thompson Canyon. Ate dinner to Cheyenne. Left Cheyenne late afternoon. Drove to Medicine Bow. Very small town. Got cabin. Ate supper in hotel.

July 31. Breakfast at Rawlins. Got Groceries. Went thru Teton National Park and entered Yellow Stone. 430 Got cabin West Thumb. Drove over to Old Faithful. 530 Came back 8 and went to hear Ranger. Show slides. Light rain and we left a little early. To bed.

7 AM, August 1, Saturday. Drove thru Park to Mammoth Hot Springs. Beautiful scenery. Colorado Grand Canyon. Rained really hard. Got Cabin. Ranger talk rained out.

Aug. 2, Sunday. Drove around area of Mammoth Springs to Old Faithful. Saw Old Faithful twice. Ate dinner at cafeteria. Left at 1240 to 100 out of Park. Made mistake. Drove 8 miles out of way. Stayed all nite Pocatello, Idaho. Went to Mormon Church.

Aug. 3, Mon. Salt Lake City. Saw capital, Mormon grounds, Salt Lake. Waded in it. Picked up hitch hiker. Stayed all night Grantsville. Saw Copper mine in Nevada. Arrived Carson City, Nevada, about 430 Decided to go to California. Drove thru Immense mountain resort. All motels no vacancy. Got on new highway thru terrific forest. Thought we would never get out. Got on New highways. Didn't even have gas stations.

1959,Aug. 4, Tuesday nite. Got to Sacramento, finally found Motel.

Aug. 5, Wednesday. Ate Breakfast. Went to State House, Sutter's Fort, Indian exhibit. Went down to Bay of San Francisco. Ate dinner. Went across Golden Gate Bridge to Fishermen's Wharf, China Town. Drove to Gilroy. Stayed all night.

Aug. 6, Thursday. Drove to Grant Canyon. Big trees. Sequoia Nat. Park. Motel at foot of mountain. 3 Bears.

Aug. 7, Friday. Left for Bakersfield, Barstow. Got to Hoover Dam took tour of dam and got motel with TV at Boulder.

Aug. 8, Sat. Got Grand Canyon view. Left about 5 P.M. Stopped Indian Res. Nice. No telephone. Went on to Flagstaff. Primitive cabin. Went to Grocery. Bad news from boys. Fire at home. Tues Aug 4.

Aug. 9, Sun. Left Flagstaff. Went to see Petrified Forest. Sand Desert. Stop in Albuquerque, Dad called Jimmy Mickel. Went on to Santa Rosa.

Aug. 10. Mon on thru edge of Texas.

Aug. 4, 1959. Tuesday. House burned at 2 A.M. Firemen came 1/2 hour after called. Boys were aroused & went out after Bill smelled smoke. We found out Sat., Aug. 6, after Sis called Bob from Flagstaff, New Mexico. Storm caused wires down at Indian Motel. We had to go 60 miles to call. Rainbow followed us across desert next day. We had stayed at crummy Motel. Had stove, but could hardly eat for thinking of what we didn't know about the fire. Got to East Alton, Tues., Aug 11. Stayed all nite at Uncle Bob's. Got home Wed. about 11 A.M.. Stop to see Bill. Mr. & Mrs. Walker had dinner for us. Sis & I stayed at Walkers & Bill & Dad at home. Next nite Sis & I slept in trailer. After fire Anton Paul slept in car. Neighbors collected clothing & everyone cooperated. They stored all our furniture in Ralph William's garage.

Fri., Aug. 14. Bro Urshan came out & promised work crew.

Aug. 15, Sat. Work Crew of Bro Stan Sliva, Cupoli, Eddie Harlan. Montgomery put front part of roof on.

Sun., Aug. 16. To church and to Urshans for dinner. In the P.M. Bro & Sis Godby & Dunwoodies came out offered to help. Also Mabel & Sol. Helen & Clarence. They took home some of my clothes. Dunwoodies loaned us clock.

Mon Aug 17 Bro Godby & Richard Engleking cleaned 1 bedroom & bath room. Joseph & Jeanette came. People from church sent us enormous amounts of all kinds of food. Chickens, pies, cakes.

Tues., Aug 18. Richard, Bro Porter work 2 hrs. Joseph came & Jeanette bought supper.

Aug. 19, Wed. Richard came 1130.

Aug. 20, Thurs. Richard came 1130.

Aug. 21, Fri. Dad & I went to store. Jeanette brought dinner. Richard came 930

Aug. 22, Joseph & Jeanette, Bro Sliva, Bro Cupoli, Bro. Montgomery.

Sun., Aug. 23. Bob & Louise went to Westfield for dinner.

Aug. 25, Tues. Bro Leonard, Rudie & Stan.

Aug. 26. In 2 days Bro Leonard, Rudie & Stan put up framework.

Aug. 27, Thursday. Bro Leonard, Rudie & Stan worked until 830 with Bill & Bob on roof. Cleaned piano.

Fri.. 28 Washed pans.

Aug. 29, Sat. Got truck from Bro Stevens, Bill, Bob & Max Wood. Sis & I cleaned yard until 530 Joseph also helped. Eddie Harlan. Jean came out to get poem for Bro Bibbs I wrote. How glade we were when the first light was turned on in the living room. We cut out the wedding dress at Carolyn's and she redid the pattern. We had to make 4 or 5 trips for her to help fit the gown which was very tight with 2 side zippers & 2 sleeve zippers. The day the man finished the floors Louise had her picture taken about 2 hrs. after the floor was varnished. The veil I made was too skimpy, so Louise decided to borrow Carolyn's. Also her Bra. Louise and Bob found house at 969 Audubon. Old man & woman 85 owned it. They made a bid which was accepted so they started buying furniture. Gufco were slow with delivery. Made Bob & Sis very disgusted. Walkers gave them 2 chairs, fireplace set & we gave them lamps. Carolyn had a family shower. Jean Urshan a shower out to Grandpa's Habigs & Rachael had one. Rachael's health very poor. Louise & Bob got tremendous amount of gifts from very unexpected people. Bro Gaertner & family made the wedding dinner at our house on Fri., Dec 18. Very beautiful with pastor & wife also Loonans.

Dec. 19. The day of the wedding was very beautiful & sunny. Beth came over and stayed so Bob had to take her home in a hurry. About 2–300 people present. It was very beautiful and successful. They took a trip to Lake Geneva. Sis & Bob gave us stainless silver wear for Xmas. We gave them 12-piece silver for Wedding present. Aunt Amelia, Wilemima & Betty came and had an accident.

1960 Jan. Mr. Plummer died.
Feb. Ida Reid–Kirkhoff's mother, Flora Trobaugh died.
Mar. 26, Sat. Mr. Walker died.
Mr. Wickliff died.
Sis & Bob went to Orleans spring.
April Rainy Easter vacation
Mr. McLinn & Mr. Young died.

May 2. Bill went to Chicago for 2 weeks Bowling school. Came home Fri., May 13. Flew to California on Jet. Took vacation went to Phoenix, Ariz. to drive his boss' Cadillac home. He came home earlier than we expected on Sat. Sun we went with Bill to take Cadillac home. Dad run out of gas on way. Bob has been painting Loonan's house & garage. Bob and Stan Sliva started putting gutters on house.

June 11. Tragedy struck our house. At 12:00 noon as I started to open screen door to call Dad & Stan to dinner scaffold slipped. Board slammed into Daddy. Mouth bleeding from nose and mouth called police. Put ice cold rags on Dad to try & stop bleeding. As I found Long Hospital no. who should call but Andy. Mrs. Harris took Dad to Community hospital. All afternoon we sat while they were trying to get doctors for Dad. Dr. Sputh packed his nose also Dr Edgbert. Sr. Thurston Smith oral surgeon.

June 14. Dad went to surgery for 2 hrs. and 40 min. while they wired his mouth. Although his face was swollen badly by Sunday nite much improved. Bruised areas left quickly. We brought Dad home Fri., June 17. at 10 A.M. He got a lovely chrysanthemum from Mrs. Elise Clark & family. Visitors in hospital, Bro. Urshan. Bro. Rose, Bro. Mercer. Bro. & Dis Wilson Sis Oakleef. Sis Blakeley, Ted Black, Bro Sliva. At home Bro Mercer 4 times, Bro Habig & Sis Jean 2 times, Bro & Sis Wilson & nephew 3 or 4 times, Bro & Sis Harris and daughter, Bro & Sis Godby & David, (They brought us green beans & green onions) Bro Hacker, Joseph & Jeannett & children. Joe cut Daddy's hair twice, Bro Sliva, Bro & Sis Castetler, Esther Hubbard & girls, Sis Heitzman, Charles, Eleane.

We had to battle an infection. Epsom salt packs in Daddy's jaw. It would heal then break out again. Louise took him to Dr. several times a week. We got a plastic bottle to feed him, instant mashed potatoes, tapioca, baby food, soft eggs, soups, etc.

July 16, Sat. I got up with my right ear stopped up. Felt so badly called Dr. Brown (prissy) them went to Dr. Russell Sage. He was very nice explaining to Andy when we got home about 330. Mary Edith & family & Aunt Amelia were there. They stayed all nite at Stuckey's, Bills friend, who had new baby. They went home Sun.

July 17, P.M. After going to Sis & Bob's a while my ear has hurt me all week. After waking me Mon. nite full of water, 2 to 3 A.M.. Mrs. Walker brought us rhubarb Mon. while I was washing. Went to Dr. July 16, July 23, Aug. 1, Aug. 9. The last my ear became open for first time following day making low singing noise. Also Aug. 11, but better. Dr. took wire off of Daddy could open his mouth.

Aug. 5. Now he can swallow without having a bottle, but still can't chew with his teeth.

July 31. About 2 after we had Bob's birthday dinner Andy on way to get girl got hit at Lowell and Ritter. Boy, 16 yr. old, Jim Morgan, who failed to stop at stop street. Bob & Sis were at our house for dinner. Insurance Co. settled for $770.00. Andy twisted his neck, hurt his head. Harry Stanley made final payment on his house. He says Patty is pregnant. We think we have good news too. Sold Andy's car for $200 to a man who lived about 3 blocks from Kirkhoffs.

Oct. 15. Andy took me to city Hospital ear clinic where friend of his head of clinic gave me a through hearing test. Also alcohol boric acid which I used 1 week. Helped me a lot. Got appointment with Dr. Ray Foster. He says I do not have sinuses trouble, but only nose trouble. But he examined Daddy and says he has bad sinuses infection. After several treatments he says he will need operation.

Nov. 18. Andy & 2 other medics went to Chicago to drive a new car to California to inspect California hospitals. Bill is building a cabin on Cordry Lake.

Thanksgiving Day. Daddy & boys went to Cabin, and I stayed home. We had supper at nite. Bob & Louise came over. I had tooth filled $9.

Dec. 5. Daddy operated at St. Vincent's by Dr. R. Foster. Louise & Bob took me at nite Tues & Wed. Billy went after him Thursday morn. Hospital bill $116.50. Dr. charged $50. I have used 7 or 8 kinds of salve in my ear. It gets better very slowly. I have lots of noise in my ear. Also got eczema on my right eye lid. Andy gave me some new salve put out by Eli Lilly, not on market yet. called Flurandrenlolne 0.05%. It is helping me.

Dec. 20. I went to town to buy **Louise** hose, panties, slip and other Xmas presents. Fell in front of our house & hurt my left arm & side.

Christmas. We went up to Louise and Bob's. Took our Christmas presents. Dad gave me a big surprise, a fur scarf for my neck. White sweater from S & Bob. We had real tree Bob got out of his mother's yard. We had S & Bob & his mother for supper.

"1961"

Jan. 12. Dad's birthday dinner at Sis & Bob's.

Feb. 1. Dad got me some gloves for our anniversary.

Feb. 9. Drain stopped up. Also Feb. 10 some more work on drain.

Feb. 17. Judy Brown got married.

Feb. 18. Louise gave me a permanent and we got new water tank. The old one leaked.

Feb. 24. Andy had final exams for medical school.

Feb. 24. big snow. Blizzard.

Sun., Feb 25. We wanted to go to church. Andy went with us. We got stuck in front of garage 30 min. 56 in children's church.

March 2, my birthday. Artificial flowers, Bill. Planter, Andy. Dad got me perfume. Aunt Helen, broach and hankie. Aunt Mabel, dresser scarf. Louise, electric scissors. Mrs. Walker, ? hose.

March 7. Andy went to California.

March 13. letter from Andy.

March 25. Helen's birthday. Laurrie Ann born at 8:15 P.M. Wt. 7–12 oz. Community Hosp.

Laurrie Ann

Our Rose bud sleeps on her rosy face
On her mother's old bed
With the sheet
Half under her head and part under her feet
She has a blue clown quilt
On top of her bed
She has golden curly hair
On her pretty round head
When she weeps
See her mother arise
When her voice it rings
To us she is the most precious of things.

"1961" April 15. Another blizzard, not affecting Indpls. so much, Heavy snow.

April 31. We had surprise dinner for Uncle Sol's 75 birthday. Helen, us, Uncle Clarence, Cleta & her husband, Guy. End of dentist work $41.

May 1. started dieting wt. 164 lb.

May 14. Mother's day dinner at Louise–perfume corsage of carnations.

May 29. Got new curtains for kitchen.

May 29. Andy came home from California on plane. Brought me a wooden bird made by prisoners of Alcatraz.

May 30. Daddy & I went to Brownstown to church. Took us 1 hr. to find church. Bro Romine preached, and we had dinner at 4 P.M. Bro & Sis Gant, Sis Miller, Bro Mercer, Harold Romine. We came home.

May. Bad rainy month. Billy had bad luck with back wall of cabin, fell twice.

June 5, Monday. Andy's graduation. We mislaid car took wrong direction. Dad brought strawberries on way home.

June 9. Uncle Sol taken to hospital.

June 12. Bob started work.

June 17. Oven door spring broke. Dad & Bob put in new one. I now weigh 152.

June 20–21–22., Andy took state board examination.

June 18, Father's day. Dinner at Louise & Bob. Dad got 2 blue shirts, pair pants, hankies, clock.

June 20. Billy bought Television from Bowling alley.

July 3. Mrs. Walker took us to dinner Joan and Finehouts.

July. Hookers came. We went to cabin for picnic with Louise & Bob.

July 15. Cynthia Coombs married.

July 31. Bob's birthday. Bob & Louise came to supper.

Mon., Aug 7. Ruth Urshan Copple funeral.

Aug. 2. Louise & Bob & baby went to California.

Aug. 4. Permanent wave. I now weigh 142.

Aug. 15. Dad, Bob & I went to Illinois, Stayed 2 nites 2 days. Came home 17.

Sept. First week Bob & Louise came home.

Oct. 8. Dad & I went out to dinner & took freeway to Shelbyville.

Oct. 12. Found **Dad had passed away** about 6 & 730 Andy came home. Left Oct.. 20 for California. also Betty. Got Lawyer Robert Girk thru John Hart.

Nov. Bill got 30 day extended leave

Nov. 23. We had Thanksgiving dinner at home with Mrs. Walker, Louise & Bob.

Nov. 25. Uncle Wm. took us to eat Howard Johnson's with Velma. Bill went to army Nov. 30.

Dec. 3. Velma Barber, Uncle Wm's girl stayed all night. Sat with me.

Dec. 16. Wm. & I went to Cincinnati. Went shopping rained all day, but warm. Saw *King of Kings.*

Dec. 17. Went to Curt's church. Children's Xmas program. Velma took us to dinner.

Dec. 18. Monday came home & found out boys had tried to break in house. Tore loose screen in back of kitchen, east.

Dec. 20. Bob came home. Went to work at Haag's.

Dec. 21. Bob caught a counterfeiter trying to pass bogus $20 for 19¢ peroxide bottle. He has to work nights 4 to 12. Wrecked his car on Burgress. Eddie Herman fixed it for $56.

Dec. 25. We ate dinner at Louise & Bob's. Gave Laurrie Ann shoe fly, blue tights', $1 in Xmas card. She gave me dresser set & perfume. I gave her blouse glasses

End "1961"

XXI—Poems by Derexa Whitcomb Brown

Our Boy Left Home Today

Our boy left home today
How full of sorrow is my lonely yearning heart;
For many days we shall not see his smiling face:
How shall we pass the hours from him apart.
He left his childhoods home today;
Things never can be quite as they have been before.
His room is dark and desolate tonight,
His hat and coat hang not behind the kitchen door.

We miss his boyish face so much;
Backward o'er months and years our sad thoughts turn;
Did we appreciate our boy when he was here?
We ask, as now our hearts for him so fondly yearn.

I try to think he will be back,
And for a visit he will only plan;
But then the thoughts that hurts comes back to me,
Our boy hereafter is a "business man."

He'll labor and gain wealth,
And then a wife and home he'll have; I must not mind,
But then the ties of childhood home will break,
And we–oh tis so lonely for those left behind!

This is the way of all the world,
One cannot have all pleasure sweet without alloy;
Sad partings come: and I can only pray tonight,
Thank God I have so good, so true a boy.

Though few in number we are strong in faith
For God is our Captain and Shield
Then onward and upwards our motto shall be
And the Scripture the weapon we wield.

Seven years we've been faithful and true
to the banner that here represents us
Sometimes the skies o'er us were blue
Sometimes dark clouds hang above us.

But still with our eyes on the goal
Like the shepherds on Bethlehem Place
We have trod on through our very Posts
Was torn with anguish and pain.

Oh! Mothers and sisters come help us
Don't you hear the Macedonian Cry
And let us stand shoulder to shoulder
Success will come by and by.

Don't you see tender hearts torn and bleeding
for loved ones that fall day by day
Can we this lesson unheeding
be indifferent and go on our way.

Oh no let us stand by the Banner
of faith and love hand in hand
Let us rally for God and his Standard
For hi and our dear native land.

A Mothers love no hand has such
A tender clasp, no voice so loyal
No eye such a tender gleam, no heart
Beats as lovingly as a Mothers.

Then why we ask are so many
Homes broken up we now see
Through a glass darkly but than we
will face to face so Gods will is good

Perhaps if we did not come in
Contact with the rough edges of the
World our attainments would
Not be so high.

6″x6″ Nettle Print by L.A. Walker, 1983

9″x9″ Painting by R.M. Sohn, 1957

Louise, APS, Betty Hooker, 378 S. Downey Ave. Indpls.., 1937

APS, Betty Hooker, Orlando, Fla., 2007. Phil, Construction, Tahoe-Donner Cabin, 1973

In 1973, we purchased two lots in Tahoe-Donner, a subdivision near Truckee. I decided to build a pre-cut Lindal Cedar Home and own a Lindal Cedar Homes franchise. I built three homes in Tahoe-Donner and one in Fallon, Nevada. We used the one on Christie Lane in Tahoe-Donner as a retreat until we decided to move to Donner Lake and remodel a home in 1982.

Eric, Phillip, David Walker, Laurrie Walker, Christie Lane Tahoe-Donner Cabin, Christmas 1974

Dad, APS, Med School Grad, 1961

APS and Arlene's 50th wedding anniversary in Woodinville, Washington, 2013.
Left: Kerry, Mark, Arlene, APS, Kris, Brady, Alex, Phil, Peter, Eric,
Liz, Sierra, and Mauriza with Isabella.

XXII—Europe with Bill, 1962. My Medical Career

On November 24, 2020, I decided to publish a book on the photographic account of my life in medicine. This book will keep my hands and brain busy and detail the second period in my life, 1957 to 2009, practicing medicine.

The practice of medicine and recording its history are my passions and are important forces in my life. In 1955, after two years of studying architecture at the University of Cincinnati, I decided to switch to pre-med to become a doctor. I told my mother of my decision. She was a public health RN and advised against my desire to study medicine: "Medicine is difficult, long, and the hours are not desirable.

My mother, Ruth M. Fulton, RN, Graduate, Deaconess Hosp., Indpls., with Red Cross Service Pin & 1924 Graduation Pin. Music box in the middle, gift from Bill to Mom

I initially consider medical illustration which was offered as a course at the University of Cincinnati, but I changed my goal to become a doctor. Because of my religious upbringing my initial goal was to become a medical missionary, but that changed as my brain matured.

Dedication to medicine came from my mother's side of the family. She and her sister; Madonna Stanley were nurses, and her brother, William Fulton, became a dentist because he couldn't afford to go to medical school. His son, Bill Fulton, graduated from Indiana University School of Medicine two or three years ahead of me. In addition, brother Bob was a Purdue University graduate pharmacist, and Eric and Kris are practicing doctors.

While studying architecture at the University of Cincinnati I took psychology and zoology courses at night school to see if I had an aptitude for biology and medicine. I aced both courses. The die was cast. Because I lived in Indiana, I decide to enroll in pre-med at Indiana University in Bloomington. I hitchhiked to Bloomington from Cincinnati and met with Associate Dean of Arts and Sciences Byron Doenges to see what classes would transfer. It was my lucky day, his wife was designing a home and needed help with structure design, which I provided. Dean Doenges got me a $125 academic scholarship for my second year at I.U. The first year at I.U. brother Bill and I rented a room in a house in Bloomington. The second year we lived in the Phi Delt house.

After completing two years of courses required for medical school, I was interviewed and accepted in the class of 1961, which was the last first-year class to matriculate in Bloomington. In 1957 I embarked on my fifty-two-year career in medicine. Five Phi Delt brothers, Bob Crist, John Heumann, Lloyd Lempke, John Records, Mike Taylor, and I rented one half of a house in Bloomington. Tom Greenberg, who was a friend of John Heumann's from Evansville joined us. Bob Crist was our leader. He was not only brilliant, but he also had great insight. Before each class examination he would sit down with us and say: "Here is what you need to know." He was right 90% of the time.

The second year was in Indianapolis at IU's Medical Center. Brother Bill rented his house in Eagledale to me and my medical school friends but didn't charge me. Jim Mount joined us.

MEDICAL SCHOOL

Anatomy and physiology were important courses our first year in medical school. The identity of cadavers was kept secret, but we knew our cadaver was an individual who died in prison. So, you don't get confused those wearing a white coat are alive.

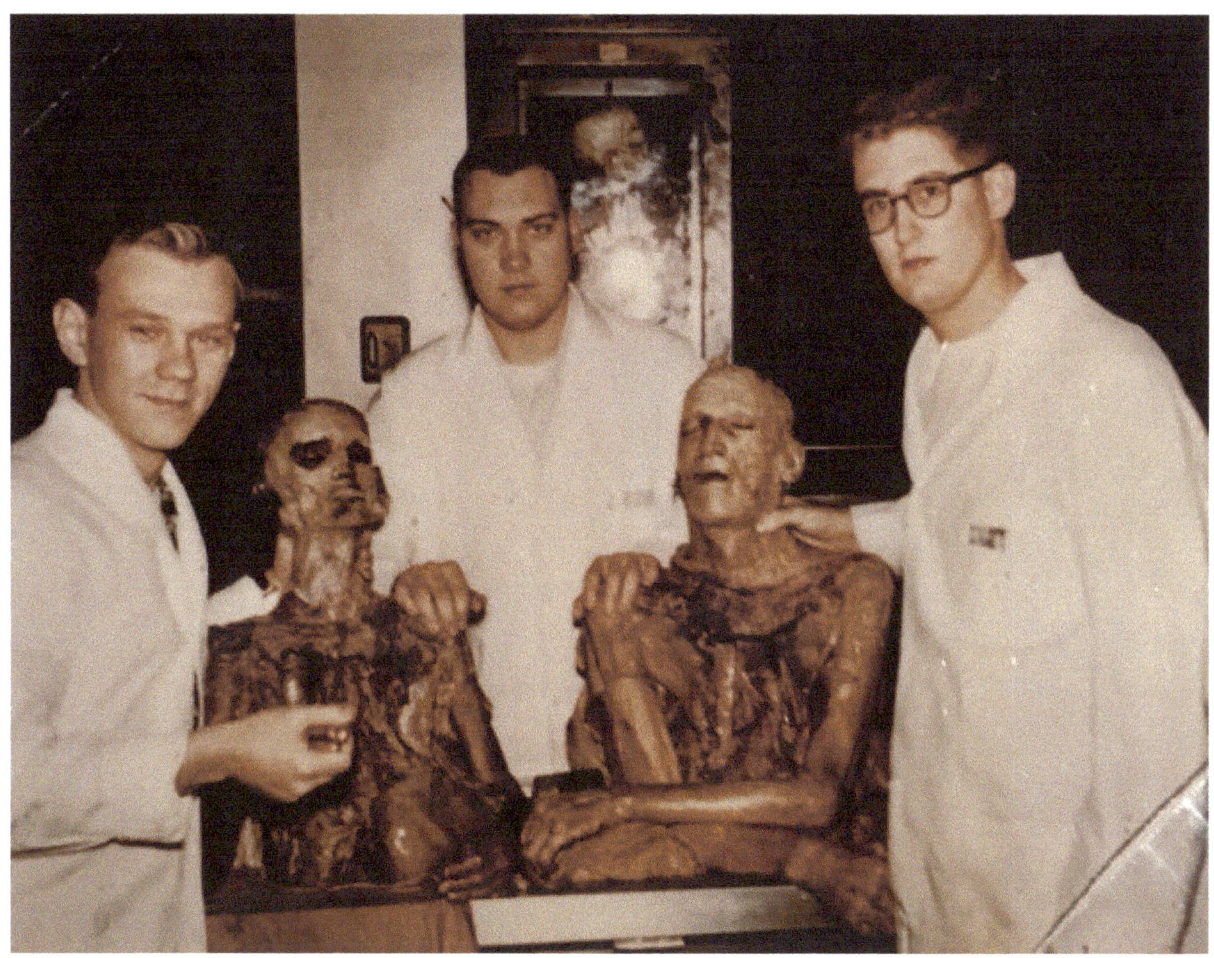

Left: APS (white coat), John Records (white coat), and Bob Crist (white coat), in anatomy lab, 1957

EL SALVADOR AND GUATEMALA, 1960

In 1958 at the end of my first year many students had to retake neuroanatomy, which was the toughest first year class. I knew I had passed, so I took a summer vacation in Europe. I climbed the Matterhorn Mountain in Switzerland and toured Europe before the start of my second year. At the end of my third year, I applied for and received a two-month fellowship with the World Health Organization (WHO) to study in El Salvador, Central America. To prepare I was assigned to Tulane University in New Orleans. Here, I had my first experience with segregation. When I boarded a streetcar, I went to the back. The conductor politely told me that is where the "colored" sit. I traveled to El Salvador and Guatemala rural areas to spray for mosquitoes that carry the malaria parasite. The rest of the two months I made rounds with doctors at the hospital in San Salvador.

Spraying for Mosquitos that carry Malaria

Women washing Clothes in a well that drains into a Creek where they get their Drinking Water

My Apartment in San Salvador

Spraying for Mosquitoes to Prevent Malaria

SAN FRANCISCO CITY & COUNTY HOSPITAL, 1961-1962

Since Indiana University School of Medicine (IUSOM) was on the quarter system, I finished medical school in April 1961 and headed to San Francisco City & County Hospital to start an internship. In June I returned to Indianapolis for my graduation ceremony. After graduation John Hironimos, who was starting an internship at Los Angeles County Hospital, drove us to Los Angeles, and I flew to San Francisco. Midway through my internship, classmate Milt Matter, who was an intern at Southern Pacific Hospital, and I rented an apartment on Twin Peaks. During my internship I rotated on emergency, psychiatry, surgical, medical, and OB/GYN services. I briefly considered orthopedics for a career, but the chief of orthopedics told me I would have to wait two years to start a residency.

My father died on November 12, 1961, and I returned to Indianapolis for the funeral. After I completed my internship my mother flew to San Francisco, and we drove to Seattle World's Fair on the way back to Indiana.

APS, SF City & County Hospital, 1961.

APS, John Hironimos, LA, 1961

Mom, Seattle World's Fair, 1962

Arlene, Tacoma, 1964

EUROPE WITH BILL, 1962

In 1962 Bill and I went to Europe, I bought an XKE Jaguar for $4,787 in Coventry, England. We toured Europe and entered East Berlin. We visited Waterloo where in 1815 Nikolaus Sohn helped defeat Napoleon. When we got back in the U.S. I called Dr. Charles Larson and drove to Tacoma for an interview for a residency in pathology.

Bill in my XKE Jaguar, Switzerland, 1962

Brandenburg Gate with Bill, 1962

Pathology Residency, 1963-1966

In Indianapolis Lloyd Lempke told me of a locum tenens job with Dr. Victor Vollrath, who had a family practice near Butler University. In 1961, I took the job and met Arlene, who was an x-ray technician in Dr. Vollrath's office. He had a patient, Mrs. Ruby Winders, who was my grade school music teacher. When I saw her as a patient, she told me: "I always knew you had it in you."

While working for Dr. Vollrath I decided on a career in pathology. I contacted Dr. Ed Smith, my former teacher and chairman of pathology at IU School of Medicine for recommendations of pathology residencies in the Northwest. He suggested I contact his "good friend" Dr. Charles Larson at Tacoma General Hospital. Arlene and I got married June 15, 1963. We drove through the Badlands of South Dakota to Tacoma, where I started my pathology residency with Drs. Charlie Larson, Jim Wicks, Charlie Reberger, and Tom Elder.

Arlene, South Dakota Badlands, 1963

Waterloo Battlefield with Bill, 1962

Dr. Charles Larson was the chairman of the residency and one of the world's foremost forensic pathologist. He was a founding member of the National Association of Medical Examiners and American Academy of Forensic Sciences, past president of the College of American Pathologists, past president of the National Boxing Association, first president of the World Boxing Association, and had done the autopsies at Dachau, WWII.

During my residency (1963-66) I accompanied Dr. Larson on forensic autopsies and testimonies. One case stands out. A young boy's death was labeled a suicide because he had a rope partially around his neck. Dr. Larson examined the scene and ruled it an accident. At the scene was an erotic picture and the boy's pants were at his knees. He died of self-asphyxia, which is thought to increase sexual gratification. As a result, he accidently killed himself. Under Dr. Larson, I became interested in forensic pathology. During my residency, we diagnosed surgical biopsies and did autopsies for all Tacoma hospitals, including Tacoma Children's Hospital and the VA hospital at Madigan Air Force Base. Later, in 1968 in Reno I became board certified as a forensic pathologist in addition to being a general pathologist.

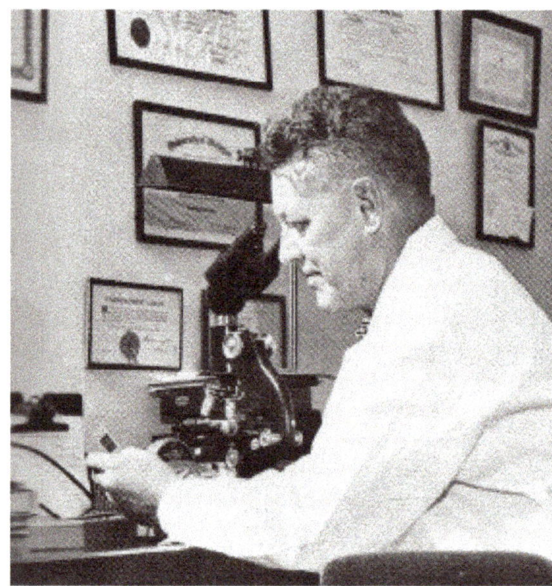

Dr. Charles Larson, Tacoma Gen. Hosp.

Arlene, Ohms Garden, Wenatchee, 1964

Louise, Arlene, Harriett, Xmas, Indpls.,

Arlene, Gladys Divide, WA, 1964

Arlene, Fort Nisqually, 1964

APS, Fort Nisqually, 1964

Arlene, Sun Valley, ID, 1964

APS, Sun Valley Village, ID, 1964

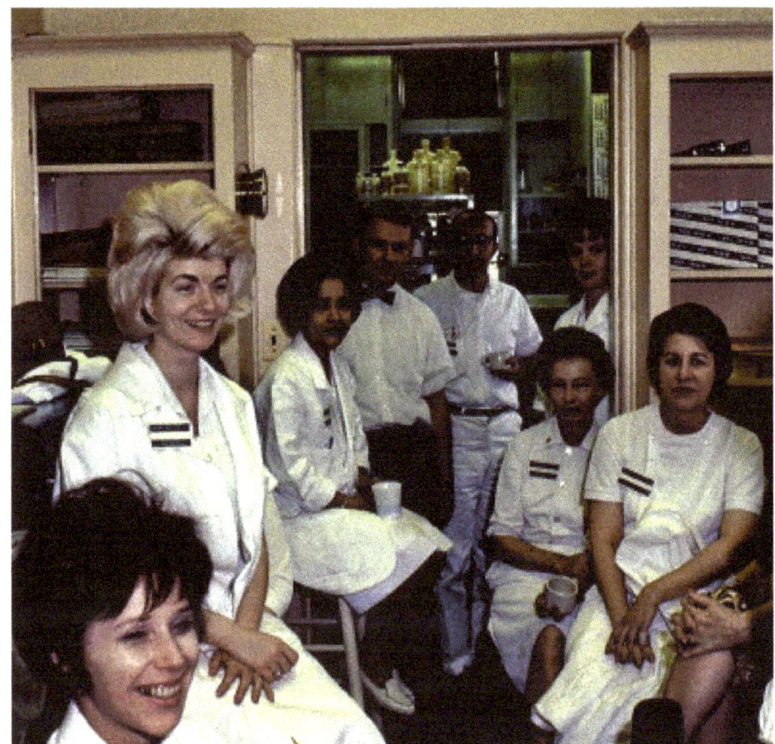

My Going-in-the-Army Party, 1966

Arlene, Columbia River Falls, 1964

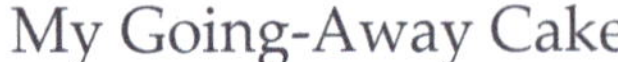

My Going-Away Cake

Arlene, Eric, Tom, Elena Elder, Phil, Lake Tahoe, 1970

U.S. ARMY, 1966-1968

In 1966, the third year of my four-year residency, I was drafted (not volunteered) into the U.S. Army. In 1966 doctors were eligible for the draft until age 35. After Phillip was born April 28, I drove to Fort Sam Houston, Texas to start my two-year tour of duty. While in Texas I met with Hal Brown and Bill Ropp for a day at the beach. From Texas I was assigned to Ft. Ord. After one year at Ft. Ord, I was assigned to the 9th Medical Lab in Saigon.

APS on a Training Exercise at Fort Sam Houston, Texas, 1966

Hal Brown, Bill Ropp, and APS on Galveston Island, Texas, 1966

VIETNAM, 1967-1968

At the 9th Medical Lab, I was appointed chief of pathology. In addition to management, my chief duties were surgical pathology and doing autopsies on non-killed-in-action service men. The most common autopsy was on individuals who died in helicopter accidents. The accidents were the result of helicopters flying at treetop level.

We did surgical biopsies for all Vietnam U.S. facilities and the Seventh-day Adventist hospital in Saigon where the most common disease was cancer of the mouth from chewing betelnut. While in Vietnam I had time to study for the pathology examination to become board certified. A four-year residency is required, and I had only completed three years when I got drafted. The board gave me one-year credit for my two years in the service. Hooray!! I only lost one year.

A Little Fun in Saigon

APS Dissecting a Fake Surgical Specimen (Cigar) in front of an Assistant, 1967
APS Diagnosing a Microscopic Slide Biopsy (Staged Helmet, Cigar, & Flack Vest) 1967

A More Serious Saigon

"Saigon On Fire" from my BOQ, 1968

Funeral in front of my BOQ, 1967

WASHOE MEDICAL CENTER

I returned to civilian life in the 1968, and we moved to Reno where I joined Physicians Consulting labs (PCL), which consisted of five pathologists. A second group, Western Pathologists Associates (WPL), included Drs. Owen Bolstad and Don Schieve and three pathologists based in California. In 1971 PCL approached WPL to jointly purchase a $30,000 twelve-test chemistry analyzer. As a result, the two groups merged and formed a clinical laboratory at 888 Willow Street, a two-story, 16,000-square-foot building. The merged group had 140 employees and twelve pathologists which served twenty hospitals. In 1993 we sold the lab to Allied Clinical Laboratories which joined LabCorp.

In 1977, Dr. Salvadorini retired as director of Washoe Medical Center's (WMC-now Renown Regional Medical Center) laboratory, and on September 1, 1977, the hospital's board of directors appointed me the laboratory director. I had the good fortune to be involved with a group of physicians who were leaders in local and state politics. Both of my partners, Dr. V.A. Salvadorini and Dr. Jack Callister, were past presidents of the Washoe County Medical Society and the Nevada State Medical Association (NSMA). However, becoming president of Reno Surgical Society was my first step in medical politics.

The society's membership required each member to give a talk and pay for dinner on a rotating basis. We also had invited speakers. Dr. Salvadorini was acquainted with Dr. Charles Larson and hosted him as a speaker. When it became my time to give a talk, I decided to discuss blood alcohol levels. At a previous meeting I asked ten volunteers to have a blood alcohol (BA) drawn and keep track of how many drinks they had. I asked another group of ten to have a blood alcohol drawn, but they were not told beforehand to keep a count of their drinks. I brought two technicians to the meeting to draw blood alcohols. The individuals who were told to keep track of the number of drinks had BAs that correlated with the number of drinks they consumed. The individuals who were not told had BAs showing they underestimated their number of drinks by one half. Conclusion: after two or more drinks most alcohol drinkers don't remember how many drinks they consume.

In 1981 I was elected Chief of the Medical Staff of Washoe Medical Center. It was my privilege to recommend and see my good friend, Maida Pringle, become an Honorary Lifetime Member of the Medical Staff. She had been Director of Nursing, Assistant Administrator and Chairman of the Board of Trustees, and the street leading into the hospital is named Pringle Way establishing her as a very important individual in WMC's history.

Another event stands out during my tenure. I was playing golf when I got a phone call from Chief of Surgery Dr. W.M. who said he got a call from a nurse, who said Dr. J.D. tried to insert a chest tube in a severely ill patient but was unable to complete the procedure and abandoned the patient. Dr. W.M. went to the hospital to complete the procedure. For that and other inappropriate actions I suspended Dr. J.D's privileges. At the next executive meeting my action was approved. Shortly thereafter I got a call from the chief of staff at the VA Hospital in another city inquiring about Dr. J.D. I told him I was prevented by Dr. J.D.'s lawyer from commenting. He said that was all he needed to know.

ELECTED—Named to the top three jobs in the Washoe Medical Center medical staff at the annual staff dinner meeting were, from left, Dr. Anton P. Sohn, Director of Laboratories, Vice Chief of Staff, Dr. Maynard Christian, Chief of Staff, and Dr. Gordon Nitz, Secretary.

APS, Maynard Christian and Gordon Nitz, 1979

APS, WMC Lab Director, 1977

In 1984 I was elected president of the Nevada State Medical Association (NSMA). My mother and family attended my inauguration.

SOCIETY OFFICERS—Dr. Anton P. Sohn, left, and Dr. Jack E. Talsma, had these cheerful looks following the annual membership meeting of the Washoe County Medical Society. Dr. Talsma was installed as president and Dr. Sohn, a Washoe Medical Center pathologist, was named president-elect of the society.

APS and Jack Talsma, 1976

Mom and Louise, Palm Springs NSMA, 1984

Scroll honors Mrs. Pringle

Maida Pringle, R.N., former assistant administrator and Board of Trustees member, accepts from Dr. Anton Sohn, chief of staff, a scroll of the resolution passed at the annual meeting in December declaring her an honorary lifetime member of the Medical Staff. Hand-lettered by Mrs. Eva Rosenauer, the document was presented at a recent award luncheon in the Board Room. The entire hospital and community paid tribute to Mrs. Pringle at a testimonial dinner sponsored by the League on May 9 at John Ascuaga's Nugget. The dinner raised $2,900 to inaugurate a nursing scholarship in her name at the Orvis School of Nursing, University of Nevada, Reno.

Maida Pringle Awarded Honorary Lifetime Member of the Medical Staff by APS, 1982

Eric and Mom, NSMA Palm Springs Meeting, 1984

APS, Pendulum of Office, 1984

Louise, APS, Mom, Arlene, Phil, and Kristin, Palm Springs NSMA Meeting, 1984

Joe Reinkemeyer flew Patty Reinkemeyer (left), Kristin, Phil (right), and the Sohn family to the NSMA Palm Springs Meeting where I was Inaugurated as President, 1984

RENO SURGICAL SOCIETY YOSEMITE MEETING, 1985

I gave a talk at a Reno Surgical Society meeting at the Yosemite Valley lodge about the 1985 Galaxy airplane crash in Reno that killed 70 people. Most died from the fire. One person was ejected and survived. He was strapped to his seat that landed on his father.

Recognition for Service

Ron Cudek, APS, Arlene, and Phyllis Cudek, 1985

UNIVERSITY OF NEVADA SCHOOL OF MEDICINE

In 1984 Dean Dr. Bob Daugherty of the University of Nevada School of Medicine (UNSOM, now University of Nevada Reno School of Medicine—UNRSOM) appointed me chairman of pathology. My 1985 faculty was Drs. Fred Laubscher, Steve Campbell, John Diamond, Sara Malin, and three California members are not shown. Also not photographed are Gussie Buyrgone, Rick Pugh, and Phyllis Cudek who were members of the department's history of medicine section. Drs. Ritzlin, Parks, and Maehara were the backbone of the department.

One of my first actions was to create a section to research history of medicine in Nevada. At the IU School of Medicine, we were required to write a history of medicine research paper for pathology. I brought this tradition to the Nevada's School of Medicine and required students in pathology to write a history of medicine 1,500-word research paper. In addition,

APS in the GBHOM Museum, 2002

University of Nevada
Reno
Anton P. Sohn, M.D.
Professor and Chair of Pathology & Laboratory Medicine,
Emeritus

Emeritus Certificate, 2009

State of Nevada
Office of Governor Brian Sandoval
CERTIFICATE OF RECOGNITION
Dr. Anton Sohn

Governor's Certificate of Recognition, 2009

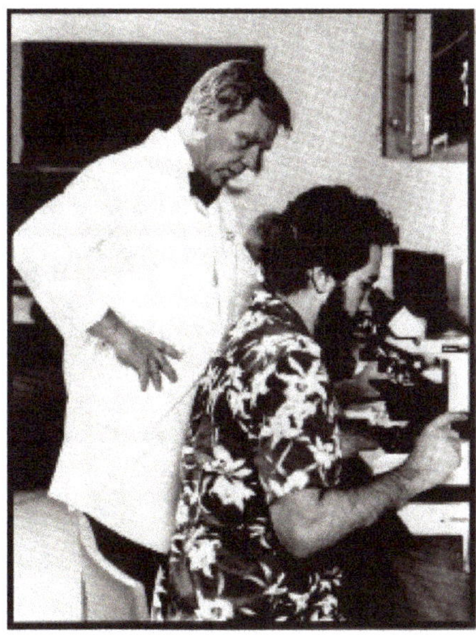

APS instructing a Student, 1986

I established a history of medicine program. Dr. Owen Bolstad and I founded a quarterly history of medicine bulletin. I named it *Greasewood,* a desert plant that Native American Piute and Shoshone had used for thousands of years to treat aliments. Owen added *Tablettes,* the French word for tablet, to give the bulletin's name sophistication. In 2021 *Greasewood Tablettes* is in its 32nd year of publication. The program includes Greasewood Press, which has published sixteen books, an oral history program with over 120 recordings, and the Great Basin History of Medicine Museum (GBHOMM) and the Doctors Hood Library. The museum and library are located in the school's Savitt Library on the School of Medicine's Reno campus. To further my knowledge of the history of medicine, in 1991 I took a one-year sabbatical at Johns Hopkins Institute of the History of Medicine in Baltimore to advance my knowledge and do research at Library of Congress.

APS & Phil (MIT Graduate), 1989

Eric (UNSOM Graduate), 1996

Kristin (UNSOM Graduate), APS, Eric, and Arlene, 2012

XXIII—PISTOL CREEK WITH FAMILY AND FRIENDS

From 1989 to 2017, four of my high school friends (Montgomery, Payne, Thompson, and Toole) took an annual trip with me to my cabin at Pistol Creek Ranch in Idaho's River of No Return Wilderness. Bob Cox and Harold Brown made an occasional trip with us. Norm Wilkens dubbed us "The Boys of Summer'. We named ourselves "The Gentlemen's Serenity Club of Pistol Creek". Our charter states, *"fishing, shooting, hiking/riding, taking photographs, reading poetry/literature, listening to fine music, smoking fine cigars, and eating and drinking merrily."*

The trip entailed meeting at my home in Reno and driving to Boise or Cascade, Idaho where we scheduled a small plane to fly us to the ranch. We made many side trips on the drive north from Reno. We frequently stopped in Silver City, Idaho to spend the night. Silver City sprang up during the 1800s and is now a ghost town with many of the old buildings still intact. We also made trips to Crater Lake, Oregon, California's wine country, and other historical sites. Unfortunately, age took its toll, and we stopped our trips 1n 2015.

Bob Montgomery, Gene Toole, 1989

Bob Montgomery, Bob Cox, and APS, 1993

Virginia City, Montgomery, Payne, APS, Toole, H. Brown, 2014

Payne, APS, Toole, Montgomery Thompson, Silver City, 2010

From 2004 to 2017, the Sohn family made annual trips to Pistol Creek. Some years our grandkids invited a friend to go along, but most years just the Sohns spent a week in the summer at the ranch. Occasionally brothers Bill and Bob flew with our family to Pistol Creek. In the fall we hunted deer and elk.

Brady and Isabella, 2015

Brady, 2017

APS, Arlene, Phil, Kristin, Alex, Brady, Kerry, Peter, Sierra, 2006

Kerry, 2006

Kerry, Brady, Eric, Phil, Sierra, APS, Peter, 2009

Brady, Sierra, Peter, 2007

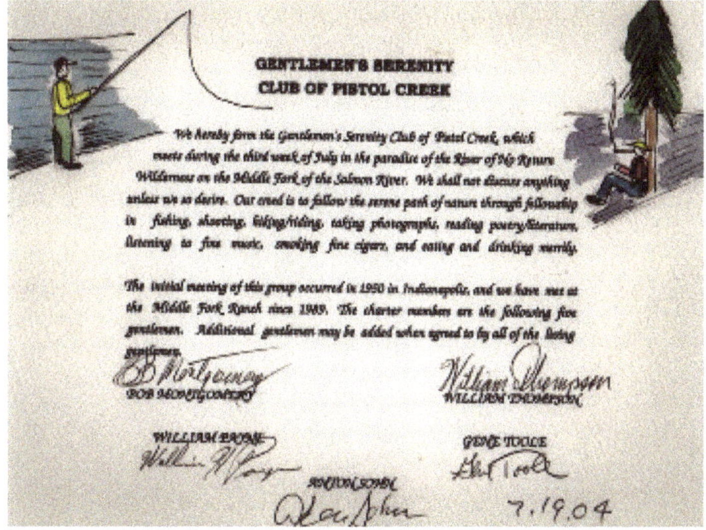

GENTLEMEN'S SERENITY CLUB OF PISTOL CREEK

We hereby form the Gentlemen's Serenity Club of Pistol Creek, which meets during the third week of July in the paradise of the River of No Return Wilderness on the Middle Fork of the Salmon River. We shall not discuss anything unless we so desire. Our creed is to follow the serene path of nature through fellowship in fishing, shooting, hiking/riding, taking photographs, reading poetry/literature, listening to fine music, smoking fine cigars, and eating and drinking merrily.

The initial meeting of this group occurred in 1950 in Indianapolis, and we have met at the Middle Fork Ranch since 1989. The charter members are the following five gentlemen. Additional gentlemen may be added when agreed to by all of the living gentlemen.

BOB MONTGOMERY

WILLIAM THOMPSON

WILLIAM PAYNE

GENE TOOLE

ANTON SOHN

7.19.04

Gentlemen's Serenity Club Charter

Toole, Brown, Monty, Payne, APS, 2014

Thompson, APS, Bill, Payne, Monty, 1992

Toole, Payne, Monty, APS, 1995

Roy Hogan, Owen Bolstad, Phil, 1989

Payne, APS, Bill Sohn, Monty, 1992

Mimi Sohn, 2004

Matt Schmitt 2016

Dave, Kara, Lois Huffman, Donner, 2003

Dave, Lois Huffman, Arlene, 2006

Kerry, 2005

Rob Sohn, APS, Chris Sohn, Montgomery, Bob Sohn, 1990

Sierra, 2004

Phil and Kerry, 2004

Brady, Kerry, and Sierra 2004

XXIV—Europe With Medical School Friends, 1958

My first adventure outside the continental North America was in 1958. I decided I needed a break after my first year in medical school. I went to Europe and met my medical school classmates, Milt Matter, Hal Navotny, and Gary Gieseke. I bought a used Volkswagen (VW) for $845 and a sleeping bag and traveled the continent. I sometimes slept beside my VW. **Dad** paid for my trip, and I used "Europe of $5 a day" as my guide. How lucky was I to have a generous father. The highlight of my trip was to I convince Gary and Hal to climb Switzerland's Matterhorn Mountain with me. Milt did not join us because the Indiana National Guard sent him to Europe, and he had to return with them. The photo of us is in front of the Brussels' World's Fair.

Matterhorn

APS on Matterhorn Summit, 1958

APS, Volkswagen, 1958

APS, G. Gieseke, H. Navotny, M. Matter, 1958

XXV—Denmark With Our Family and Arlene's, 1973

ARLENE'S HERITAGE, DENMARK, 1973

In 1973 Arlene, Phil, Eric, and I flew to Europe and bought a Mercedes-Benz sedan in Germany. Then, we drove to Denmark where Arlene's father was born and met up with her family (father, mother, and Uncle Sven and his wife, Flo). We also visited with Arlene's brother Mark, who was studying in Denmark. While in Denmark we made excursions to Sweden and Hungary. Hungary was still behind USSR's iron curtain, and we were required to leave our passports with authorities whenever we left our hotel in Budapest.

Pop, Arlene, Phil, Eric, Gram, Flo, Sven, Mark, Frederiksberg, Denmark..

Phil in our new Mercedes roof window, Denmark

Phil (no hat), Eric (no gun), Queen's palace guard, Frederiksberg, Denmark.

Phil, APS, Eric at Legoland, Copenhagen.

Phil and Eric on a defused WWII mine, I hope. Martin Hedegard, Arlene's grandfather.

Arlene, Phil, Gram, Pop, Eric, Sven, Flo, and APS in a Danish beer garden.

Jelling church where Arlene's relatives are buried.

Pop and Sven at the side of the house where they were raised.

Front of the house where Pop and Sven were raised.

Eric & Phil on a "slow boat" to Sweden.

Phil and Eric at Jutland preparing to shoot a canon.

Phil, Einger, Arlene, & Eric.

Phil, "unhappy" Eric, & Arlene
boarding a bus to Budapest, Hungary.

XXVI—Puerto Rico To Visit Bob And Mimi, 1980

In 1980 we went to Puerto Rico where Brother Bob was directing a pharmacy division of Eli Lily. We spent a week visiting with Bob, his wife, Mimi, and their two children, Chris, and Rob.

Arlene, Rob, Phil, Kristin, Bob, Chris, and Eric going boating.

Eric and Kristin in Old Town, Puerto Rico.

XXVII—HAWAII WITH FAMILY, 1983, 1986, AND 2010

HAWAII-TO RELAX IN THE SUN, 1983, 1986, & 2010

We took several trips to Hawaii over the years. In 1983 Phil went on an exchange student program to Germany. He stayed with Patrick Kretz family. In turn, Patrick carne to Reno for a visit. We decided to treat him with a trip to Hawaii. We visited Pearl Harbor National Memorial, where the sunken USS Arizona with its war dead has been made into a memorial. In 1986 I was invited to give forensic pathology lectures at the University df Hawaii Burns School of Medicine. Arlene's mom went with us for a week-long vacation in Honolulu.

Eric, Phil, and I took scuba diving lessons at the YMCA in Reno. After we were certified we took <living trips to Hawaii and the Yucatan peninsula in Mexico. In 2010 Arlene and I accompanied Eric and Mauriza to Honolulu to see a USC/University of Hawaii football game

HONOLULU

Patrick, Phil, Kristin, Eric, Arlene, & APS ata WWII War Memorial, 1983.

Eric, 1983.

Eric and APS scuba <living, 1986.

Eric, Mauriza cuse v Hawaii football game) 2010.

XXVIII—MEXICO WITH FAMILY, 1985

MEXICO-TO SCUBA DIVE, 1985

In 1985 we flew to the Yucatan Peninsula for a vacation. Phil, Eric, and I took a boat to Cozumel Island to scuba dive. We also took a bus trip to tour the Chichén Itzá ruins and the Temple of Kukulcán (pyramid) where we went up a narrow passage to the sacrifice altar.

YUCATAN PENINSULA

Eric going scuba <living at Cozumel Island.

Eric parasailing.

Phil & Eric in front of the Kukulcán Temple.

Sacrifice altar inside the Kukulcán Temple.

XXIX—Caribbean Cruise, Arlene, Louise & Russ, 1997

PUERTO RICO, SAINT THOMAS, P ANAMA CANAL, COSTA RICA, & ACAPULCO-WITH RUSS & LOUISE, 1997

Day 1, Jan. 8: We left Dallas with Louise and Russ for San Juan, Puerto Rico. There were Royal Caribbean agents at the gate. We had a small sitting balcony with our cabin on The Legend of the Seas. **Day 2**: We docked at Charlotte Amalie on Saint Thomas Island. Russ' birthday is January 11.

Russ' 65th birthday

Arlene and Louise at Charlotte Amalie

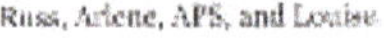

Russ, Arlene, APS, Louise, Caribbean, 1997 Glenda, Arlene, Fishing in Alaska, 1997

Front: Bob Sohn, Arlene with Phil, APS, Bill, Bob Walker with David
Back: Mimi, Harriett, Mom, Laurrie, Louise, 1968 (Front Cover)

XXX—Fishing In Alaska, Arlene, Gene, Glenda, 1997

Salmon & Halibut Fishing in Alaska, 1997

Gene & Glenda, Guide, Arlene & Andy

Andy's 52 lb. King Salmon

XXXI—ENGLAND, ARLENE, GEORGE, ROBERTA, 1997-8

In Mid-1997 the Prutzmans (George and Roberta) and the Sohns (APS and Arlene) signed up for a two-week Holiday London Theatre Tour led by Professor of English Phil Boardman and Theatre Professor Jim Bernardi. We saw a series of performances and afterward, the professors led discussions. In 2021 the tour is in its 31st year. Decembeu 28, Sunday: We left San Francisco in the evening for London's Heathrow airport. We sat next to David and Becky Seibert, whose daughter, Sarah, went to Wooster with Phil. Sara and her husband, Paul, were also on the trip. Monday: We arrived in London anda bus took us to the York Hotel. The hotel was located in Kensington on Queen Bourgh, two blocks from Queensway.

Roberta and Arlene.

George (on the left in a gray coat) in the museum

Arlene, "Little Dancer", Roberta, George in London

Arlene at Stonehenge

XXXII—GREECE AND TURKEY WITH ARLENE & KRIS, 1999

On May 25 Arlene and I flew to Athens. Kris got in the next day to start our 12-day excursion of Greece, its Islands, and Turkey. We toured the Acropolis and the Parthenon. We went to Delphi, took a boat to Santorini. We sailed to Turkey and visited Ephesus.

Mykonos

APS, Kristin, and Arlene at the Parthenon

EPHESUS

Kristin, APS, and Arlene

XXXIII—Tahiti With Arlene and Kris, 2001

In the 1970s I had an Edna Valley wine for the first time at an NSMA meeting in California. I was so impressed with the wine that I bought stock in the company. In 2001 they featured a Tahiti cruise, and I signed up for Arlene, Kristin and me. On March 12 we met a Radisson Seven Sea agent in LAX and were escorted to the gate of our Tahiti fligh.t. We splurged for first class, which gave us access to the first-class lounge in the airport. We later heard the other passengers complain about lack of leg room in the back of the plane. In Pape'ete, Tahiti, we took busses to our ship, *Paul Gauguin.*

Kristin and Arlene, Tiare behind right ear, single; behind the left, married

Our cruise ship, Paul Gauguin.

Arlene, Kristin, and APS

The seas were like glass. When we awoke at 5:30 AM on March 18, we were off the shore of Raiatea. A group of children carne on board to sing and dance for us poolside. Edna Valley Wine Company hosted a cocktail party and only Mondavi wine was served. On the island of Taha'a, we took an open truck tour, going up mountain trails and, visiting a pearl farm and a vanilla plantation. We then visited Radisson's private island to snorkel and kayak, followed by a BBQ. We celebrated Kris' birthday in Bora Bora, where we walked around Viatape and took another bumpy island tour, visiting a pineapple farm and craters from WWII that our troops built.

Arlene and APS at Raiatea dock

Kristin on a Raiatea tender

Kristin at a Vanilla Plantation

Kristin, Radisson's private island to snorkel and ride in kayaks

Kristin and our driver, Bora Bora

Boxing Boys

Kristin's birthday cake

Tahitian dance instructors

Kristin and APS, Cook's Bay, Moorea

APS, Kristin & Arlene, Kristin's birthday

Poerani Pearl farm

Arlene & Kristin at Black Pearl Gem Co

Kristin at Rocky's pineapple farm

Kristin, Cook's Bay, Moorea

XXXIV—Ireland With Arlene, Bill & Harriett, 2001

After the wedding reception for Stephanie and Kurt on June 9, arlene and I drove to the airport for the flight to Ireland. Bill and Harriett got there just before boarding. We arrived in Shannon, Irland at 6:00 AM.

June 10, Sunday: the odyssey began. Bill started out driving. We were on the left-hand side of the roan and round-about the jajor intersections. The road to Miltown-Malbay was barely wide enough for two cars. As I was yelling at Bill to look out for the stone fences at the edge of the pavement, Harriett and Arlene were yelling for Bill to look out for oncoming cars. We clipped the rock wall and put a few scratches on the left rearview mirror and ran over a curb. The rest of our trip was constantly marred by flat tires. From the Shell Staten we drove the short distance to the Cliffs of Moher, which are sheer cliffs 700 feet above the ocean. We than, drove to Galway for the night.

June 11: We drove to Clifden and Kylemore Abbey, a school run by the Benedictine sisters.

APS in Guinness Brewery gift shop

Bill, Harriett, and Arlene, Dublin bar for lunch

Bill. Harriett, Arlene, APS

Arlene, Bill, and Harriet, Cliffs of Moher

Arlene, Harriett, & Bill, Kylemore Abbey.

1,000-year-old runs of Clonmacnoise

Harriett, Bill, and Arlene in Dublin

Site of Blarney Stone, Blarney Castle.

Blarney Castle

Bill's whiskey taste test, Arlene & Harriett

Arlene kissing the Blarney Stone

XXXV—EGYPT WITH ARLENE, 2005

Carol Mousel told us about the Overseas Adventure Travel, an organization that conducted trips around the globe. When they advertised a trip to Egypt, we signed up.

Day 1, October 7: Up at 4:00 AM, Kent, our next-door neighbor, took us the Reno airport.

Day 2, Saturday: In Cairo we met with guide assam Gamal and the eleven in our tour group.

Day 3: We visited the unknown solder's tomb and went to the Egyptian Museum, which cost 35 LE or $6.09 U.S. (5.75 LE = $1.00 U.S.) per person. We saw items from King Tutankhamun's tomb, an exhibit on Akhenaten, and Royal Mummies. The four sarcophagi from King Tut's tomb and the mask were impressive.

Day 4, October 10 We took the buss to the airport for the flight to Luxor and Karnak. Armed guards were assigned to our bus because there had been a recent armed attack on some German visitors. We checked in the Winter Palace Hotel (Sofitel). We met for a night tour of the Luxor Temple.

APS

APS and Arlene at Karnak

Day5, October 11: We took a boat ride across the Nile to site of outdoor breakfast for sunrise. It was wonderful to see the orange sun come above the trees. After the sunrise we visited the Valley of the Queens. The main attraction was Queen Nefatari's tomb, which was closed. I visited one Ramses III's Tomb and it had well preserved colors on the carvings. Arlene visited another tomb and we both visited Amenherkhepshefs tomb that had a f-month fetus mummy. From there we went to the Valley of the Kings. I visited Tutomos III's tomb that had some steps and ladder that Arlene didn't want to try. It had a res sarcophagus without a mummy. Arlene visited Ramses I tomb.

King Djoser's step pyramid

Arlene at the Great Pyramid

Day 11, October 17: We took a boat across the Nile for a camel ride to St. Simeon, a fourth century monastery that lasted until 1920 when they moved to new quarters.

Day 12, Tuesday: We flew to Cairo via a stop in Luxor. It was a one-hour flight to Luxor and one hour to Cario. We took the bus to Mena Hotel near the pyramids. In the afternoon we went to the cotton house and bought shirs for the boys and one for me. We got a towel for Kris. For dinner we went to an upper middle-class home for husband-and wife interior designers. The husband was in Saudi Arabia making a trip to Mecca. We bought the chocolates for the hostess. This was one of our better dinners.

Day 13, October 19: After breakfast we went King Djoser's step pyramid, the first pyramid in Egypt. Then we went to King Mereruka's tomb that was built in 2300 BC. Next, we visited a rug factory that was the only industry of the village. It was started to employ and teach children a skill. At the three pyramids, Cheops, Khafre, and Menkaure, we went in the building that housed the Solar Khufu, a 144-foot boat that was discovered in 1954. It was well preserved. The next stop was the great pyramid. I went up the smaller pyramid and was disappointed as there was nothing to see and it was a short passage. I was out of the passage in 20 minutes. We drove to a vantage point to photograph the three pyramids. We bought pink granite pyramids and canopic jars.

Solar Khufu discovered in 1954

Day 14, Thursday: We attended lecture on Islam by a professor at the Cairo University. We visited a Coptic church, St. Barbara and Ben Ezra Synagogue, and the Hanging Church built on a tower of a Roman fort. We went to the Muhammad `Ali Mosque which contains his Crypt. We visited the church, Abu Serga, or Saint Sergius, over the room of housed the holy family when they went to Egypt.

Day 15, October 21: We got in NYC at 2:30 AM.

Day 16, Saturday: We were in atlanta on time and had a two hour wait before boarded for Reno.

Tutmose III, Luxor Museum

APS' Birthday

APS, Nose of Sphinx Damaged by Napoleon's Troops

XXXVI—AUSTRALIA WITH ARLENE, 2006

Our trip to Australia was our second trip with Overseas Adventure Travel.

Day1-2, November 21, Tuesday: Traveling through LA, the Quanta's shuttle took us to their business class lounge. After boarding and dinner we slept five hours in a fully reclined chair. Since we crossed the international date line, we lost a <lay and landed at 0930 in Melbourne after a 15-hour flight.

Day 3, November 23: Melbourne was 72 degrees and delightful. We met our tour guide at 1230-Paul Kennedy, a 40-year-old Australian with a great sense of humor.

Day 4, Friday: We took a bus for a city tour with our group of fifteen. We visited the Old Melbourne Gaol where many incarcerated prisoners had been executed by hanging. Other prisoners did the cruel deed. I pointed out to the guide that many choked to death and didn't die immediately from a broken neck. This was obvious to me because their faces were swollen. After executions, autopsies were performed, and the body was decapitated. Death masks were made. Prisoners that didn't die immediately from a broken neck had swollen faces. This results when the neck is not broken, but the noose cuts off the venous return to the heart with the carotid artery still pumping blood to the head. Months later a Reno friend from UNR made the same tour of the Gaol. The tour guide informed the group that a forensic pathologist from Reno, Nevada, was the source of this information. The photo of Ned Kelly's deathmask (below) shows a swollen face.

We went to St. Patrick's Catholic cathedral, but a service was in progress so we couldn't go in. It is Gothic designed with flying buttresses. We visited the botanical garden with Captain James Cook's cottage which had been moved from England. Cook is credited with making the first recorded European contact with the eastern coastline of Australia. Next, we visited the Koala compound and Victoria Market, a large open-air market with many vendors. We bought 5 T-shirts for $25 for the grandkids.

Gaol Deathmask

Old Melbourne Gaol

St. Patrick's Catholic Cathedral. Arlene in Captain Cook's Cottage

Captain James Cook (1728-79) & APS (the person wearing a vest), and Cook's cottage
His cottage was moved from England to Australia

Day 5, November 25, Saturday: We flew to Adelaide, a one hour and twenty-minute flight. We took a bus tour of the city and the mountains. Adelaide is a city of parks surrounding the city.

Day 6, Sunday: We went to the Barossa wine country, which not included in 'our tour and cost $105 Au ($80 U.S.) each. The valley appeared to be four times as wide as Napa Valley, and is only one of several wine growing areas in Australia. We were informed there is a glut of Australian wine and it will be three or four years before the demand catches up with the supply. We found the same wine is more expensive in Australia than in the US. We bought four bottles of wine from Langmeil winery. They have the oldest vines in the world-160 years.

Fairytree

Arlene (on the right)

Arlene on a visit to Australian wine country

Day 6 continued: The roots go down 60 feet and don't need irrigation. For dinner I had kangaroo steak with a juniper berry sauce. To get catsup one has to ask for tomato sauce and they charge you $0.50 Au ($0-40 U.S.) for a small thumb size container.

Day 7, November 27, Monday: We took a two-hour flight to Alice Springs, another one-hour time change. We toured the Flying Doctor's service, which takes care of patients in the outback. I donated some money to them by buying over-priced hatpins. Then, we took the bus to the old telegraph station dating from the 1800s. Alex, a mixed blood aborigine, who appreciated the care his people got at the station, showed us around. He was in his 70s and had great stories on how the children survived during WWII when the Japs threatened. The students from the school far aborigines hiked through the desert and coast jungles to avoid the Japs. We saw our first wild kangaroo in a dry riverbed. We had a hosted dinner at the Red Ochre Grille. Arlene had emu and I had camel. The emu was fine-grain red meat very much like antelope. Camel on the other hand is like <leer, moose or elk in texture.

Alex, a mixed blood aborigine, and Arlene at the telegraph station

Emily Gap poster

Emu steak dinner

EmilyGap

Day 8, November 28, Tuesday: We took an outback cultural "optional" tour with Lindsey, who was brought up in the old traditional way. When he was a teenager, he went through a ritual where they burned his flesh, knocked out his two front teeth with a rock and made him a man. Men who don't' go through this ritual are not considered men, even though they are much older. The tour took us to Emily Gap, Jessie Gap, and other areas sacred to aborigines. We looked at rock paintings, some which had been partially removed by thieves.

Lindsey, a mixed blood aborigine guide

Linear rock carvings by ancient aborigines

Arlene with an aborigine and her painting, which we bought

Arlene and a Yipirinya aborigine grade school student

Day 8 continued: We visited the Carroboree Rock with two holes high on the face. It was posted off-bounds to hikers. We walked to the other side of the rock and looked up to see tourists climbing through the holes. We visited the Amoongung village and were served Billie tea. The ladies and children carne out to sell their paintings. We bought one for $40 Au ($30 U.S.). (The prices in the shops were two to three times what we paid.) We returned to Adelaide and visited the Yipirinya Aborigine grade school. We interacted with the students by reading to them. I read to a little hoy who told me he had a headache. He was about 6 and couldn't read, but he would repeat words after me. Next we visited the outback radio school for children on remate stations. For dinner we chipped in for food for a BBQ by our tour guide, who cooked kangaroo, lamb, and emu to perfection

An Emu being raised for its meat

Arlene in an aborigine art gallery

Arlene at Kata Tjuta

Kata Tjuta

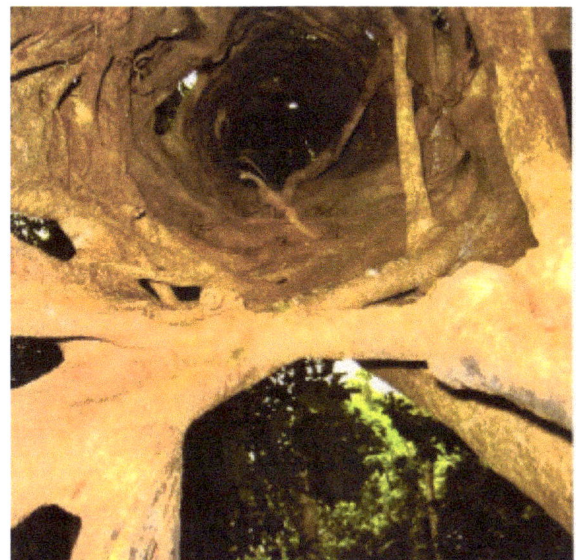

Hollow Melaleuca tree

Sydney Opera house

Arlene on a boat in Sydney Harbor

Aborigine musicians

Opera house stage

XXXVII—SCOTLAND AND ENGLAND WITH ARLENE, GENE, AND GLENDA, 2007

Glenda went on a choir tour of Ireland with tour director Melanie. Melanie invited Glenda and Gene to hear about her next tour to England. They told Arlene and me about the tour and we also signed up.

Day 1, Friday: We arrived exactly on schedule in Edinburgh at 8:55 AM. Burt Dyer, who lives in Scotland picked us out of our group of fifteen and asked if we were the Sohns. On the way to Stirling Castle, we stopped at the Battlefield of Bannockburn where Robert the Bruce, the first king of Scotland, defeated England's King Edward II in 1314. We met up with Gene and Glenda and toured Stirling Castle. We spent two hours and-saw tapestries with a unicorn, which is the symbol of the monarch of Scotland, amour, and paintings. Melanie, our tour guide, bought us a pass to historic landmarks of England. On the way back to Edinburgh we missed several turns and got back to Thistle Hotel at 5:15 PM. The thistle is the national flower of Scotland. According to mythology invading Vikings stepped on the thistles and their yells alerted the Scots to the invasion.

Glenda, Gene, Arlene at Edinburgh Castle

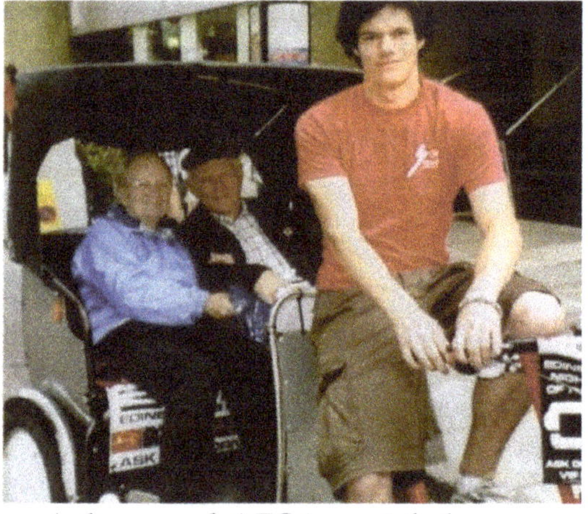

Arlene and APS in a rickshaw

Arlene, Melanie, Burt Dyer at Bannockburn

Glenda and Arlene at Stirling castle

Much of the information and many photographs in this chapter were supplied by L.E. Toole.

Day 2, Saturday: We walked with the group to the Edinburgh Castle and visited the main castle, a dungeon used as a prison since 1480, a weaving room, and adjoining buildings. St. Margaret's Chapel was built in 1100. We stopped at a woolen mill where Gene bought a cap with Scotland's pattern and I bought a vest for $70 with the same pattern. We walked the Royal Mile and hired rickshaws to take us to a lunch area called Maison Blue. Sunday: We drove to St. Andrews, the birthplace of golf. We visited the ruins of the cathedral and the Castle. We drove to Glamis Castle at 1430. It is still used as a house for the grandnephew of Queen Elizabeth. Parts of the castle are over 400-years old.

Day4: We left Edinburgh and headed to England, where we visited Bowhill House, dating from 1812, and its great art collection-Canaletto, Reynolds, Gainsborough, proofs of Sir Walter Scott's books, and Monmouth's execution shirt. We visited Melrose Cathedral where Robert the Bruce's heart is buried. We visited Bamburgh Castle with its torture chamber and checked in the Belford's Blue Bell Hotel for 2 nights.

Day 5, Tuesday: We toured Holy Island, which we had to cross at low tide, and visited Lindisfarne Castle. We visited Alnwich Castle where Harry Potter, Robin Hood, and other movies were filmed.

APS and Arlene at Melrose Cathedral

Gene at Bamburgh Castle

APS and Arlene at St. Andrews

Arlene, APS, and Glenda at St. Andrews

Alnwich Castle

Lindisfarne Priory

Alnwich Castle with Lindisfarne Castle in the distance

APS at Lindisfarne Castle

Hotspur (Sir Henry Percy), Alnwich Castle

Glenda and Gene at Hadrian's Wall

Day 5 continued: Alnwich Castle dates from 1096 but was rebuilt in 1309.

Day 6, August 1: We drove south to Birdoswald, a Roman fort on Hadrian's wall. At Birdoswald we walked about the ruins and a 17th-century house. Sheep were wandering amongst the ruins. We had lunch in the Village of Brampton, then, we drove to the waterfalls and Cathedral Aysgarth. We spent the night in Leyburn at the Golden Lion.

Day 7: We drove to the Bolton Abbey and Harrogate where we stopped for lunch at Betty's. This restaurant was a focus of Melanie. We were allowed 15 pounds ($30 U.S.) each for lunch, and it was pretty good. At 7:30 PM we got in York where we would spend the next three days.

APS at Birdoswalci

Glenda, APS, and Arlene at Birdoswalci

Arlene and Glenda at Betty's Tea Room

Glenda and Gene in York

Arlene at Buckingham Palace

APS at the Royal College of Surgeons

John Hunter (1728-1793)

Gene and Glenda in Harrods Georgian Tea Room

APS at town of Whitby

APS at the War Museum

XXXVIII—Disney Cruise With Family, 2013

March 29: We met Eric and his family in Salt Lake City. When we arrived in Orlando, Eric hada Limo meet us. It was a one-hour dive to Cape Canaveral. We checked in the Radisson.

Day 1, Saturday: We toured the ship with Eric, Mauriza, and the kids. We had dinner and it was a four-star meal. March 31, Easter: The boys were gone all day to the teenager's lounge. We watched a play of Aladdin. Isabella hada rousing great time watching the play.

Day 3, April 1: We landed in Grand Cayman at around noon. Eric, the kids, and I took the launch to the capital, Georgetown. From there we took a 15-minute bus ride to the tender to go out to swim with the stingrays. There were four or five boats and over a hundred people in waist high water to pet the rays. Eric, Sierra, and I went to four or five shops and got Sierra a tank top and some pins.

Day 4, April 2, Tuesday: We arrived in Costa Maya at noon and took the bus to Chichén Itza.

Arlene and APS in front of cruise ship

Eric, Kerry, and Brady with stingrays

Kerry, Brady, and Sierra at Chichén Itza

Kerry, Brady, Sierra, and APS

Day 5, April 3. We docked in Cozumel. Sierra had a cough at the start of the trip and the rest of us got it on day three. We left the boat at noon to go swim with the dolphins. Eric and the kids swam and had great fun while the re t of us watched. Before dinner there was a pirate production at the swimming pool. Most of the kids and adults were dressed in pirate gear.
Day 6, April 4, Thursday: We saw a Disney stage show that was comparable to a Broadway show. Isabella was fussy and Eric later said he was up with her for an hour in the night.
April 5: Arlene and I started having some back pains with our URI. When we got to Castaway Island the ship had trouble docking due to "strong currents" and we set off to sea to kill the time before docking. After about one hour the speaker system said they were going back to Castaway Island. We docked, and they said they were going to stay until 5:00 PM. We walked the beach, Brady and Sierra got pins and a tank top. The glass bottom trip was cancelled. Back out to sea. The crew brought us a special Mickey Mouse Cake for our 5th-wedding anniversary.

Brady with a dolphin

Pirate APS

Pirate Isabella

Sierra, Isabella, and Mauriza with Pirates

XXXIX—My Books

Greasewood Press Books & Newsletter Founded by A.P. Sohn MD

1. *This Won't Hurt a bit (The Life and Practice of Reno Dentist Harry Massoth)* Barker, 1995.
2. *The Healers of 19th-Century Nevada (19th-Century Chinese, Indian, Midwife, and Physician Healers)* A.P. Sohn, 1997.
3. *People Make the Hospital (The History of Washoe Medical Center)* Now Renown Regional Medical Center; A.P. Sohn & Carroll Ogren, 1998.
4. *Good Medicine (Four Las Vegas Doctors & the Golden Age of Medicine*) Interviews: Drs G. Sylvain, J. George, L. Kreisler, & J. Barger; Editor, Annie Blachley, 2000.
5. *Serving Medicine (Nevada State Medical Association & The Politics of Medicine*) History of the Nevada State Medical Association; R.G. Pugh, 2002.
6. *Pestilence, Politics, and Pizzazz (Public Health in Las Vegas)*
7. History and Interview: Dr. Otto Ravenholt; Annie Blachley, 2002.
8. *Cutting Edge (Reflections & Memories of Doctors on Medical Advances in Reno*) Interviews: Nineteen Leading Reno Physicians; Editor, R.G. Pugh, 2002.
9. *Better Medicine (The History of the University of Nevada School of Medicine)* Now UNRSOM; Phyllis Cudek & A.P. Sohn, 2003.
10. *Nevada Veterinarians (Profiles of Doctors in a Caring Profession*) Interviews: Twenty Leading Nevada Veterinarians; Editor, R.G. Pugh, 2007.
11. *Frontier Surgeon and Georgetown Medical School Dean (Reminiscences of George Martin Kober)* Editor, A.P. Sohn, 2008.
12. *The Birthplace of Nevada Medicine (Carson City)* The Practice of Medicine from 1850 to Present; R.G. Pugh & A.P. Sohn, 2009.
13. *Doctoring in Nevada (Inspiration, Dedication, and History)* Interviews: Fifty-two Nevada Doctors; Editors, A.P. Sohn & R.M. Daugherty, 2013.
14. *150 Years Of Nevada Medicine (and more) (Nevada's Men and Women Healers)* A.P. Sohn & R.M. Daugherty, 2014.
15. *Medicine is History (Nevada's Great Basin History of Medicine)* Great Basin History of Medicine Museum & Program; A.P. Sohn, 2017.
16. *Idaho Wildflowers in the River of No Return Wilderness at Pistol Creek (Medicinal use of Wildflowers & Pistol Creek Ranch History)* R. Montgomery, W. Payne, A.P. Sohn, W.J. Thompson, and L.E. Toole; 5th edition, 2018.
17. – 20. *With These Hands (A lifetime of Art and Crafts), Growing up in Irvington, My Honor to Serve Mankind, Traveling the Globe, Call of the Mountain,* A.P. Sohn, 2020.
18. 21. *Vietnam War* (TotalRecall Press, 2022, A.P. Sohn)
19. 22. 1,000 Years of Medicine in Nevada's Great Basin (TotalRecall Press, 2022, A.P. Sohn)

Quarterly Nevada History of Medicine Newsletter

20. *Greasewood Tablettes* (1989 to present) Founding Editors: O.C. Bolstad & A.P. Sohn. Present Editors: A.P. Sohn, R.M. Daugherty & P.C. Usera.

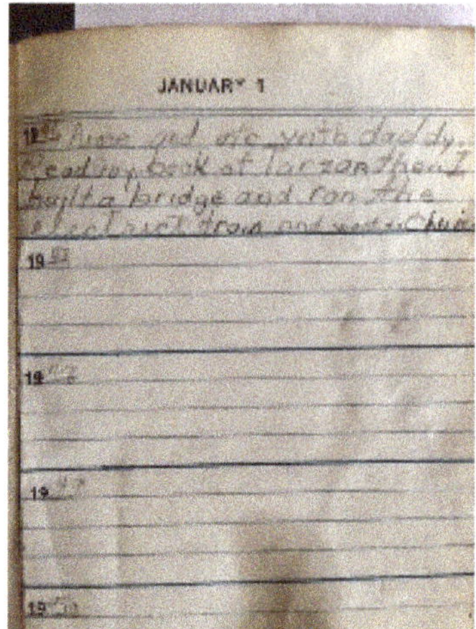

APS 1945 diary; my first recorded written words

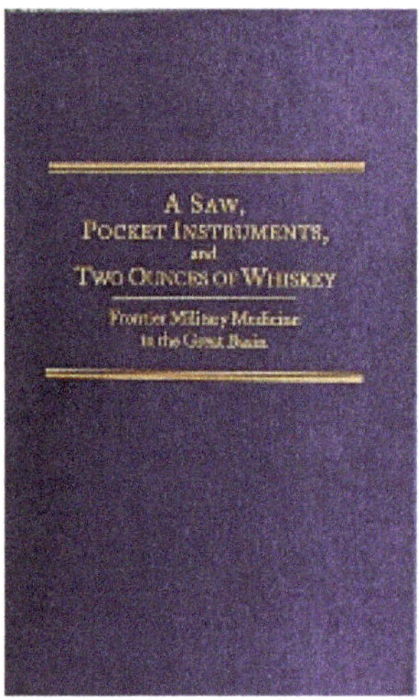

A.H. Clark, Spokane, 1998

Greasewood Press, 1998

Greasewood Press, 2003

Self-published, 1992

Greasewood Press, 1997

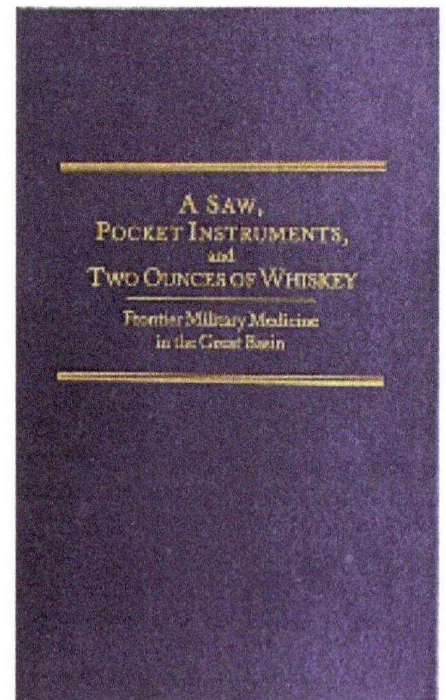

A.H. Clark, Spokane, 1998

XXXX—My Handcrafts

Table Top with Ceramic Pieces, 1964

Tahoe Donner Cabin,
Stained Glass Window, 1970

Portable Bar, given to Phillip in Woodinville, Washington, 1965

Small Table and Bench made from Trex Decking and Tree Limbs
with Bark from our Reno Backyard Sugar Maple Tree, 2013

36″ Clock made with Eric, 1983

Wall Clock made with Kristin, 1985

Left: Table Legs made from Maple Tree Limbs and Support between Legs from Donner Lake Cabin Manzanita Bush.
Right: Table Tops and Bench from Walnut Doors from Remodeled Reno Kitchen, 2009

Left: Bedside Stand from Hardwood Drawers with a White Shelf Inserted, 2009.
Right: Lamp Bases from Redwood Burls, 2002

36″ x 8″ *Burnt Pines Lodge* attached to Broken Canoe Paddle.
Placed above Interior PC Cabin Door, 2004, Photo by Bill Brace, 2020

Dollhouse for Kristin, 1978

APS & Kerry, who helped make the Table, 2012

Outdoor Patio Table Top provided by Dave Dewey from Ponderosa Pine. Table is Bolted to Roof Supports. Stools Legs made from Maple and Oak Limbs from Reno. Stool Seats made from 16″ x 16″ x 4″s (2012)

Left: Painted Table Top made from Walnut Doors from our Reno kitchen. Legs made from Maple Limbs that are supported by Manzanita Limbs, 2016.
Right: 40″ x 30″ Table Top by Dave Dewey from Ponderosa Pine, 2006

Mallard Ducks, 14″ x 6″ Wood, Reno, 1985

Dave Dewey & Bill Payne at Ranch Workshop, 2012

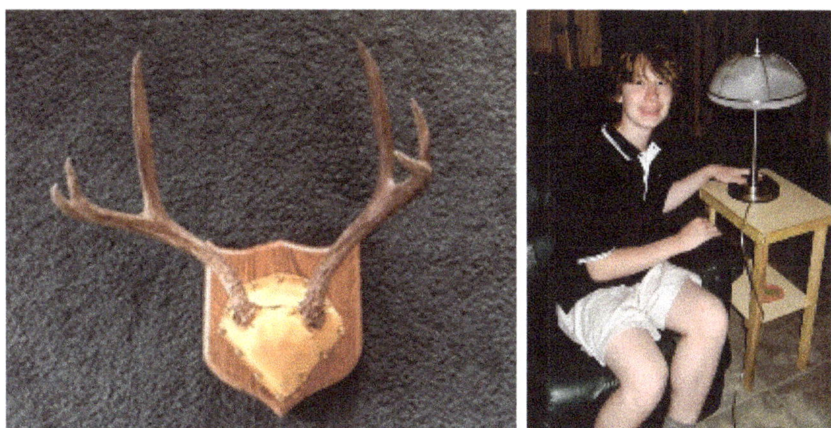

Left: Shield with Deer Antlers made hunting partner, Matt Schmitt, 2012.
Righr: Lamp Table Top and Shelf cut from a Yellow Plastic Counter Top with Peter, who signed it on the Under Surface, 2009

Phi Delta Theta Shield (30″ x 24″) cut from Linoleum for Music Room at the Indiana University Chapter and Installed with my Brother Bill in 1955. The 10″ x 10″ Wood Shield made for Donner Lake Cabin in 1990

Left: Phil, 1981 with Bald Eagle I Carved for our Tahoe Donner Cabin.
Right: I took the Eagle to Pistol Creek and placed it on a Bench in the Pistol Creek Cemetery. Bill Payne helped make the Bench. APS is next to Bertie Boyd and wife Karen. On the right are Ranch Managers, Chris and Dave Dewey, 2013

Kentucky Flintlock Rifle and Flintlock Pistol made with
Eric and moved to our Pistol Creek Cabin, 1982

Left: Boxing Bear carved from 20″ x 11½ x 3⅝ Wood, Reno, 1985 and Bolted to Bench at Pistol Creek. Right: Table from Unused Lumber, 2012

Left: Table Top made from two Walnut Doors from our Reno Kitchen.
Right: Table from Unused Lumber, 2014

16″ Handcrafted Table Clock,
APS & Kristin, 1983

80″ Handcrafted Grandfather Clock
APS & Eric, 1983

XXXXI—My Art

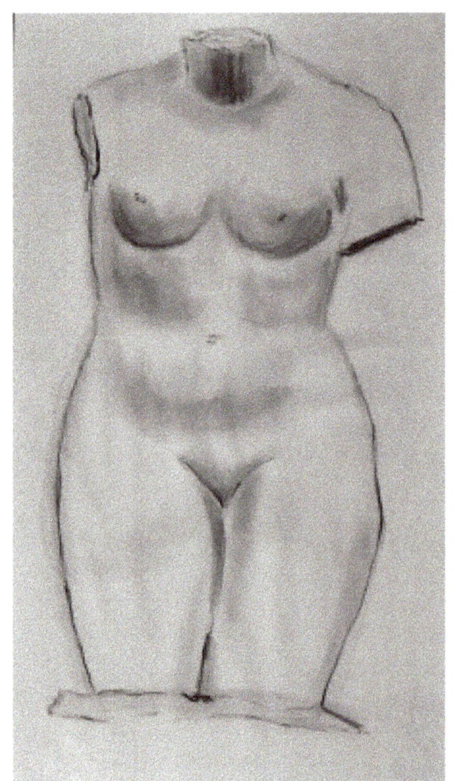

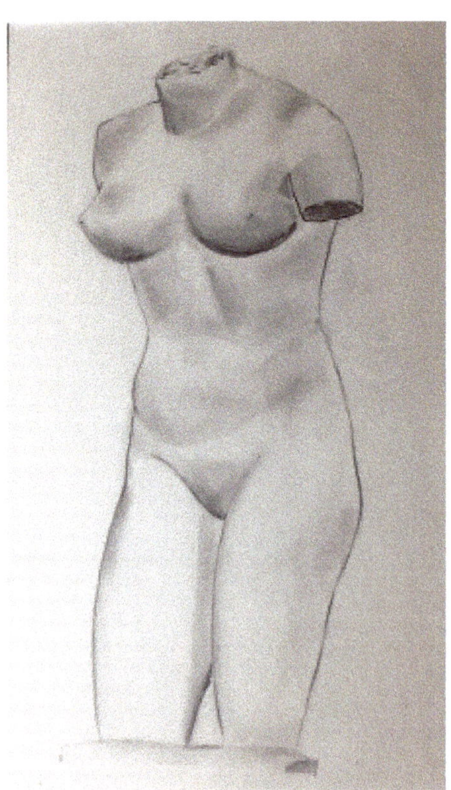

20″ x 12″ Pencil-Charcoal Drawings, 1954

20″ x 18″ Pencil-Charcoal Drawing, 1954

24″ x 12″ Pencil-Charcoal Drawing, 1954

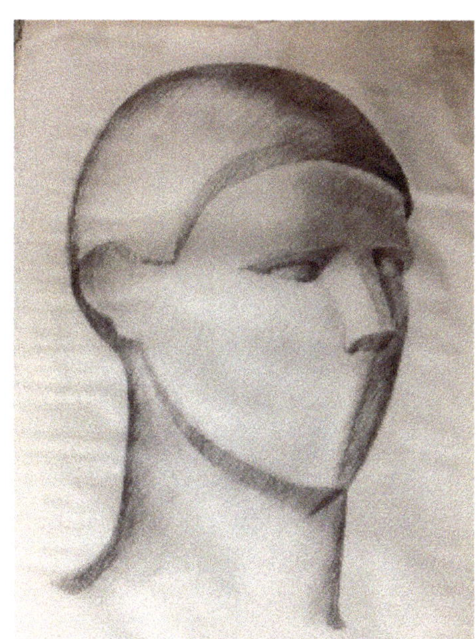

24″ x 18″ Pencil-Charcoal Drawings, 1954

Posters for Pitstop for the Little 500 Bicycle Race at Indiana University won Best Design Award. The Phi Delt Team was Co-sponsored by Pi Beta Phi (Pictured are Two Members of Pi Beta Phi and APS) 1957

1800s Artifacts (Horse Shoes, Ox Shoe, Chisel, Mouse Trap, Hand-Made Square Nails, Tuxedo Tobacco Box, etc.) found on the Donner Emigrant Trail, near our Tahoe-Donner Cabin. Placed on Burlap Covered 18″ x 24″ Board, 1982

Idaho Wildflowers in the River of No Return Wilderness,
5th Edition, each 13″ x 10″ 2018

WATERCOLOR PAINTING—RENO

Crimson Columbine at Pistol Creek, 10″ x 14″ (2011)

Golden Columbine at Pistol Creek, 10″ x 14″ (2005)

Elk in Goldenrod, 15″ x 24″ (2005)

Brown County Indiana State Park, 15″ x 24″ (2011)

Water Tank, Sumpter, Oregon, 14″ x 20″ (1999)

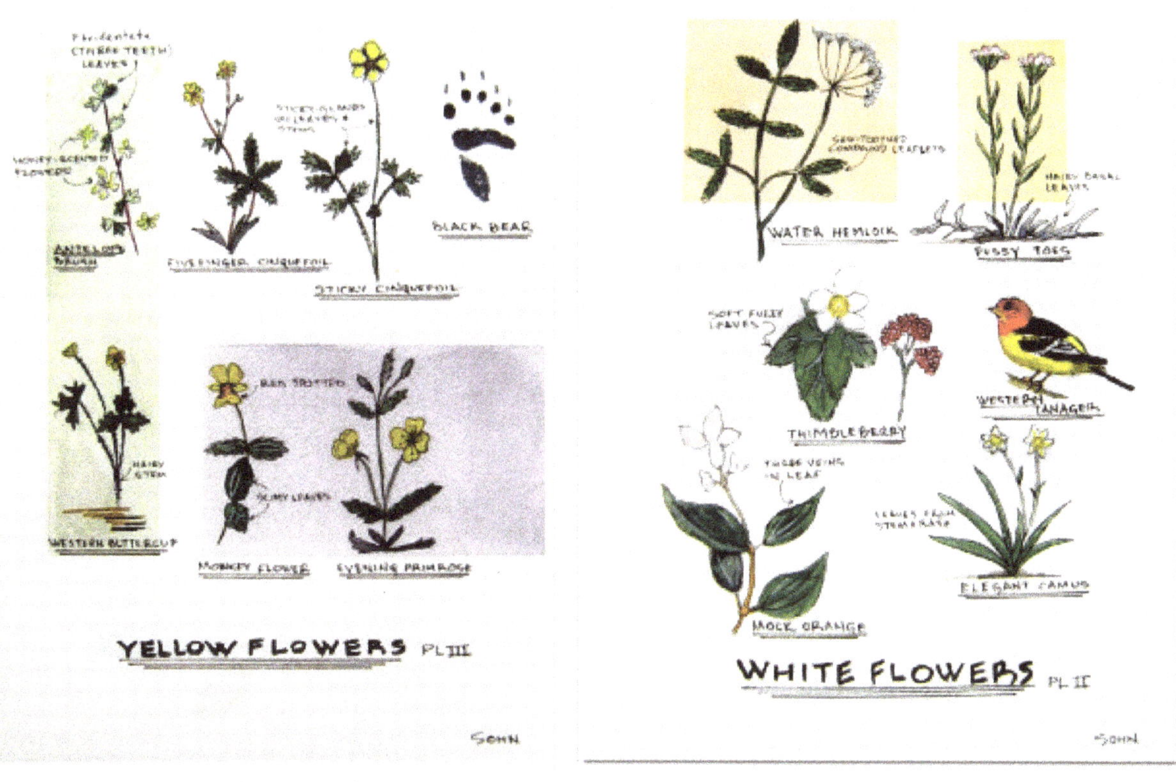

Idaho Wildflowers in the River of No Return Wilderness,
5th edition, each 13″ x 10″ (2018)

Truck, Tuscarora, Nevada, 14″ x 20″ (2006)

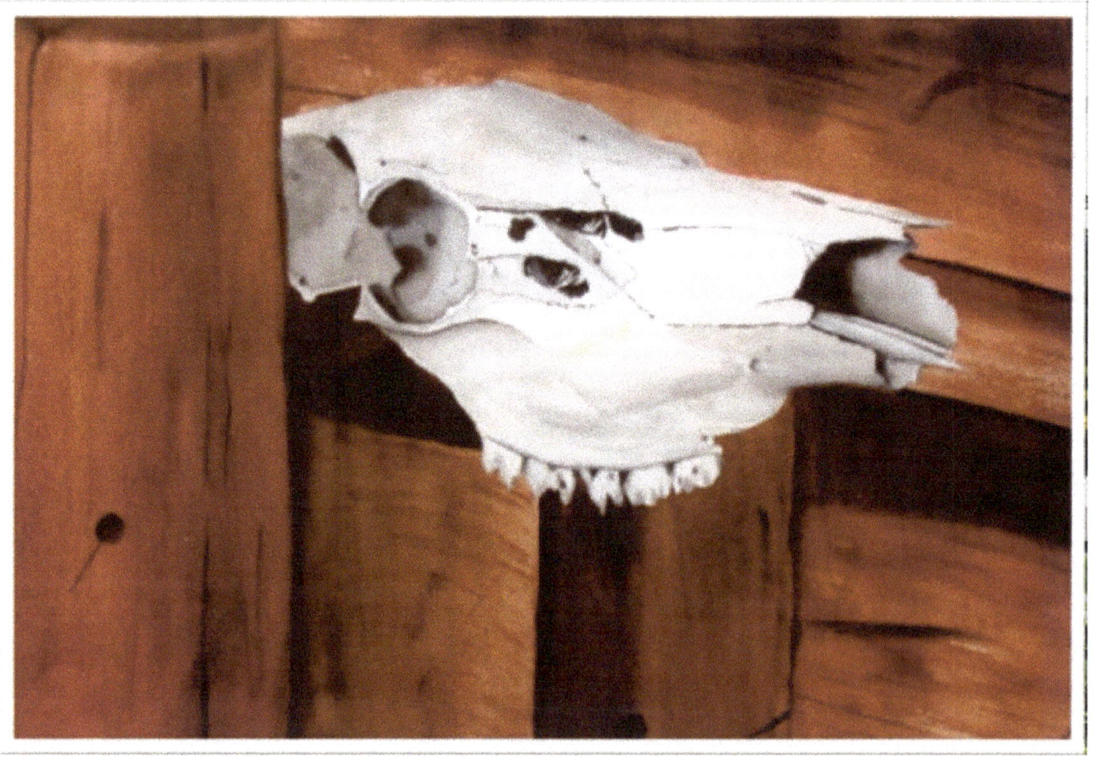

Elk Skull at Pistol Creek Lodge, 15″ x 24″ (2005)

Arlene at Truro Lighthouse, Cape Cod, Massachusetts, 15″ x 24″ (2005)

Lake view from Donner Lake Cabin, Pogonip on Trees, 15″ x 24″ (2009)

Fawn Lily (Glacier Lily) 10″ x 14″ (1991)

Spotted Saxifrage and Beautiful Sandwort, 10″ x 7″ (2005)

Winter Scene, 15″ x 24″ (2013)

Maple Leaves, 10″ x 9″ (2005)

"A Rose is a Rose is a Rose" (2005)

Pistol Creek Ranch Runway. Lodge on the left, Barn and Corral on the right, Abe in righthand corner, 15″ x 24″ (2013)

Ken Maehara, 20″ x 12″ (2009)

Moss Covered Tree, 12″x 10″ (2009)

Red Oak Leaves and Acorns, 18″x 24″ (2010)

Fall in Indiana, 15″ x 24″ (1980)

Geese Flying South, Oil Painting, 50″ x 24″ (1980)

Reflected Lights, Oil Painting, 24″ x 28″ (1965)

WATERCOLOR PAINTING
4 BUDDING LEONARDO DA VINCI'S

Left: Bill Payne, Bob Montgomery, Bill Thompson, and Gene Toole, 2006

Their art work—good enough for framing, 8″ x 12″ (2006)

APS Giving Instructions, 2006

Their art work, 8″ x 12″ (2006)

OIL PAINTING

Mount Rainier, 24″ x 30″ (1964)

Mount Rainier, 24″ x 30″ (1964)

APS, Indiana University (1957)

IU Friend "Buns" 20″ x 16″ (1956)

APS, Indianapolis (1959)

30″ x 18″ Humpty Dumpty and Jack & Jill for our Kids' Bedrooms (1973)

Grand Canyon, 24″ x 28″ (1966)

Italian Riviera, 29″ x 36″ (1969)

Van Gogh's Flowers, 24″ x 20″ (1970)

Indian, 22″ x $11\frac{1}{2}$″ x $3\frac{5}{8}$″ Wood (1985)

ARCHITECTURAL DESIGN—UNIVERSITY OF CINCINNATI

House Interior, 15″ x 12″ (1954) Staircase Design, 12″ x 8″ (1953)

Abstract House Floor Plan, University of Cincinnati, 16″ x 9″ (1953)

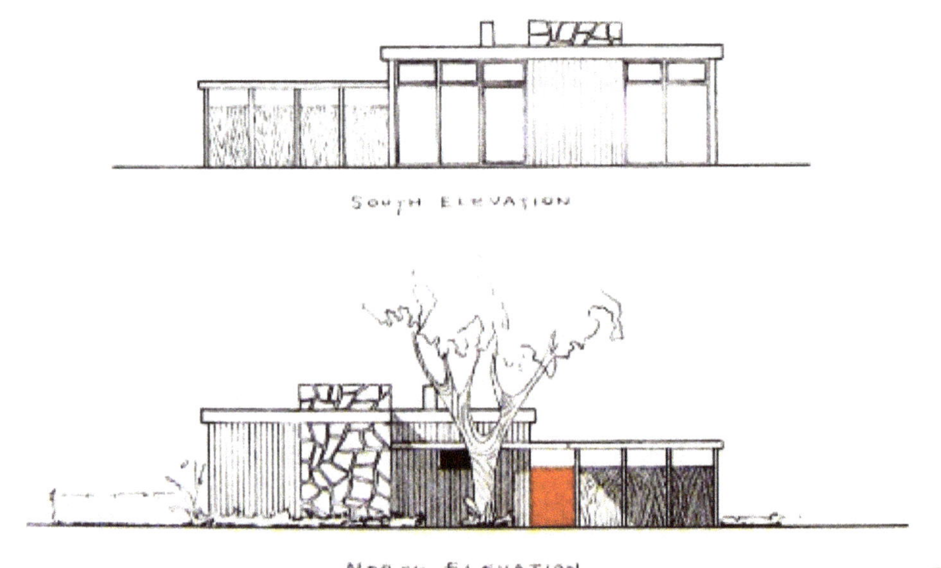

House Elevations, 1954 (See Previous Page, House Interior)

BALSA WOOD MODEL—UNIVERSITY OF CINCINNATI

St. Sophia, 20″ x 30″ (1954)

Playhouse Constructed by APS in 1975 (8′ x 9′)

Architectural Design

Cabin on Cordry Lake, near Nineveh, Indiana, for Bill, 1955

Cabin on Cordry Lake, Under Construction, Photo by Bill, 195[illegible]

Donner Lake Cabin

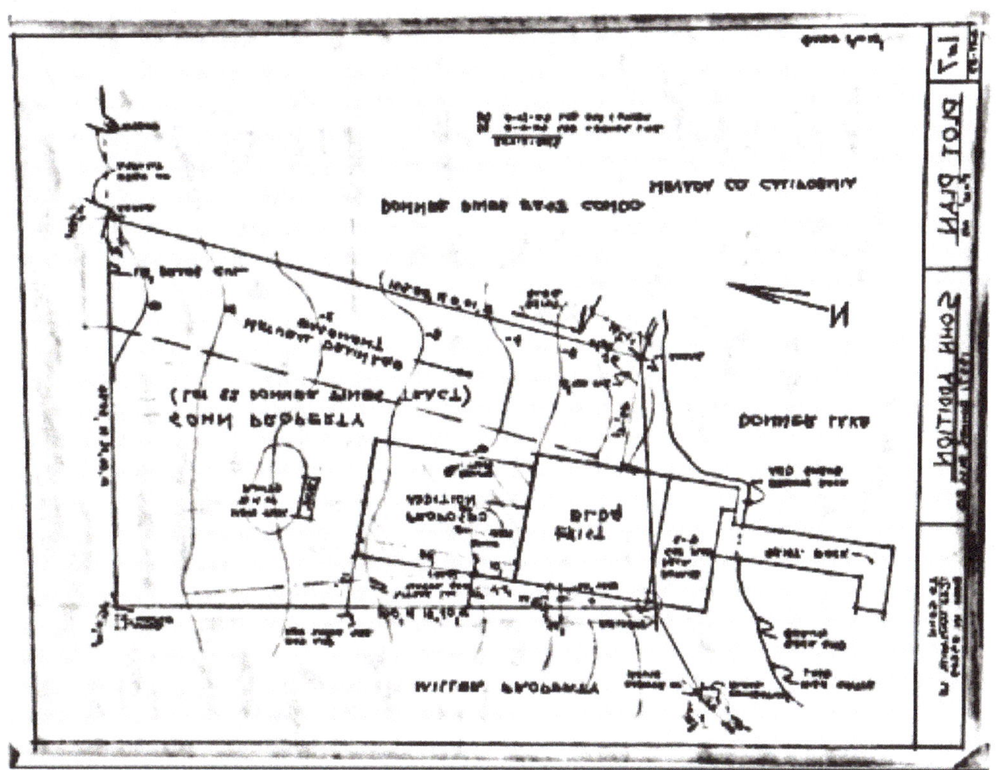

Plot Plan

Donner Lake Cabin, Built in 1983. Drone Photo by Kerry (in Doorway) 2007

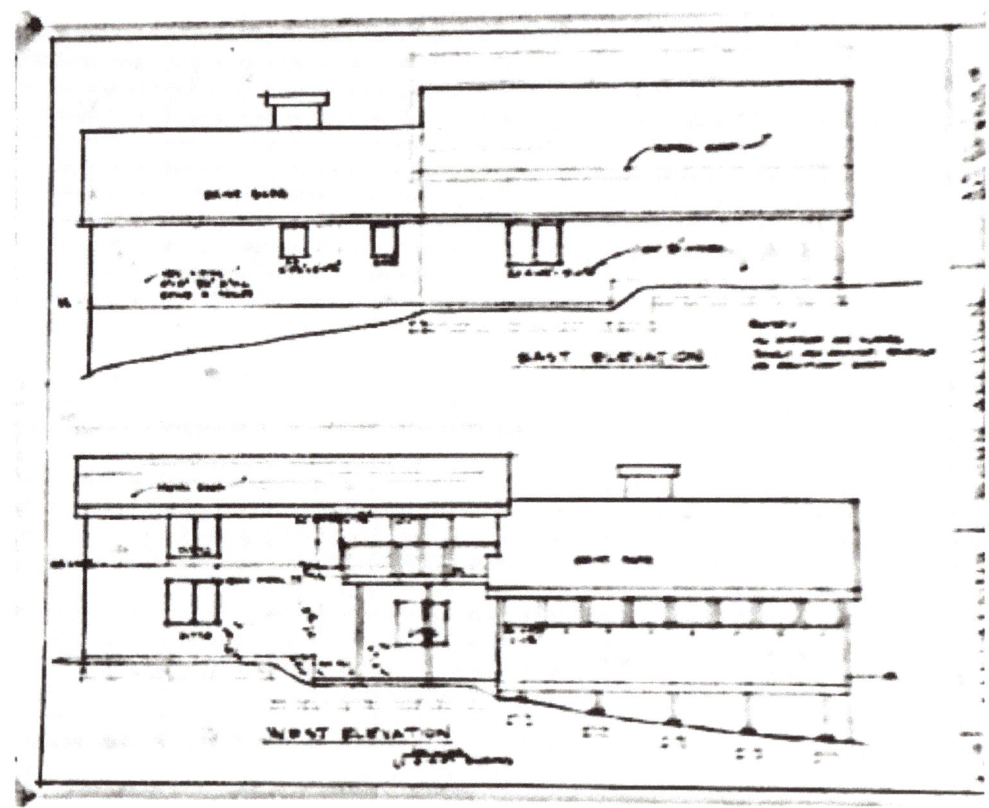

Donner Lake Cabin Side Elevations

Pistol Creek Cabin

Built in 2002, Northeast Side, 2012

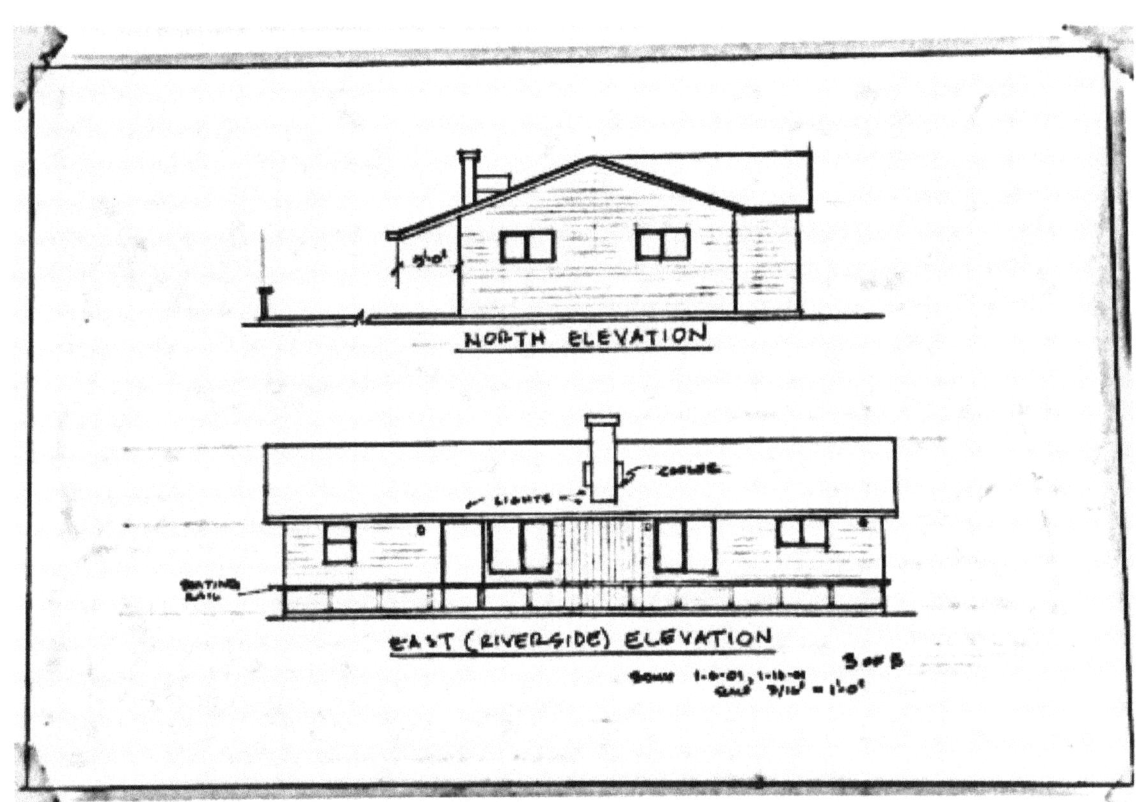

Pistol Creek Cabin Side Elevations

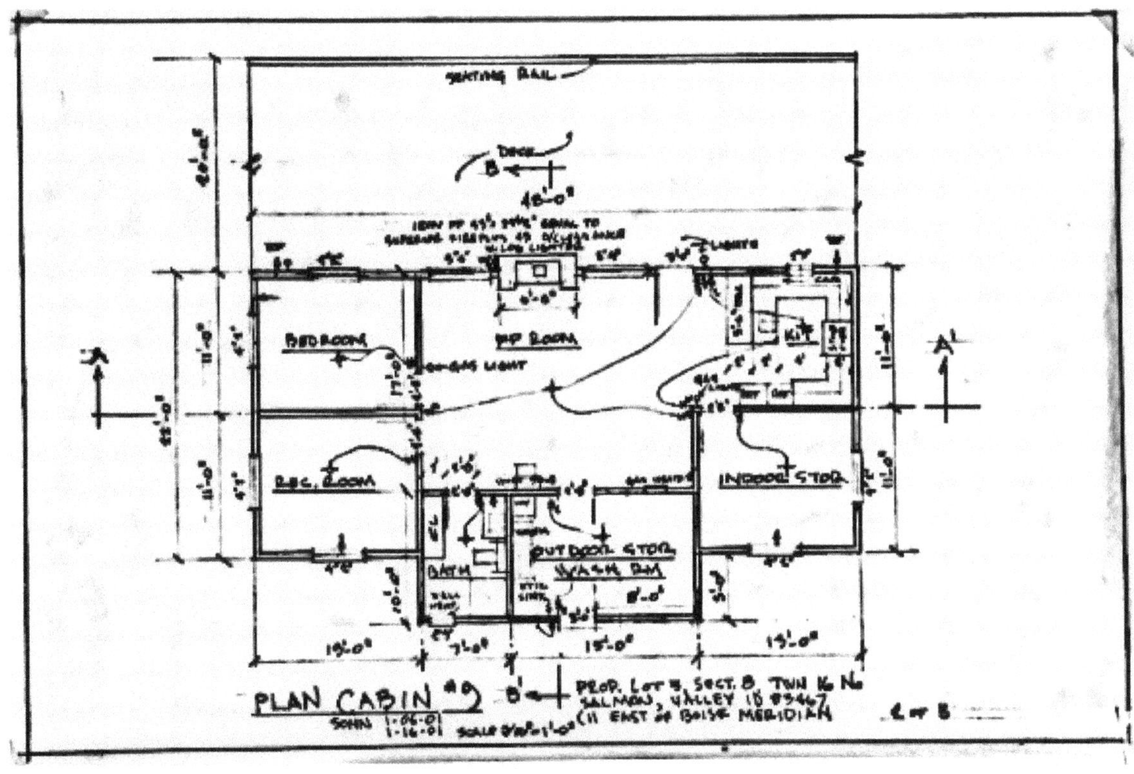

Pistol Creek Cabin Floor Plan

RENO RESIDENCE

Front Entrance, 2022

Built in 1971, Southside, June 3, 2020

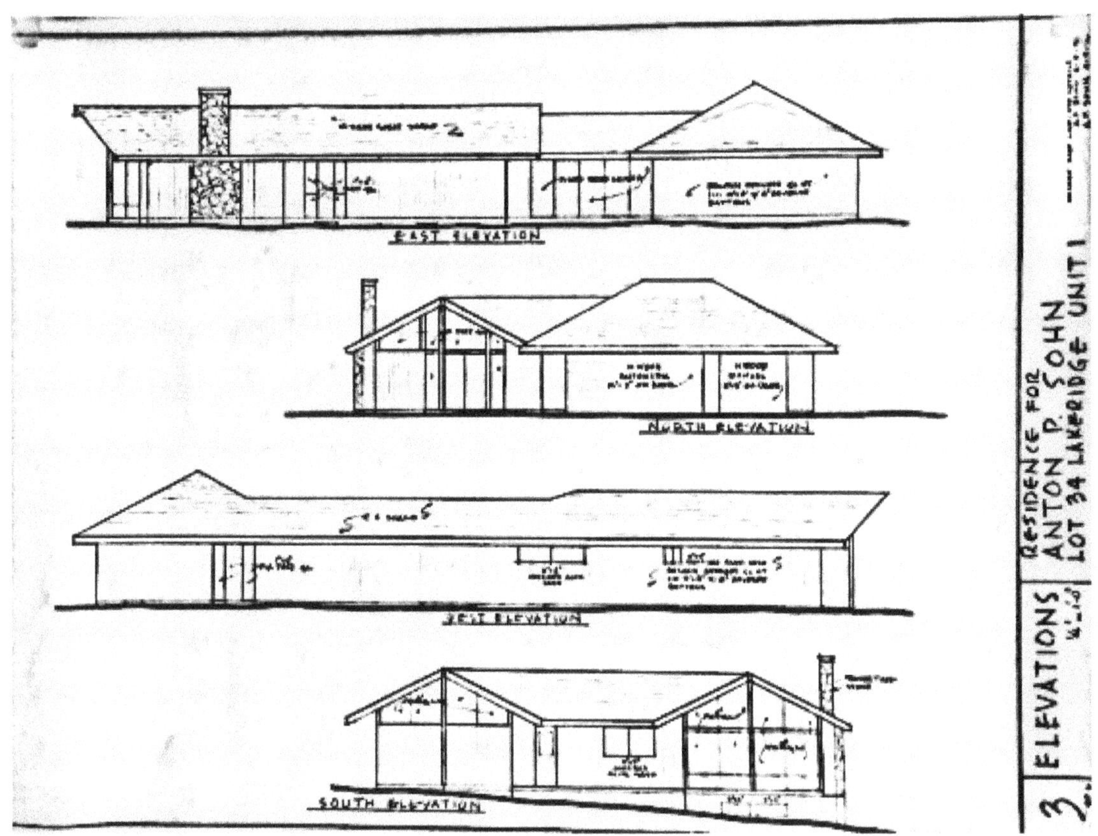

Reno Residence Elevations

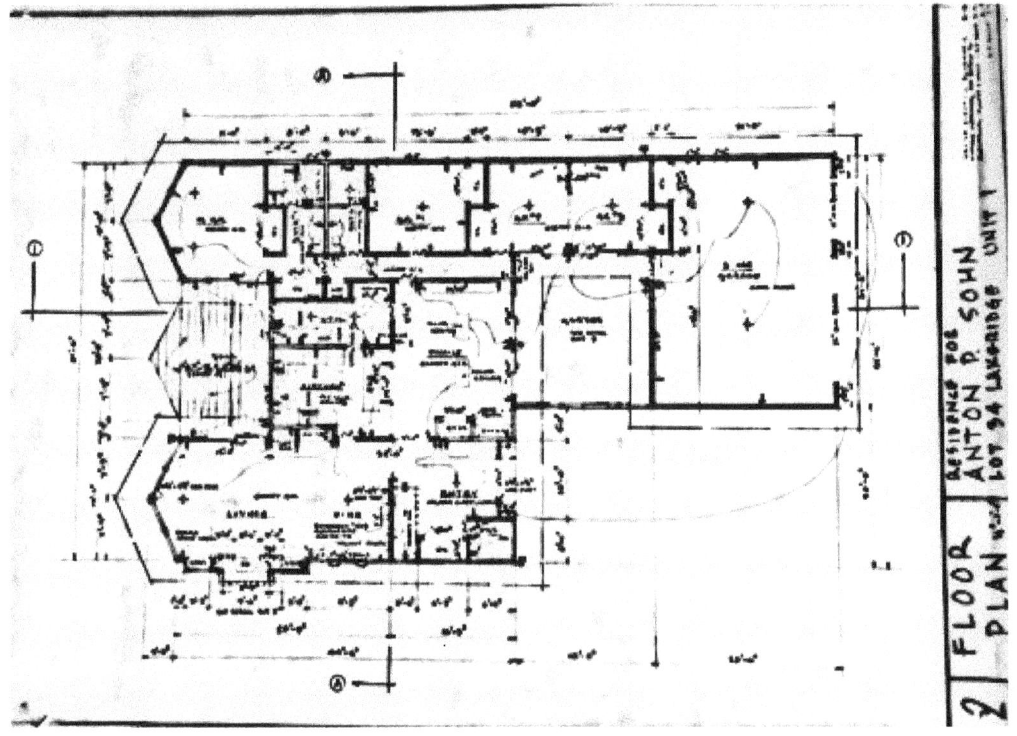

Reno Residence Floor plan

XXXXII—Sohn Obituaries and Tomb Stones

Anton P. Sohn Was Founder of Church

By BESS WATSON

Reading the Bible and working for his church were the favorite avocations of Anton P. Sohn, 74, retired grocer who died in his sleep yesterday at his home, 378 S. Downey.

He always kept his Bible on the kitchen table and would arise at night, go to the kitchen, drink a glass of milk and read the Bible.

Mr. Sohn was a founder and charter member of Calvary Tabernacle Church, at 902 Fletcher, an Apostolic church which has grown to be one of the largest of the denomination in the country and which has had as many as 1,200 Sunday school members. At the time of his death he was a deacon and trustee of the church. For years he seldom missed Sunday school and was a member of the adult class.

Born at New Albany, Mr. Sohn lived in Indianapolis since 1905. For 50 years he was a grocer, retiring eight years ago after operating a store 30 years at 1034 Fletcher.

Since 1905 he had 14 stores in different locations here. Once he owned three at one time.

Mr. Sohn was a sympathetic person and no one in need ever left his store without food because he had no money.

During World War I, Mr. Sohn maintained a farm in Jackson County.

Services will be at 10 a.m. Monday in Calvary Tabernacle Church, with burial in Washington Park Cemetery East. Friends may call from 7 to 10 p.m. tomorrow and from 2 to 4 and 7 to 10 p.m. Sunday at Shirley Brothers Irving Hill Chapel.

Survivors are the widow, Ruth Marie Fulton Sohn, a great-great-niece of former Governor James Whitcomb; three sons, Robert F. and William P. Sohn, Indianapolis, and Dr. Anton P. Sohn Jr., San Francisco; two daughters, Louise Walker, Indianapolis, and Betty Hooker, Orlando, Fla.; a sister, Amelia Webber, New Albany, and three grandchildren.

Annlouise (Sohn) Walker Parke

INDIANAPOLIS, IN - August 29, 1934-April 1, 2018

Loving mother, grandmother, and sister, Louise passed away peacefully on April 1, 2018. She is survived by son David Walker and wife Geralyn, stepsons Kevin and Neil Parke, 6 grandchildren, and siblings Anton, William, and Robert Sohn.

She attended Howe High School and Earlham College graduating in 1956. During her teaching years she obtained an M.S. in Special Education from Butler University. Louise developed a wide circle of friends while Education Director at President William Harrison Home, a position from which she retired in 1993.

Louise lived a life of quiet grace and dignity with a dedication to Christ. She taught us how to live, love, and respect others. We are blessed and proud to have been a part of her life. She will be greatly missed.

Friends and family are invited to gather 4:00-8:00pm on Monday, 9 April 2018 at Flanner Buchanan- Memorial Park. A funeral service will take place, 10:00am on Tuesday, 10 April 2018 at the funeral home. She will be laid to rest at Memorial Park Cemetery.

Memorial contributions in her memory may be made to East 91st Street Christian Church, 6049 E 91st St, Indianapolis, IN 46250.

To view the full obituary please visit www.flannerbuchanan.com

Ruth Marie (Fulton) Sohn Indpls, Ind — March 2, 1903–September 12, 1986.

Loving mother and grandmother passed away peacefully. Ruthwas a devote Christan and member of the Calvary Tabernacle, an Apostolic church, one of the largest in the US.

Born at Hindsboro, Illinois, Ruth has lived in Indianapolis since 1921. She graduated from Deaconess Hospital at Ohio and Capital Streets, 1924. She was a Public Health Nurse in Indianapolis before she married Anton Peter Sohn in 1933.

Services were at Calvary Tabernacle church with burial at Washington Park Cemetery East.

Survivors are four children, William P. Sohn, Robert F. Sohn, Anton P. Sohn, Annlouise (Sohn) Walker Parke; and multiple grandchildren.

Aunt Amelia, Mary, Steve, Joe Roth, 1975
George Peter & Mary Elizabeth Sohn's Grave
Saint Mary' s Cemetery, New Albany, Ind.
Tomb Stone Carved by George Peter Sohn

Nikolaus Sohn (1797-1882)
Saint Mary' s Cemetery
Paid by APS & Bill Sohn
Photo by Bill Sohn

Dad & Mom's Grave
Washington Park Cemetery, Indpls..

Nikolaus Sohn's Children on
Back of Nikolaus Sohn's Stone
Saint Mary' s Cemetery

Photos by Bill Sohn

Index

G

H

I

J

K

My honor to serve   Cpt. A.P. Sohn, Ret.

On the way to Monterey
Where sea otters play,
The Sun flashes
Like lightening over the Sierra
To splash like thunder in the sea.

While serving Uncle Sam
Two-year-old Phil played in the sand
Near Monterey Bay.
I was physician at Fort Ord
Awaiting the Vietnam order.

In the lab and emergency room
Seeing patients with disease,
Putting them at ease,
I learned military honor.
Next stop, Vietnam.

I managed the lab in Saigon
For one year until I was gone
To the good ol' USA.
Until I was gone
To the good ol' USA.

Saigon was restless
While Vietnam was deadly.
Autopsies and surgicals
Seven days were the norm,
Occasionally a day of rest.

Daily a Letter to home.
Often treats from home,
Which I shared with GIs
Who had no treats
Or contact with a home.

Vietnam Warriors,
T. Brady, R. Ganchan, W. Myers,
T. Cafferata, heroes and friends,
Who fought the war
With honor and valor.

I made trips up country
To testify in military courts
On noncombat deaths.
The best was yet to come,
Vacation in Japan.

On vacation in Japan
During Vietnam's monsoon
I met Arlene for a second honeymoon.
It was a welcome relief
And a battle tension release.

I made a trip to Da Nang in haste
To testify on a murder
Of a girl by a GI off base.
At the demilitarized zone
I spent time at a marine base.

I saw with sadness
The mountains in the distance
Where my 1961 San Francisco
Intern roommate was killed
In a navy helicopter accident.

Also in Da Nang
I was invited by a marine
To go on a Search and Destroy mission
And be safe near the machine gunner.
Guess how I replied?

During Tet, Saigon was ablaze
With fire and smoke haze.
I went to Hong Kong on a run
For Rest and Relaxation
And to have some fun.

Day is done, Gone the sun.
No battle wounds, just a Bronze Star
For valor. A free flight to Indpls. from
California, if I joined the army reserve.
Guess how I replied?

Day is done, Gone the sun.
My call to duty is done.
No Sohn or Fulton ever
Refused serving Uncle Sam.

www.ingramcontent.com/pod-product-compliance
Lightning Source LLC
Chambersburg PA
CBHW040259100426
42811CB00011B/1318
9781590951323